Surveillance and Film

Surveillance and Film

J. Macgregor Wise

Bloomsbury Academic
An imprint of Bloomsbury Publishing Inc

BLOOMSBURY
NEW YORK · LONDON · OXFORD · NEW DELHI · SYDNEY

Bloomsbury Academic
An imprint of Bloomsbury Publishing Inc

1385 Broadway	50 Bedford Square
New York	London
NY 10018	WC1B 3DP
USA	UK

www.bloomsbury.com

BLOOMSBURY and the Diana logo are trademarks of Bloomsbury Publishing Plc

First published 2016

Library of Congress Cataloging-in-Publication Data
Names: Wise, J. Macgregor (John Macgregor), author.
Title: Surveillance and film / J. Macgregor Wise.
Description: New York : Bloomsbury Academic, 2016. | Includes bibliographical references and index.
Identifiers: LCCN 2016005485 (print) | LCCN 2016007811 (ebook) |
ISBN 9781628924848 (hardback) | ISBN 9781628924824 (ePDF) |
ISBN 9781628924831 (ePub)
Subjects: LCSH: Electronic surveillance in motion pictures. | Voyeurism in motion pictures. |
BISAC: PERFORMING ARTS / Film & Video / History & Criticism. |
LANGUAGE ARTS & DISCIPLINES / Communication Studies.
Classification: LCC PN1995.9.E38 W57 2016 (print) | LCC PN1995.9.E38 (ebook) |
DDC 791.4302/3–dc23
LC record available at http://lccn.loc.gov/2016005485

ISBN: HB: 978-1-6289-2484-8
PB: 978-1-6289-2485-5
ePub: 978-1-6289-2483-1
ePDF: 978-1-6289-2482-4

Cover Design by Eleanor Rose

Typeset by Integra Software Services Pvt. Ltd.
Printed and bound in the United States of America

For Donna McGregor Wise,
Who always encouraged me to write

Contents

List of Figures

Acknowledgments

I first taught a class in surveillance, media, and culture in the summer of 2000. The four-hour time blocks of the summer session loaned themselves to the use of films as a means of exploring the issues at hand, more than enough time to lecture, watch, and discuss in a single session. That summer, the magazine *Brill's Content* had declared the "Summer of Surveillance," primarily because it marked the American premiere of the groundbreaking reality TV shows *Survivor* and *Big Brother* (and *Time* magazine also featured *Survivor* on its cover). Between reality TV, the rise of the internet, greater awareness of sophisticated marketing techniques (like customer loyalty cards), and new surveillance systems being put in place on city streets (CCTV) and in offices (tracking typists' keystrokes), it seemed a good time to start exploring not only what these various surveillance systems did but how we were representing them to ourselves through our popular media, especially film. That first summer, we watched Krzysztof Kieslowski's *Red* (1994), Michael Radford's *1984* (1984), Francis Ford Coppola's *The Conversation* (1974), Tony Scott's *Enemy of the State* (1998), Peter Weir's *The Truman Show* (1998), and Irwin Winkler's *The Net* (1995); we read work by David Lyon and George Orwell, and talked about privacy, Foucault and panopticism, Baudrillard and simulation, Deleuze and control, consumerism, the global spy network Echelon, and many other topics. As I've taught the class again and again through the years, the topic has become increasingly relevant, especially after 9/11. The readings have expanded and we've added (and dropped) films: Steven Spielberg's *Minority Report* (2002), Andrew Niccol's *Gattaca* (1997), Alfred Hitchcock's *Rear Window* (1954), Michelangelo Antonioni's *Blowup* (1966), Florian Henckel von Donnersmarck's *The Lives of Others* (2006), Michael Haneke's *Caché* (2005), and Michael Powell's *Peeping Tom* (1960) all made it on to the syllabus at one time or another.

So, first of all, I would like to thank my students at Arizona State University for all their insights and contributions to our class discussions and for keeping me on my toes and up to date. I would also like to thank my colleagues (past and present) in Communication Studies at ASU's west campus, a better group of folks than I could ever hope to work with. And thank you to my colleagues in the broader field of communication and cultural studies for supporting my extensive work on culture and technology (with its consistent thread of surveillance studies nearly always present): Jennifer Daryl Slack (my co-author and dear friend), Lawrence Grossberg (teacher, mentor, and inspiration), Norm Denzin (who, as a teacher, inspired creativity), Toby Miller (who published my paper on the *Truman Show* long time back), Greg Seigworth, John Erni, Steve Jones, James Hay, Hille Koskela (my co-editor for a volume on new visualities and technologies), Mark Andrejevic (for helping fill in missing episodes of the first season of *Big Brother* that my VCR had forgotten to record, and for his inspirational work), Bob Swieringa, and everyone in the Conjunctures group for their constructive support and feedback on my early work on webcams, control, and the attention economy. My thanks to John Erni, Keehyeung Lee, Vamsee Juluri, Dietmar Kammerer, Esther Cheung, Lori Way, Ilana Luna, and many others for suggesting titles that I should look at (and putting out inquiries on my behalf). And thanks to John Erni and Yi Sun for comments on the procedurals chapter.

My thanks to Arizona State University for the sabbatical leave in the Spring of 2015 that allowed me to complete this book.

My thanks to the editorial team at Bloomsbury Academic, especially Katie Gallof, for believing in this book. And to the anonymous reviewer for the suggestions and support.

My thanks to Petra Peper for her enthusiasm for this project for many, many years.

And my thanks and love to my family, for putting up with the teetering stacks of DVDs and books and papers in the living room. Elise, Brennen, and Catherine, you all are my touchstones.

Parts of Chapter 3 appeared in J. Macgregor Wise. 2002. "Mapping the culture of control: Seeing through *The Truman Show*." *Television and New Media* 3(1): 29–47.

Introduction:
Mapping the Surveillant Imaginary

Figure I.1 Bolt and Deranian watch the children. *Escape to Witch Mountain.*

We start with a scene from the 1975 Disney film *Escape to Witch Mountain*. This is a scene that I had never paid much attention to when I watched it growing up, but now I see it with added significance. The film is about two young children, Tony (Ike Eisenmann) and Tia (Kim Richards), who are survivors of an alien shipwreck passing as human children until they can be reunited with their people again. They have been captured by the evil billionaire Aristotle Bolt (Ray Milland) and his henchman, Lucas Deranian (Donald Pleasance), who seek to exploit the children's psychic powers for financial gain. Bolt has adopted the children and has set them up in a seeming children's paradise in a mansion on the California coast. The scene in question shows Bolt and Deranian in front of a bank of video monitors. They have installed surveillance cameras throughout the children's quarters in order to learn the extent of their powers. Deranian boasts that he will be adding more cameras soon.

Despite a certain creepiness to the image of two middle-aged men watching children in their bedrooms via closed circuit television (CCTV), the voyeurism in this case is simply an act of power, operating out of a need to extract information from/about the children, and to control them to make sure they cannot escape. The cameras have their place within the array of security features on the property (guards, guard dogs, high walls, and so on). The children have their own forms of surveillance: the ability to see and hear events happening at a distance. In one scene, Tia, using her psychic powers, listens in on a conversation between Bolt and Deranian in another part of the house.

I begin this book about surveillance and film with this scene not because it is exceptional, but precisely because it is not. In 1975, CCTV was enough of a common technology not to merit much notice. It becomes a simple plot point in a family film to emphasize the power and immorality of the villain and the tightening noose of control encircling the children. This is a short scene. The camera does not linger on the monitors or otherwise call out the technology as unusual or new. Of all the possible ways that Bolt could have attempted to glean the information (eavesdropping, personal spying, interrogation, and so on), this technology was chosen. The hidden surveillance camera that does not just record, but provides a live feed to a monitor in another location, is a symbolic as well as pragmatic and efficient choice. CCTV systems have come to be understood as meaning power, usually power to control. There is something we feel is sinister in such systems, though they are set up ostensibly for our protection. They are unintrusive, unnoticed, but not wholly unexpected. By 1975, audiences had been trained to expect to be on surveillance cameras for almost three decades, ever since hapless adults were caught on candid cameras for popular entertainment.

As a further example of what we could call the banality of surveillance, in 1974, the year before *Escape to Witch Mountain* was released, the popular British sitcom *Are You Being Served* broadcast an episode entitled, ominously enough, "Big Brother." The show is set in a London department store in the men's and ladies' fashions department. This episode begins with Mr. Rumbold (Nicholas Smith), the department manager, announcing that due to a rise in theft, the store was going to install CCTV cameras on the floor and that he would be monitoring them from his office. The staff, after grumblings about invasion of privacy, begin to change their behavior when they know the camera is on. They begin to perform for the camera (adopting posh accents with customers, dressing up, making particular comments which they hope are heard favorably by management, and so on). On Mr. Rumbold's part, in the meantime, he moves on from watching for shoplifters and begins watching the staff, making obsessive notes about any infraction (from smoking on the floor to excessive tea and bathroom breaks). The staff finally get fed up with Rumbold and his cameras. They devise a performance for the cameras to convince Mr. Rumbold that he is deathly ill and that the cameras are the cause. Trusting that the cameras had brought him the truth about the behavior of his department, he believes the charade since it is played out on camera (he believes what the staff say on camera over what the doctor tells him in person), and has the surveillance cameras removed.

The show was known for its farce and broad (and low) comedy and not its political critique, so it is safe to assume that the issues raised in this episode were well-worn and comfortable enough for sit-com fodder. Nonetheless, the episode sets out a number of key issues surrounding visual surveillance. First is reference to George Orwell and Big Brother, the idea that behind security cameras lurks an authoritarian dictator bent on crushing human freedoms, and this is indeed a popular frame through which we have viewed surveillance.[1] Second is that while there are valid justifications for surveillance (crime prevention), there is also "function creep" and the cameras get pointed at others (like staff) and used for other purposes. In this case, the cameras meant to prevent crime are used to enforce department rules and people who were not the initial targets of surveillance find themselves in the camera's eye. Third, behaviors which people assume are private become public through surveillance. Fourth, people change their behavior when they know they are being watched; they become more aware of their own behavior and how it varies from expectations or the norm. Thus such observation can be used to help (or force) subjects to internalize normative attitudes and behavior. Michel Foucault called this "discipline," and that is another framework through which surveillance has been theorized and understood.[2] The fact that Mr. Rumbold is taking detailed notes of each infraction (or at least makes his exasperated secretary take such notes) is part of the disciplinary regime. Fifth, monitoring CCTV leads to voyeurism (Mr. Rumbold zooms in on a young attractive staff member adjusting her pantyhose) and voyeurism is linked with obsession and illness. Surveillance is a slippery slope: if we *can* watch for something, then we *must* watch for it, and it becomes imperative *not to miss a thing*. Sixth, when faced with a problem, we seek a technical fix, a machine to solve the problem. In this case, it is the installation of the camera system rather than relying on human intelligence (meaning, the eyes and ears of the employees themselves). The store has hired a private detective who is personally surveilling the department in disguise, but the staff, in a state of heightened paranoia, attack him after he pretends (supposedly) to steal something to test the system. And, seventh, we tend to treat the images from surveillance cameras as somehow providing us the truth; they seem objective, mechanical, and impartial and can observe others when they have let their guard down. That's why accidents and crimes seem more shocking in grainy CCTV or cameraphone images, or monsters seem more frightening or sex more erotic.

Surveillance is a common feature of popular films and has been for as long as there has been popular film. The body of films about surveillance has a long history. As film scholar Catherine Zimmer has put it, "[e]ven before narrative forms began to dominate cinematic practice, imagery we have come to associate with surveillance has been with film from the beginning."[3] Thomas Levin, a media studies scholar, has even pointed out that one of the first films by the Lumière brothers in 1895 is of workers leaving the Lumiere brothers' factory; the bosses were watching their workers.[4] Film itself is a form of surveillance: using film cameras to document public and private moments. This was much of the fascination of early cinema, before narrative came to dominate, and continued in the use of cameras to capture everyday life in documentary film, anthropology, and so on.[5] Zimmer continues that "as soon as narrative began to make its way into these films, surveillance thematics soon followed," such as voyeurism and the capturing of crime and sexual escapades and more.[6] The body of films about surveillance has expanded more rapidly in recent years. To take a non-scientific measure, let's look at IMDB.com, the online database of film, television, and videogame titles. When I looked at IMDB in the Spring of 2014, it listed 601 feature films that have been tagged with the term *surveillance*. Only 21 titles appear between 1915 and 1949 (the year George Orwell published *Nineteen Eighty-Four*), which probably says more about the limitations of the IMDB database (a bias toward recency and audience familiarity over comprehensiveness) than actual numbers of such films. However, it lists 300 films in the fifty-two years from 1949 to 2001, and 279 in the thirteen years since September 11, 2001. These numbers can roughly indicate a couple of things. One is that surveillance is much more part of the culture post-9/11, and the second is that we identify certain contemporary events and practices as being surveillance, but do not use the label (and the conceptual framework) of surveillance on earlier practices. That is, surveillance as it is understood today is a relatively recent concept.

Partly, the reasons for this increase could be because surveillance is a common feature of everyday life, from private detectives and spies to warrantless wiretaps, massive NSA surveillance, and what Hal Niedzviecki has called the culture of peeping.[7] We are used to CCTV cameras in businesses and on street corners, the files kept on us by doctors, employers, insurance agents, the government, marketers, and more. Indeed, media scholar James Carey once wrote that "the sense that someone is always watching, potentially at least, is part of the structure of feeling of modern life."[8] It is not surprising then that surveillance has been well represented in feature films, and indeed throughout mass media. The question I will be pursuing in this book is *how* has it been represented in film. What is the *surveillant imaginary* that the films present?

By *surveillant imaginary* (a term developed by Dietmar Kammerer, David Lyon, and others[9]) I mean the collection of stories, images, ideas, practices, and feelings that are associated with surveillance at a particular point in time. The imaginary is closely tied to popular culture: the popular films, programs, songs, comics, advertisements, and so on. Following Stuart Hall, I see the popular as a site of struggle, a place where understandings of politics, identity, ethics, and more get reinforced, debated, and transformed.[10] Surveillance itself is not the same as the surveillant imaginary; the latter is our way of understanding surveillance practices and technologies. But the surveillant imaginary is not something secondary to actual surveillance, simply how it is represented. As Dietmar Kammerer has stated it, "the surveillant imaginary is not external to the working of surveillance, but intrinsically linked to its functioning."[11] Kammerer's statement echoes film scholar Catherine Zimmer's conclusion that "Ultimately I would argue that cinematic (and televisual) narratives of surveillance serve as such specific structural models of the dynamics within a culture of surveillance that they should be viewed not just as 'reflections' of an increasing surveillance-centered media, but themselves as *practices* of surveillance."[12]

Surveillance is many things. It encompasses a great variety of processes, technologies, intentions, and outcomes. Some surveillance systems support public health or safeguard citizen's rights, while some manipulate and oppress populations; some are personal and others are impersonal; some document abuse and others perpetuate abuse. We can use, as a baseline, sociologist David Lyon's definition of surveillance as "any collection and processing of personal data, whether identifiable or not, for the purposes of influencing or managing those whose data have been garnered."[13] Lyon structures the definition in this way to emphasize that surveillance is more than individuals watching others (which is often seen as voyeuristic), but the collection and use of myriad data (including visual data) for the purposes of control. This collection would include such practices as marketers gathering demographic data on consumers to better sell products to them and DNA and biometric databases being used by governments to keep tabs on their populations. Surveillance is therefore more than just voyeurism, though voyeurism can be part of surveillance. Voyeurism is the obsessive desire to look, usually, sexual in nature. The film *Gattaca* (2007), for example, is about a society surveilled down to the genetic level, but it is not a film about the obsessive sexual gaze. And though a police procedural provides many opportunities for officers and agents to act voyeuristically (sometimes almost in an off-hand way), that is not necessarily the nature of the mission or plot.

Although surveillance is many things, that is not the way that it is portrayed in feature film and other media: Films about surveillance have a much narrower range of representations, a much narrower *problematic* (a problematic is a limited set of issues or questions available to a text or genre). Most films about surveillance are about individual voyeurs or legal or extralegal investigations, or struggles against totalitarian societies. We can quickly bring to mind the stereotypical images from surveillance films: a man looking through a telescope or binoculars, men in a surveillance van monitoring transmissions, or men surveilling a bank of video monitors (the gender in this sentence is deliberate). The act of surveillance, both in actual practice and in feature films, raises questions of ethics, trust, power, and control (as well as race, gender, class, sexuality, politics, economics, culture, and society). How our films represent these themes is important to understanding the character of contemporary culture and society. How they represent these themes we will call the surveillant imaginary.

I am looking at films, rather than surveillance in everyday life more generally, because I would argue that our feature films are important sources of our understandings of the capabilities of surveillance in society (what can be done), the context of surveillance in society, and the culture of surveillance (even when we realize that the capabilities on screen are fictional fantasies and don't represent actual technology or practices). These media texts are some of the few places in contemporary society where issues about surveillance are widely addressed. Surveillance is usually the domain of (apart from practitioners of surveillance) policy analysts, privacy lawyers, and a handful of academics. Historical events may push surveillance into the news, everyday discourse, and popular consciousness: revelations of the FBI's surveillance of the counterculture and political movements in COINTELPRO and Richard Nixon's wiretapping in the 1970s, or whistleblower Edward Snowden's revelations about the extent of the NSA's surveillance capabilities in 2013, for example. But narratives provide structures of ideas through which to understand these events. Often it is the narrative, or a character, or a scene, or a phrase that remains with us long after the particular events fade.

The surveillant imaginary is a regime of representation, an attempt at a coherent and seamless narrative about how the world is. Psychoanalytic film critic Todd McGowan, following the work of Jacques Lacan, calls this the symbolic order, the rules and codes of society. Film can reveal the symbolic order and even "works to secure the rickety construction of the symbolic by giving it an image of wholeness that it doesn't have on its own."[14] This "illusion of plenitude" provided by the film is termed *the imaginary*. However, the symbolic order is not coherent, but contradictory, and is constantly troubled by the real. The importance of the role of film in understanding surveillance, then, is not just the ways film maps out and supports what Nicholas Mirzoeff calls complexes of visuality[15], but the ways it can reveal its constructedness as well. What Lacan called the gaze is that which troubles the symbolic, the nice neat narrative, that reveals its constructedness.[16] The tension in film is between the ways it papers over the contradictions and antagonisms of the social and the ways it can reveal those antagonisms.

Surveillance and Film takes as its object of study the body of films that takes surveillance itself as its primary topic of concern. The book is more selective than encyclopedic in scope. It is not my purpose to cover every such film, or to identify every representation of surveillance in popular film. Indeed, such a survey would be pointless as the instances would be too many and too banal: every voyeur, every nosy neighbor, every police stakeout, every kook with a camera, every thief casing a job, every spy plying his or her trade, every maniac stalking a camper, every private detective digging for clues, every reporter pursuing a story, every CCTV camera, every microphone, and so on. My intent is to engage with key exemplars that raise issues pertinent to the body of films at large. At times this will involve a more literal approach to the subject, that is how, when, and why technologies and practices of surveillance appear in a film, but at other times it will involve how the film camera itself takes on the perspective, aesthetic, and characteristics of surveillance and how films contribute to broader complexes of visuality.

The book is not just concerned with whether or not surveillance is represented in film, but *how* surveillance is represented in film. The images and stories we get about surveillance indicate anxieties, concerns, topics of interest, and even just everyday experience. This narrower problematic of surveillance is also shaped by the medium itself—especially the structure and affordances of feature film—a way of telling stories, of editing sequences and combining sound and image. For example, for a medium that emphasizes image and sound it is easier to tell a story about cameras and watchers than databases and algorithms. Films can also tell different types of stories from television. Television's role in the surveillant imaginary is quite prominent because it involves not just popular fictional serials (from *Dragnet* to *CSI* to *Person of Interest*), but also reality television programs that feature surveillance and news and documentaries that rely on surveillance footage. As with the example of *Are You Being Served* above, we will occasionally discuss televisual texts in relation to the themes we are pursuing. But even though feature films now circulate readily on the same home and mobile screens as television serial programs, and become intermixed in popular discussion of surveillance, I retain a focus on feature films because they are a particular type of text (of a certain length, with particular emphases on singular conflict and resolution, whereas television serials can work through the repetition and difference of multiple episodes over years), and that may help this particular book retain a certain cohesion.

Revelations about surveillance, such as the Snowden leaks about the NSA, always make surveillance feel like a new phenomenon. Truth is, surveillance has been part of culture and society for as long as there has been culture and society, but we just get accustomed to it. If we look at Lyon's definition of surveillance again, "the collection and processing of personal data, whether identifiable or not, for the purposes of influencing or managing those whose data have been garnered," then the origin of surveillance lies with the birth of accounting, trade, tribute, and taxation.[17] From the biblical Book of Numbers to the Domesday Book of 1086 to nineteenth-century surveys of London's poor to the growth of bureaucracies, surveillance has been part of social life and governance.

Surveillance history is not just a history of technologies, practices, and documents, but how we are entangled in dynamics of visuality, regimes of representation, or, rather, what Mirzoeff calls complexes of visuality. Complexes of visuality concern how practices of visuality are caught up in arrangements of power and the management of populations through "classifying, separating, and aestheticizing" authority.[18] His work examines what he calls the Plantation Complex, the Imperial Complex, and the Military Industrial Complex. For example, look at the plantation complex in terms of surveillance. The primary authority in the plantation was aptly named the Overseer. Mirzoeff and other scholars, such as Christian Parenti and Simone Browne, each argue that accountings of the slave trade, from organizational diagrams for slave ships to the rules and regulations of the US plantation, originated influential forms of surveillance in order to label and control African slaves.[19] Arun Kundnani and Deepa Kumar argue that "patrols set up to capture runaway slaves [were] arguably the first modern police force in the United States."[20] Practices of surveillance were pioneered not just on plantations but in colonialism more generally (part of Mirzoeff's Imperial Complex). For example, the British occupation of their colonies, like India, led to the creation of forms of racial categorization and identification documentation such as internal passports and permits, and the first use of fingerprinting to track individuals.[21] The procedures of surveilling the private lives of dissidents, the use of agents provocateurs, and "spreading disinformation in the media" were piloted in the American occupation of the Philippines.[22] Surveillance has a long, global history.

Film cameras have their place within genealogies of surveillance. From documenting individuals and populations by name and description, authorities moved on to the photograph as being the authoritative proof of identity (and, later, the fingerprint as another unique image of the individual). As both Simone Browne and Christian Parenti have set out, portraits of slaves and rogues galleries contribute to this history.[23] Motion pictures document not only individuals but also populations. Early films were not just used for entertainment but also by anthropologists to study other cultures (and at times these functions of science and entertainment blurred in disturbing ways).[24] And as early as 1914, the British newspaper *The Daily Mirror* was worrying about the possibilities and consequences of cinema cameras blanketing

London, recording all aspects of daily life and tracking individual behavior, making individuals accountable for their movements.[25] But while film is a surveillance technology, it is a medium that reflects upon practices of looking in society and the desire to look.

In psychoanalysis, the term for the general pleasure in looking is *scopophilia*. This is a normal part of sexuality and also relates to general curiosity and inquisitiveness.[26] *Voyeurism* in this approach is the aberrant, pathological version of this drive, when scopophilia becomes obsessive. Scopophilia obviously plays an important role in cinema viewing: we take pleasure in the images projected before us in the theater, and the sounds that surround us. Even when the images are not seemingly aesthetically pleasing (think of horror films), there is a curiosity and fascination in watching, seeing images that we would not otherwise have seen. Even with the most innocent, non-sexual film, the camera provides us with intimate images of others' lives, and their private moments and private spaces. By providing us with a particular image, shot from a particular distance and angle, focused on only specific aspects of the scene, films guide our own vision—indeed, we have no choice, save looking away from the screen at the rest of the theater and its inhabitants, than to take the camera's gaze as our own. This is the basic idea behind Norman Denzin's argument that cinema taught us how to look at the world and each other; and cinema allowed us to bypass culturally inflected interpersonal rules of when and how we can look at other people.[27] Cinema allows us to stare at other people, often in close-up, intimate distance, in ways that are not allowable in everyday life. We can stare without guilt because, in the case of fictional film at least, the actors have assented to be stared at in this manner.

In the selection of images it shows, cinema teaches us how to regard what we are looking at: Is it important? Amusing? Scary? And it teaches us what to think about it or them. Should we respect them? Fear them? How should we look at them? Cinema is therefore deeply entangled with ideologies of race, gender, sexuality, and class as its gaze reinforces ways of looking at the world that we must participate in if we are to watch the film.[28] This does not mean that we have to accept these images, or agree with their portrayal, but we have to consume them to watch the film. If we do not question the views we are given, then we are accepting that way of seeing the world and others.

The field of surveillance studies itself is relatively recent.[29] It has its origins in the 1970s and many point to Michel Foucault's study of the development of new forms of discipline and power in the nineteenth century using information to manage individuals and populations as being particularly influential (though many of the key concerns of the field were already being mapped in James Rule's earlier work).[30] The field of surveillance studies itself is quite diverse, ranging from the sociology of crime and policing[31] to reviews of government programs of global surveillance,[32] the uses of CCTV cameras[33] and biometric identifiers,[34] the management and tracking of individuals through consumer data,[35] the uses of the internet to track and profile individuals,[36] the monitoring of children in the education system,[37] and more.[38]

But alongside the sociological, economic, and political analyses of surveillance has been a continuing call to consider the *culture* of surveillance as well: What does surveillance *mean*, what is the *experience* of surveillance, and how does a society present surveillance to itself through popular culture? As Gary T. Marx has argued, "as important as historical, social, philosophical, legal, and policy analyses are, they are insufficient for broad understanding. We also need cultural analysis to understand how surveillance is experienced."[39] David Lyon has also noted, "[f]ar more likely [...] that we know about surveillance because we have read about it in a classic novel such as *Nineteen Eighty-Four* (1949) or that we have seen a film depicting surveillance such as *Enemy of the State* (1998). Such movies and novels help us get our bearings on what surveillance is all about and—because they are usually negative, dystopian—give us a sense of the kind of world we wish to avoid."[40] And Thomas Levin insists that "a socio-political understanding of surveillance at the dawn of the new millennium must also include an analysis of the striking proliferation of the *rhetorics* of surveillance—at both the thematic and the formal level—in virtually all contemporary media ranging from cinema and television to cyberspace."[41] In answer to these calls there has been a growing literature on surveillance in popular culture, especially film, to which this book hopes to contribute.[42]

The importance of a cultural analysis of surveillance is in part because the domain of popular culture is one in which understandings of the world are presented and contested, a site of struggle. But it is also crucially important because culture is not simply a site that reflects on surveillance practices, but surveillance has become a part of our culture. A number of scholars now refer to a *surveillance culture*.[43] This is not just a sense that our culture has gotten used to being tracked and spied on in various ways, but that surveillance has become part of the way we begin to understand our world and interact with others. The practice of watching others, in the form of reality TV, has been a dominant cultural form since the 1990s, and the practice of self-surveillance has become the norm: continually posting information and images about ourselves first on the world wide web (through blogs and webcams) and now on social media (with updates and selfies and tweets). Mark Andrejevic termed this *lateral surveillance*: that rather than Big Brother surveilling us, or us surveilling back at the institutions of power (what has been termed *sousveillance*[44] and *sub-veillance*[45]), we surveil each other.[46] Indeed, monitoring the streams of personal information from our social network contacts across multiple social media platforms as well as through person-to-person communication (like calling, texting, and so on) become important forms of social bonding: how we live, interact, and otherwise socialize with our cohort in a form of constant contact. Also included in this culture are how we manage and negotiate these streams of data (like privacy settings on social network sites) and the awareness of being watched by others. Surveillance has become an important form for both our popular and interpersonal culture. This is not to say, Lyon (and others) would be quick to argue, that other powerful structures of surveillance don't persist; they do. State surveillance (especially around security from the national to the local levels, around the movement of bodies and the circulation of communication, and so on) and private surveillance (especially ever finer capacities of marketing data) expand, pushing "surveillance more and more into the tissues of everyday life."[47]

Through an examination of popular film from the last half century, we can trace different ways that surveillance has been understood and key ideas related to surveillance. In the chapters that follow I will expand on some of these ways. There have been three key models of how surveillance functions in society (and many variations on these), and each becomes a way of understanding surveillance and how or why one should respond to it. The most common, still, is the evocation of Big Brother. Based on George Orwell's novel *Nineteen Eighty-Four*, this perspective sees surveillance as being a means of social oppression by an authoritarian regime.[48] We are surveilled to keep us under control; surveillance is a threat. The second model is based on the work of French philosopher Michel Foucault who also saw surveillance as a form of social control, but through the self-disciplining of the subjects of surveillance.[49] If we know we are being watched, we change our behavior accordingly, internalizing norms. This form of control he termed *discipline*, but this form of surveillance is termed *Panoptic*, because he used as a model of discipline's functioning Jeremy Bentham's idea for a prison, The Panopticon, in which prisoners are kept under control not by brute force or bars, but by knowledge that they are always possibly being surveilled by guards in a central tower. The third model of surveillance is from another French philosopher, Gilles Deleuze, who argued that the social regime of discipline that occurs in institutions (prisons, workplaces, schools, hospitals, and so on) is breaking down: control now occurs throughout the society; it is now constant.[50] And we are constantly being managed and manipulated, though we might not be aware of how or when. This is accomplished through the proliferation and circulation of data by and about us, which is modulated, not necessarily by a central authority, but by logics that work across institutions and the society.

These models and ways of understanding surveillance highlight a number of themes including those of visibility, identity, power, trust, risk, privacy, voyeurism, and control. In this book, I will explore the surveillant imaginary of contemporary feature film. I do so not to present the final interpretation of what these films mean and do, but to inspire additional analysis of other films and popular texts. I approach these films with a loose set of critical questions (inspired by a more comprehensive set of guiding questions set out by Gary T. Marx).[51] What activities constitute surveillance? What devices constitute surveillance? What are we meant to feel about these practices and devices? How are they presented to us or how are they depicted? Are they presented as moral? Legal? Are there particular images, symbols, sounds, or music associated with these depictions? Who carries out the surveillance? Who is subject to surveillance? Is surveillance the concern and practice of an individual or an organization? Who benefits from the surveillance? What are the limits of surveillance and who or what places those limits? Is there a proper use of surveillance, as depicted in the text? Is surveillance a problem in the film, and if so what is the problem of surveillance? Is the problem the technology, the system, an individual, or something else? Who or what is blamed? What is the solution to that problem? What solutions to that problem are not posed? Who does not surveil? Who is not subject to surveillance? How is resistance to surveillance represented? Whose view of the world is this text presenting? Does it assume a race, gender, class, sexuality, nationality, morality, politics? Who or what is missing from this story? Does the working of surveillance match one of the key models of surveillance? Do we see instances of key themes?

Let me give you two examples to help set the stage for what is to come. These are two films by the filmmaker Wim Wenders in which, in contrast to each other, we can trace an important dynamic of surveillance: care and control. David Lyon has argued persuasively that surveillance has two faces. It is not only about watching over as a means of control of the other, but one can watch over someone in order to care about them. Many instances of surveillance take place in order to care for individuals or populations (e.g., medical surveillance of contagious disease), to protect rights, to keep from harm. We will see how this aspect of surveillance plays out in the film *Wings of Desire* (1987), and how surveillance as control plays out in *The End of Violence* (1997).

Wim Wenders's film *Wings of Desire* provides us with an angel-eye perspective on Berlin. The premise of the film is that angels are among us; they watch over us and try, subtly, to help us if we are distressed, to comfort. The film opens with a close-up of a hand with a fountain pen writing a poem about childhood. A voice-over reads the poem as it is written. This is followed by the titles and then, in black and white (as is most of the film), a shot of clouds and then a close-up of an eye. We then get an aerial shot of buildings, Berlin. Coming through the clouds we are the eyes that watch, that circle the city. The next image is of a man standing on a rooftop looking down. He has large angel wings, but these fade into invisibility. This is the angel Damiel (Bruno Ganz) whose story we will follow. Damiel, his friend and fellow angel Cassiel (Otto Sander), and other angels move about the city, invisible to all but children, watching and listening, recording, and trying to comfort. They can go anywhere (an airplane, a building, the street) and listen in to everyone's thoughts. This perspective of divine surveillance allows us, the audience, to follow the angels into people's apartments and lives, to listen to their inner monologues of worry. The camera moves fluidly from room to room, in and out of buildings, into cars and busses, across space. This is a powerful, intrusive, and intimate surveillance, but it is a surveillance with the intent to record and to care and to comfort.

But as powerful as this surveillance is, it is not all powerful or omniscient. This is true of any surveillance system. The angels only observe at a remove—they cannot actually touch or physically interact with people and they cannot experience the world as humans do; they lack access to the full sensation of the world. The film contrasts the world of angels—filmed in dreamy black and white by a camera that moves silkily anywhere, a world of pure observation—with the world of humans—filmed in rich color by firmly grounded cameras, a world felt as well as seen. The plot involves Damiel's increasing dissatisfaction with watching and recording, taking notes in a small notebook, for eternity, "forever hovering above," and his increasing desire to experience the world fully as humans do. He has also fallen for a young trapeze artist, Marion (Solveig Dommartin), in a down-on-their-luck circus. She too flies above her audience wearing wings. She is troubled with thoughts of suicide and death, which draws Damiel in to observe and help. He follows her into her dressing room and watches as she changes, his desire turning the surveillant gaze of care into the gaze of the voyeur. The camera lingers on her bare shoulder.

Figure I.2 Surveillance as care: Damiel listening in to Marion's thoughts. *Wings of Desire.*

The idea of a total system of surveillance is one that we will encounter in a number of films. But it is important to remember as we move on that even complete observation cannot really know its subject, or feel what they feel. That if the intimacy of angels is still at a remove from the subjects of their surveillance, then the surveillance of CCTV or any technical means must be always more so.

Wenders's later film *The End of Violence* involves a more earthly form of surveillance. Ray (Gabriel Byrne) is a former NASA engineer who has been hired to help build an extensive, super-secret network of surveillance cameras in Los Angeles. The system is meant to prevent crime, to end violence, by being able to observe everyone everywhere and respond immediately. While its purpose is protection, there is always the danger of abuse by nefarious individuals. The project is a technical challenge for Ray, but he is increasingly worried about what the system will really be used for. He watches the cameras out of care for victims, but worries that it may end up controlling the population. Ray tries to leak details of the surveillance system to a Hollywood producer he once met. One evening he spots what looks like a kidnapping and attempted murder, but suddenly finds his surveillance feed blocked by the system. This smacks of a coverup to Ray. He is later able to track down the recordings of that event and sees the two kidnappers seemingly targeted by the surveillance system itself, and killed. Their victim escapes.

The producer to whom he had mailed the system plans, Mike Max (Bill Pullman), known for making popular violent films, is having his own crisis of conscience. He was the victim of the kidnapping and only barely escaped the assassination attempt. It is hinted that he was targeted because he received the plans for the surveillance system. Mike goes into hiding with a family of Mexican gardeners and has a change of heart about violence. His violent films had always come out of his own paranoid

Figure I.3 Surveillance as control: Ray watches Los Angeles. *The End of Violence.*

worldview, but he realizes that his view is incorrect, and that not everyone is as cut-throat as he assumes.

The film is full of references to seeing and surveillance: the CCTV system is housed in an old observatory, where Ray uses the telescope to scan the heavens when he is taking a break from scanning the citizens of Los Angeles; we see the voyeurism of film production; while on the run, Mike slips into his old house and spies on his wife; Ray's housekeeper at the observatory turns out to be a spy planted to keep an eye on him; and in the end a young girl talks about the sky and heavens, stating that (in a nod to *Wings of Desire*) they are watching us. We see the dynamic of care and control: Sam watches the screen in order to help people (though he is powerless to do more than watch), but realizes that the system can be used for control. And we are given reassurances that such pernicious systems can be defeated. The agent in charge of the surveillance system states that it must remain secret until Congress approves it, because, it is implied, the public would never stand for it if they knew, and it would have to be dismantled. This is why they go to such lengths to keep knowledge of the system from falling into the wrong hands. The film ties the problem of surveillance to the problem of violence, the regime of fear and paranoia reinforced by the violence of our popular culture (especially feature film and gangsta rap). In this film, we see the issues of watching, of control and voyeurism, and of being watched; of building a system of total surveillance and of hiding from such a system; and of trust in the veracity of what the cameras reveal. These are all threads we will pursue in the coming pages.

Further Reading

Kirstie Ball, Kevin D. Haggerty, and David Lyon (eds). *Routledge Handbook of Surveillance Studies*. New York: Routledge, 2012.
Norman Denzin, *The Cinematic Society: The Voyeur's Gaze*. Thousand Oaks: Sage, 1995.

Rachel E. Dubrofsky and Shoshana Amielle Magnet (eds). *Feminist Surveillance Studies.*
    Durham: Duke University Press, 2015.
John Gilliom and Torin Monahan, *SuperVision: An Introduction to the Surveillance Society.*
    Chicago: University of Chicago Press, 2012.
Sebastien Lefait, *Surveillance on Screen: Monitoring Contemporary Films and Television
    Programs.* Lanham: Scarecrow Press, 2013.
David Lyon, *Surveillance Studies: An Overview.* Malden: Polity, 2007.
Garrett Stewart, *Closed Circuits: Screening Narrative Surveillance.* Chicago: University of
    Chicago Press, 2015.
Catherine Zimmer, *Surveillance Cinema.* New York: New York University Press, 2015.

1

The Watchers

Figure 1.1 Jeffries watches Thorwald. *Rear Window.*

One of the most recognized types of surveillance film could be referred to as the voyeuristic film. These are films that focus on the perspective, actions, and experiences of one who watches. A wide variety of films fall into this category, encompassing a wide variety of surveillors: the pervert in the bushes watching through the window as someone undresses; the monster or criminal in the bushes watching through the window to choose the time to murder someone; the detective or spy who follows and watches; the security guard or officer who monitors CCTV cameras; and others. To call these all voyeuristic, however, is a bit limiting as not all are about watching because of sexual desire. There are a number of reasons why surveillors watch, including power, control, or care. What holds this category together, gives it its coherence, is the positing of surveillance as an *individual* issue: It is about a single surveillor, as opposed to team or organizational surveillance (characteristic of the procedural—see Chapter 4) or films about pervasive surveillance societies (see Chapter 3).

Voyeurism and film

What do we mean by *voyeurism*? In a general sense, we use the term to refer to the act of watching someone else for our own pleasure. A *voyeur*, then, is, as Norman Denzin has put it, someone who "takes morbid pleasure in looking at the sordid, private activities of others."[1] Voyeurism is a pathological version of the general drive *scopophilia*. Obsessive voyeurism is more specifically sexual and about power and control over the desired other. Scopophilia is also related to *exhibitionism* in that with the latter the drive to look at others becomes a desire to be looked at, perhaps as a way of affirming one's identity and existence, to be accepted by another.

Laura Mulvey's influential and controversial article "Visual Pleasure and Narrative Cinema" draws on psychoanalysis to discuss how narrative film is structured in such a way as to reinforce patriarchal ideology.[2] According to Mulvey's argument, there are two ways of looking in narrative film. The first is scopophilia, as discussed above. The person on screen being looked at is seen as an object of pleasure. This can at times be a stronger version where the person is overtly the object of sexual desire: a voyeuristic gaze. Key to this psychological process is the separation of viewer and viewed; the voyeur does not want to close that gap, they just want to watch unobserved. The second way of looking is *narcissism*. Narcissism focuses the gaze on human forms: we want to see ourselves on screen, that is, we seek out bodies and faces we can identify with. Psychoanalyst Jacques Lacan argued that people form their sense of identity, a sense of coherent self, in the mirror stage of development, when an infant sees an image of itself, or sees its mother or other adult and recognizes (or, rather, misrecognizes) that image of a coherent body as itself: "that is me." Identity, the first articulation of "I," is based on an image external to us, not an inner sense of self. The ego ideal is an image. Cinema gives us lots of ego ideals for us to identify with: stars. We want to be like them, be them. The narcissistic gaze sees the character as an ego ideal; we wish to identify with what we see. Key to this psychological process is the collapsing of distance between observer and observed.

Both processes and ways of looking are evident in narrative film. But they are contradictory. One wants to watch at a distance; the other wants to collapse that distance. Narrative cinema, in a patriarchal culture, deals with this contradiction, Mulvey famously argues, by splitting the look by gender. In a patriarchal ideology, the normative viewer is male; the camera shows us the world and the people in it as a heterosexual male would see it. Women on screen are then the object of the voyeuristic gaze—they are seen as objects of pleasure, often as objects of desire. Women on screen are regarded as sexual objects and the camera films them as such, perhaps focusing on their legs (many female characters are introduced to the audience legs first). Minimally, they are objects to be looked at. Men on screen are then the object of the narcissistic gaze. We, the audience, are meant to identify with them (even if we are female). These contradictory looks, Mulvey goes on to say, structure the stories narrative cinema tells. Men carry the action forward; women are passive objects or, if active in the plot, are eliminated or punished in the end (and are not an ego ideal to be emulated).

Mulvey's theory was influential, controversial, and much argued with and corrected.[3] Whether such a patriarchal narrative structuring applied to all films, just classical Hollywood films of the 1940s and 1950s, or relied on particular and partial readings of the films, has been debated, as has the passivity of the audience in this theory, or the limiting of the male gaze to either narcissism or perversion.[4] And what of the female spectator, might they not identify with both passive object and active subject?[5] But the idea that the camera can have a voyeuristic look, that it positions audience members as voyeurs, is especially germane when the subject of the film is voyeurism itself. When are we asked to identify with the look itself, and when are we asked to identify with the person looked at?

However, we must complicate things a bit. Lacan argues that in the mirror stage the infant *misrecognizes* itself in the image. When we identify with the subject on screen, we participate in the imaginary and share its sense of social plenitude. What is important is to locate in cinema the ways this identification is disrupted, our positioning disturbed. According to some psychoanalytic theories of cinema, this is the interruption of the real into the symbolic through the gaze (being that which cannot be represented, the blindspots films try to ignore).[6] We can take this point more broadly to consider the times when the surveillant gaze itself is disrupted by desire—but not the desire of lust but desire that is driven by what is *not* in what is offered in the surveillant image (be it a film or TV screen, or monitor, or even data), desire driven by what is *lacking* in the image, which is the real that eludes the representation. These are moments when we question the correctness or completeness of the view of the world we are presented with in the surveillance image: what is missing? But there are also times when the surveillant gaze is disrupted by revealing *too much*, an *excess* rather than a lack, by revealing the inadequacy or contradictions of the surveillant imaginary or the complex of visuality. Deleuze and Guattari, contra Lacan, argue that desire is not based on lack but is productive.[7] Not only this, desire is productive of the social, not just the individual. According to this perspective, the surveillant imaginary on film is not reflecting on individual desires, say that of a voyeur or exhibitionist, but participating in desiring production that organizes populations, structures of power, and disruptive flows. So while I will be using some psychoanalytic film theory for the insights it allows into film and the questions it raises for surveillance studies more generally, I wish to acknowledge its limits as well. The surveillant imaginary is not just about individual desires and meanings but broader social forces and relations of power.

The voyeur on screen

Rear Window

Of the numerous films which focus on the activities of the voyeur, Alfred Hitchcock's *Rear Window* (1954) is perhaps the best known—and most analyzed.[8] Denzin refers to Hitchcock as "the voyeur's director" and points out that "the gaze ... in all its forms" is ubiquitous in his films.[9] *Rear Window* is a masterful, complex, and subtle film, and I cannot do justice to all its nuances here. We will return to this film later in the chapter, and throughout the book, to highlight various aspects of it. But to start, let me set out its scenario.

Rear Window is about L.B. Jeffries ("Jeff") (James Stewart), a professional photographer with a penchant for action, who is laid up in his New York apartment with a broken leg after an accident on a shoot. Bored, restless, and immobilized, Jeff has little to do but look out his apartment window into a courtyard and at the apartments across the way. He is visited by a nurse, Stella (Thelma Ritter), and his fiancée, Lisa Fremont (Grace Kelly), who works in high fashion. Both of these women criticize his hobby of watching his neighbors. The events of the film take place during a heat wave, so windows and curtains are open, making his neighbors more visible than they otherwise might be.

The film can be (and has been) read as Hitchcock's reflections on cinema itself. As the film starts, curtains open on the rear window and the scene is from Jeff's apartment. His window is our cinema screen; we are the immobilized Jeff, watching little stories play out in all these other windows (each a little screen).[10] Almost all of the shots of the film are either filmed within Jeff's apartment or from his window. The events of the courtyard and apartments unfold at a distance, the distance of a voyeur.

Both Lisa and Stella tease Jeff about his voyeurism, Stella making reference to Peeping Toms. Jeff defends himself by stating that his watching is harmless and that his neighbors are free to watch him as well. However, when he is actually in danger of being looked at, he pushes himself out of view and into the shadows. Indeed, Lawrence Howe has argued that the film is as much about avoiding being seen (scopophobia) as scopophilia.[11] Jeff has been following the ongoing dramas in the other apartments

Figure 1.2 The courtyard as cinema screen. *Rear Window.*

(as he interprets the events therein), even giving them his own names such as "Miss Lonelyhearts" or "Miss Torso." He does not know them, and has not met them, but he presumes to know them based on what he sees. While a good number of neighbors are visible to him, at the start of the film his gaze is most arrested by the woman he dubs Miss Torso, who tends to dance around her apartment in her underwear. I should note that "Miss Torso" is an ominous moniker to assign to a woman in a film where a woman is dismembered, but it is a name that emphasizes the ways the male gaze objectifies and fragments women into body parts. The male composer is also seen doing housework in his underwear, but this is not portrayed as being sexually provocative and does not capture Jeff's (heteronormative) gaze.

The plot really begins when something else draws his attention away from Miss Torso. One of the apartments houses a salesman and his invalid wife who is always scolding and mocking her husband. One day Jeff notices that the wife is missing and becomes convinced that the salesman, Thorwald (Raymond Burr), has killed her. Uncovering her murder becomes his mission. And in fact, his surveillance of his neighbors only intensifies while pursuing this mystery. From simply watching, he turns to binoculars and, finally, to a high-power telephoto lens to watch the salesman. He had not subjected his other neighbors to this level of scrutiny until this point.

There are a number of forms of surveillance represented in the film. The key is obviously Jeffries. Jeff has an itch to scratch, both literally (an early scene has him desperately searching for a means to scratch his leg under his cast) and figuratively. As a man of action, he desires excitement. His action frustrated, he turns those energies to voyeurism, compensating for his broken leg with his phallic telephoto lens. As a professional photographer it is his job to watch and photograph others. His job justifies his voyeurism to a certain extent. Jeff's aberrant desire even undermines his relationship with Lisa, to whom he is reluctant to commit and marry.[12] He would rather watch his neighbors, and obsess about them, than kiss her. This begins to change when, looking out the window herself, Lisa begins to agree with his theories. She goes into the courtyard, and later into Thorwald's apartment, becoming an object of Jeff's surveilling gaze. However, this is more a gaze of care and protection than desire and control (more on this below).

In the end, the film seems to recuperate Jeffries. Thelma says that everyone should go outside and take a look at their own house once in a while. Thelma and Lisa do this. They go out into the courtyard and look back at Jeffries (though we do not see him, in his window, from their point of view). And Jeffries is finally forced out of his apartment. His voyeuristic viewing position is disrupted first by Lisa, who reinterprets his readings of his neighbors with her own surveillance and insight, challenging his interpretations of them and their actions (empathizing with Miss Torso, for example). Jeffries's position is also disrupted by Thorwald, who throws him out the window.[13] In the final scene, Jeffries is asleep and smiling, with two broken legs in casts but facing away from the window. And Lisa is there, reading a book about travel and adventure, and keeping an eye on him. Jeffries's actions are not corrected, however. He is not essentially transformed by the events of the film. The excitement and action have satisfied his itch, his frustrated desire has found an outlet, and he is satisfied; however, he still has not really met his neighbors. His voyeurism is justified by uncovering the murder. He seems to have transformed Lisa, a bit, perhaps, but she seems to have achieved what she wanted as well (both Jeff and fashion).

Besides Jeffries's activities, there are other forms of surveillance in the film. Lisa, for example, recognizes the power of being the object of the gaze, as a model. In the film she does her best to get Jeff's attention, to get him to look at her and her fashions. She later becomes an active player in his investigations, joining him in his surveillance.[14] There are other mentions of everyday surveillance. For example, the opening shot of the film includes a helicopter hovering over the apartment building opposite, the men in it ogling the women sunbathing on the roof. And mention is made of the apartment superintendent's watchful gaze, knowing what goes on in each apartment. But, significantly, we also see the role of police surveillance. Jeffries calls in the assistance of Detective Lieutenant Doyle (Wendall Corey), a war buddy of Jeffries who does some investigating based on Jeff's suspicions. As an aside, Doyle and Jeffries served on a reconnaissance plane in the war, another form of surveillance.[15] Doyle's character emphasizes the legal limits on surveillance. Legal surveillance, both in terms of the information Doyle is able to provide—countering Jeff's theories of murder—and in its inability to act without probable cause, frustrates Jeffries's desire, forcing him to turn to extra-legal methods (vigilantism), and inspiring Lisa to break into Thorwald's apartment. Jeffries and Lisa are ultimately justified in breaking the law by uncovering the murder. However, consider how guilty and unethical their actions would be considered if Thorwald had ended up being innocent. The ends justify the means.[16]

Rear Window presents us with a solitary voyeur, with whom we are meant to identify, driven by frustrated desire to voyeurism that is sexual, at first, and then obsessively investigatory, even resorting to extra-legal methods in pursuit of the knowledge he was so certain of, knowledge provided by his surveillance. He is a professional voyeur who prefers to act alone but is immobilized. In many ways, Lisa and Stella actively take on (and over) his investigations.[17] The film raises a number of aspects of surveillance from the casual surveillance of neighbors to the professional surveillance of the police and, to an extent, the building superintendent.

Peeping Tom

Let us compare the representations of the voyeur in *Rear Window* with another film, similar in some ways but radically different in others: Michael Powell's controversial *Peeping Tom* (1960). They are similar in that they both focus on individual voyeurs, professional photographers each, and both films use psychoanalysis as a means of explaining the voyeurism. Both comment on the ways that cinema itself is voyeuristic: *Rear Window* by presenting the view out of Jeffries's window as a cinema screen and suturing us into his viewing position, and *Peeping Tom* by its focus on cameras, photography, and filming throughout the film as it follows Mark (Carl Boehm) at his work at a film studio, as a freelance photographer, and in his extracurricular activities. And both speak to the social context of the 1950s, though in very different ways. But beyond these features, they are quite different films, most obviously in that in *Rear Window* Jeffries uses his voyeurism to solve crimes, while in *Peeping Tom* Mark uses his voyeurism to commit them.

To call *Peeping Tom* controversial is an understatement. When it was first released in 1960, critics at a preview screening were so shocked by the film, and so vitriolic in their reviews, that the film received only a limited distribution before disappearing for decades. The event marked the end of director Michael Powell's distinguished career. Powell, and screenwriter Leo Marks, wanted to make a film about Freud, but given that another film on the psychoanalyst was in the works decided to write one instead on Freudian themes.[18] The film is about Mark, a voyeur with a film camera who, rather than watching and filming at a distance, has rebuilt his camera to kill the women he is filming. He then watches the films of his kills. The film *Peeping Tom* is commenting forcefully on the violence implicit in voyeurism as well as the violence implicit in the camera itself.

This is a film about voyeurism that makes us aware of our own voyeurism. Denzin calls this type of film "reflexive cinema" and we will return to this theme in Chapter 5.[19] Classical Hollywood film utilizes what has been called the historic mode of narration.[20] The audience should be unaware of the camera filming and the film is edited so as not to remind us of the conditions of its production, especially the camera itself, so we can lose ourselves in a film. Despite its opening parallel of the window to a cinema screen, never in *Rear Window* are we made aware that we are watching a film and we are not aware of the camera itself. But in *Peeping Tom*, we are made aware of the filming camera from time to time. As Jeremy Hawthorn has pointed out, there is a theme of double observation in the film, of watching watching.[21] We see through the point of view of Mark's camera, at times losing focus, and we watch Mark watch a film, or watch someone watching another, making us aware of our own role as a spectator. There are various types of surveillance depicted in *Peeping Tom*, beyond Mark and his camera. The family house that Mark still lives in has been broken up into apartments, with Mark as the landlord. However, the house has been wired for sound, allowing Mark to hear what is going on in any room. In addition, Helen's mother is blind, which has sharpened her hearing, making her acutely aware of movements and activities in the rooms around her.

Peeping Tom is an exploration not just of the fruits of voyeurism (violence against women) but its roots as well. It examines Mark's childhood and the trauma that caused his perversion. Mark's father, a psychologist, filmed Mark incessantly, using Mark as a research subject on the topic of fear. He would terrify his son and film his reactions (and write up and publish the results, to great acclaim). Mark, given his first film camera by his father, follows in his father's footsteps, creating a documentary to capture the ultimate fear—that of impending death as well as the moment of death itself. Most terrifying though isn't the impending death, but that Mark has attached a mirror to his camera so that his victims watch themselves as they are killed (the ultimate mirror stage: they can only see themselves being killed and not their murderer; they then misrecognize the murderer as themselves). In

Figure 1.3 The view from murderer Mark's camera. *Peeping Tom.*

the flashbacks throughout the film (scenes from his father's home movies), Mark's father is played by the director himself, Michael Powell, and young Mark is played by Powell's own son. The film director is the father who terrorizes with his camera. Cinema itself is a voyeuristic psychological experiment to manipulate the audience, turning us all into voyeurs watching distorted reflections of ourselves as if they were spectacles of an other.

What horrified critics at the time wasn't just its subject matter of terror, murder, and sexuality (including the first brief nude scene in a mainstream British film), and not just the fact that the film sutures us into the uncomfortable position of the voyeur and murderer (we watch the crimes from the perspective of the murderous camera), but that the film portrays Mark somewhat sympathetically, as a shy, almost innocent boy who had been abused and is living with the consequences. He is aware of his condition and even seeks out a colleague of his father's to talk about a cure for scopophilia. One might argue that Mark is portrayed with more sympathy than his victims. Partly this is because of the role of Helen (Anna Massey), one of the tenants in Mark's house, who wants to get to know the reclusive Mark and be his friend. Her response to the discovery of the films of Mark's childhood is more intellectual than emotional. She does not react in fear or horror or as a victim or potential victim. "Explain this to me," she says. "I want to understand what I am shown." Intellectual approaches to matters of affect, like fear, are at the root of the issue, however, given Mark's father's rational, distant study of fear. But, on the other hand, Helen shows empathy that Mark's father does not. Helen becomes an entry point into the film's investigation of male voyeurism and violence. She wishes to understand him. But the film also points out that it is not just Mark who is the issue (an isolated monster) but a whole society that victimizes women via the male gaze

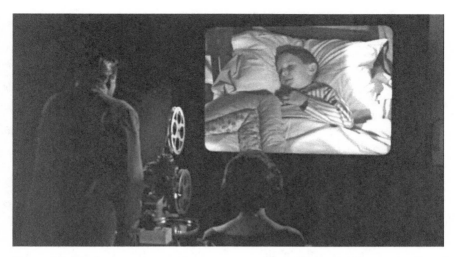

Figure 1.4 Watching people watching someone watching: Mark and Helen watch a film of Mark as a child being watched by his father. *Peeping Tom.*

and male violence: film actresses are abused by directors, abused women pose for nude photos, and members of the establishment support industries of pornography and prostitution.

Jeremy Hawthorn writes:

> It would be bizarre to categorize *Peeping Tom* as a feminist film, and yet it makes available insights central to that second wave of feminism that was to flourish at the end of the decade in which it was first shown. Before the arguments of second-wave feminists gained currency, the idea that prostitution, pornography, or even the work of the glamorous female film star were linked both symbolically and directly to structures of violence in society seemed absurd. And yet such a link is to be found clearly delineated in *Peeping Tom*.[22]

In addition, Tania Modleski argues that a similar critique of the theme of male violence against women can be found in *Rear Window*.

> Lisa's increasing absorption in Jeff's story, her fascination with his murderous misogynist tale, is accompanied by a corresponding discovery of women's victimization at the hands of men. At one point in the film, Lisa can be seen staring even more intently than Jeff: that is, when Miss Lonelyhearts picks up a young man at a bar and brings him home, only to be assaulted by him.[23]

Not only is Miss Lonelyhearts assaulted and Thorwald's wife murdered, Miss Torso is almost constantly harassed by men, and Lisa herself is assaulted by Thorwald.

Care and control

As we see from both *Rear Window* and *Peeping Tom*, the represented motivations for voyeurism vary, as do the consequences. This goes to a matter at the heart of surveillance studies. As David Lyon has put it, surveillance is a relationship.[24] It is a connection between watcher and watched. This relationship is one of power: the power to see, to know, to be seen, to be known, to be in control. Establishing surveillance says something about a relationship and can transform it. Surveillance often connotes a lack of trust. For example, what does the proliferation of means of tracking and monitoring children and adolescents say about the state of contemporary family relationships? When surveillance is established in a workplace how does that change the relationship between management and staff? How is this related to increased stress and tension? I know from experience that when surveillance technologies are implemented, employees feel untrusted, unvalued, and reciprocally have less loyalty to the company. The question when looking at surveillance relationships is the quality and nature of the relationship. Does it involve trust, love, fear, suspicion, hostility, or something else? Lyon states that surveillance relationships range on "a continuum from care to control."[25] Surveillance could be about protecting the other, making sure that they come to no harm. Or surveillance could be about control of the other, protecting oneself from the other or attempting to dominate the other. Often, it's complicated and feature films become sites for working out these dynamics.[26] We saw these dynamics play out in the examples discussed in the Introduction: *Wings of Desire* and *The End of Violence*.

Mark in *Peeping Tom* is clearly on one end of the continuum: he wishes to produce fear and death through his surveillant activities. Jeffries in *Rear Window* exhibits a number of relationships. When he watches Lisa cross the courtyard into Thorvald's apartment, he watches out of care and concern. When he watches Thorvald, he wants to know him and his activities to uncover the truth, to control his actions so that he cannot get away or commit another murder. As to Jefferies's watching of Miss Torso and the other "bathing beauties" in his courtyard it is not out of care and not out of an explicit intention to control or do harm, but by objectifying them and intruding on their solitude (even in a public space) there is harm nevertheless. A key point here for *Rear Window* is that Jeffries's lack of relationship with his neighbors enables his voyeurism. If he had met them, gotten to know them, would he be as comfortable watching from the shadows, or so casually intruding into their everyday lives?

Blowup

Control is evident in both *Rear Window* and *Peeping Tom* in another significant way: their surveillance is in part justified by their profession as photographer. Photography, Susan Sontag has convincingly argued, is about control.[27] Taking a picture is an act of claiming what is seen as one's own and transforming it. Photography, she states, is an act of violence. Photography is a way of managing the environment (framing it in certain ways, focusing only on particular aspects, reducing the world into an image ...). The camera, by intervening between the photographer and the subject, allows the photographer to detach, to be less involved, to become simply an eye, to be left alone (just as the voyeur wishes to watch and be left alone). Culturally, photographers are often given tremendous scope to intervene in others' affairs, to rearrange people, to take their images for their own purposes. Observing from a detached distance is part of a day's work, almost habit, for the professional photographer and filmmaker. We see this as well in another film of the era, Michelangelo Antonioni's *Blowup* (1966). In *Blowup* we see how Thomas, a professional photographer, played by David Hemmings, appropriates images of the working class for his own career; we see his sexually aggressive use of his camera as he photographs models; and we see a general air of empowerment, entitlement, and control. When a mysterious woman desperately wants some photographs he took of her in a park, he begins to investigate the images, blowing them up to examine the minutest of details, and seems to uncover a murder. This film, however, unseats its protagonist and undermines his confidence in what he is seeing. He goes to the park, but the body is gone. His photographs are stolen. The very last scene in the film begins with a point of view shot (which we presume to be Thomas's) looking up into a tree, but as the camera swings down we see the protagonist in front of us. We are unsure who the camera now represents. In the background, a tennis game is being mimed by students without rackets or a ball, yet we hear the sound of the game, the thwack of the racket. To photograph is to capture reality in order to understand it, to freeze it so that one may blow it up, examine it minutely.[28] *Blowup* questions this impulse, the modernist certainty that reality can be studied. Images beget images beget images. And understanding, once so sure (a figure in the bushes with a gun! A body!), slips away.

Arguably, most surveillance films featuring the solitary voyeur emphasize the control end of the spectrum of relationships. Culturally, surveillance has been articulated to aspects of control. For example, a classic surveillance study by Clive Norris and Gary Armstrong of a CCTV operation in the UK showed that while publicly CCTV was touted as promoting safety, in particular the safety of women in downtown shopping districts, there were very few instances of CCTV operators watching individuals out of a sense of care.[29] Indeed, women were more likely to be targeted voyeuristically by the (predominantly male) operators.

Gigante

Notable is a film that plays with gendered stereotypes of the stalker voyeur. This is the Uruguayan film *Gigante* (2009). *Gigante* is about Jara (Horacio Camandule), a 30-something, introverted quiet giant of a man. His size and strength make him a threatening-looking figure. He works as an overnight security guard at a supermarket and occasionally as a bouncer at a club. His job as a guard is to watch surveillance monitors, which he does passively (as he passively watches most of his life go by). The most animated he gets is playing videogames with his young nephew. We get the sense that under this threatening frame is a kind-hearted kid. While he watches his bank of surveillance monitors, he does not participate in the voyeurism of his co-workers (all men, who use the cameras to ogle the women in the store and speak about how "hot" someone they are watching is). But Jara just watches and notices. When one of the cleaning staff is stealing, if it is minor he will let it go, but if it is expensive he will venture down to the floor to have a quiet word of warning. Not fully care and not fully control, Jara's surveillant gaze occupies a middle ground.

One night he spots Julia (Leonor Svarcas) and begins watching her, though not in the leering ways of his comrades. For example, he will rewind a tape just to watch her walk around a corner. He begins to follow her on the street, but seems unable to approach her to speak to her. The key tension in the film is not knowing whether the film will follow the conventions of the voyeur stalker so generically evident, with his sexual frustration turning to violence. The film relies on the audience's knowledge of these stereotypes and the standard plots of the average thriller. He is large and threatening; he is watching and following her without her knowledge; and he does have a violent streak: he beats up a cabby who propositions Julia and also causes a scene at work, going berserk, trashing part of the store, and attacking a manager. The film does not let up on this tension (between his shy playfulness and his violence) as, like the director puts it in his DVD liner note, the film "walks the boundary between falling in love and obsession." In that Jara seems to have difficulty expressing himself verbally, but only through violence, we as an audience are concerned what will happen if he finally decides to meet Julia face-to-face.

It is the CCTV camera that proves the solution, just as it was the CCTV cameras that brought Julia to Jara's notice. Once, when Jara is following Julia, he ducks into the entranceway to a store to avoid notice while she shops at a market stall, only to discover that his face is being displayed on a bank of TV screens for sale in the

Figure 1.5 Jara caught on CCTV by Julia. *Gigante.*

shop window, negating his attempt to hide. Julia, however, appears not to notice him. Toward the end of the film, Jara is hiding in the back of a store while Julia buys something up front. He is unaware that he is, again, on CCTV and that the monitor is up at the register where Julia is. He notices the camera at last and looks at it in surprise. Julia, at the counter, watches his reaction on the monitor and smiles. This may be the first time she has actually seen him (it is, in any case, the first time the film shows us her watching him). And, as his first glimpse of her was on a monitor, so is her first glimpse of him. Her smile, I think, emboldens him to approach her, which he has been trying to steel himself to do. The film in many ways is about overcoming the distance between images and reality, especially in a culture dominated by screens. As the audience tries to figure out who Jara really is based on his image and the tropes of popular film, Jara himself has his own image of Julia, and tries to piece together who she is from a distance (often making incorrect assumptions about her, like when following her into a theater that is showing two films, he looks for her first in the auditorium showing the romance, when she is next door watching the horror film). Characters at a distance are images, especially when mediated by screens like CCTV, and onto these screens the audience projects fears and hopes. The surveillant images are like blind dates. At one point in the film Jara has a drink with a man who just had such a blind date with Julia, who says that he won't see her again because "you build up unrealistic expectations of the other."

Red Road

Red Road (2007) presents us with scenes of surveillance as care, but then shows how quickly the technology, and the surveillant gaze, turns to control. An independent film written and directed by British filmmaker Andrea Arnold, *Red Road* follows the work of Jackie (Kate Dickie), a single woman who works as a CCTV operator in Glasgow. Sitting in front of a large bank of CCTV screens she watches pedestrians go by. Her gaze is one of care—she is watching over the population to keep them from harm. For example, she spots a woman walking hurriedly down the street looking worried, and follows her with the cameras until she is safe. In another case, she spies a young woman crying in an alley and calls the police in to assist her. Jackie seems to know these streets, and gets to know some of these people. For example, there is a man she often sees walking an elderly bulldog, which seems quite ill. When she is off of work, she sees the man and the dog on the street. The man is looking at ads in a shop window. Jackie stands next to him, reading the ads as well. She has seen him do this on camera, but is unable to make out what he is reading. On the street, next to the man, she has crossed from one side of the screen to the other, but still cannot bring herself to talk to him or even pet the dog. Later, on camera, she spots the man carrying the dog wrapped in a towel, to a car. She seems to share his sadness at the dog's death. Jackie is not a neutral watcher. We see her emotionally react to what she sees. She worries for the woman in the white jacket, is amused at the late night office cleaner dancing and singing as she works, and has a caring smile for the man and his dog.

Figure 1.6 Jackie watching. *Red Road*.

But Jackie's surveillant gaze is not simply one of care; we also see her tempted by voyeurism. After calling the police to protect the crying woman, she spots another woman running away, being followed by a man. She begins to call the situation in to the dispatcher, but stops and cancels when soon it becomes clear that this is a consensual tryst behind a garage. However, she does not pan away from their lovemaking but hesitates, glancing guiltily over her shoulder to see if anyone else in the control room is watching her, or watching her watching. She watches, her breathing heavier. Her guilty glance confirms that she is breaking the rules. There is a close-up of her hand resting on, almost caressing, the control knob. This is surveillance for desire: voyeurism (even Wim Wenders's surveillant angels felt desire). The shot of her hand on the control knob emphasizes the haptic aspect of CCTV cameras.[30] They are not simply disembodied views, but controlled and active: one moves a knob or joystick and manipulates the view. Surveillance is embodied, that is, it involves action, motion, and physical participation.[31] As embodied, surveillance also entails bodily reaction, affect, desire, and an orientation of one's body with regards to the surveilled other.

Jackie up until this point has been quiet and relatively subdued, if not sad. Her own affair with another officer seems to be more of convenience than passion. In this scene in the control room, we see a hint of her desire. This revelation of desire at this moment is important for the film because it is at this point that she recognizes, with shock, the man behind the garage and frantically tries following him with the cameras, but loses him in the darkness. The man with red hair seems to turn into a red fox she sees darting furtively away. This is the turning point of the film, and the impetus of the plot, as Jackie obsessively pursues the man on camera, taking surveillance tapes home for review (also breaking the rules), and asking other officers to keep an eye on him for her. She becomes so single minded in her pursuit of him, bending the surveillance apparatus to her will, that she neglects her duty of care and almost misses the stabbing of a young girl (which, it is implied, she could have prevented had she been paying proper attention).

Jackie becomes an obsessed stalker, not only watching but integrating herself into this man's, Clyde's (Tony Curran), life and using the city's surveillance system to not only watch him but ultimately to frame him for a crime. Surveillance at this point is clearly that of control. She has crossed an ethical line in this need for personal revenge. But as Jessica Lake has argued, Jackie has crossed from the optic space of CCTV surveillance to the haptic space of interpersonal surveillance. "[S]urveillance is represented as an excruciatingly intimate and subjective act driven by individual voyeuristic desire."[32] We see that same movement, the crossing of the female voyeur from detached observation to physically engaged surveillant interaction, in the narrative arc of the first season of *Homeland* (2011) as well where Carrie (Claire Danes) goes from obsessively watching the surveillance cameras she has had implanted in the home of Nicholas Brody (Damian Lewis), whom she suspects is a terrorist, to meeting him and starting a relationship. In the end, in *Red Road*, Jackie is able to forgive Clyde and drop the charges against him. But can we, the audience, so easily forgive Jackie her ethical abuses of power and use of the surveillance system to punish Clyde? And what are the implications regarding our own ethics of surveillance if we do?[33]

Consider the ethical question played out in Krzysztof Kieslowski's acclaimed film *Red* (1994; part of his Three Colors trilogy of films). In that film, a young model, Valentine (Irene Jacob), meets a retired judge (Jean-Louis Trintignant) whose hobby is to sit in his house on a hill listening to the phone conversations of his neighbors. He has equipment to intercept the cordless phones' transmissions. She cannot sit by passively and listen to a married man arrange an affair, or a drug dealer plan his business. Valentine goes down the hill (crossing from the surveillant site, above the neighbors into the embodied everyday) to inform the wife of her husband's infidelity, but once there she spies his children listening in on his conversation and giggling. She questions her own desire to intervene, and retreats.

We can't ignore the fact that *Red Road* is one of the few contemporary films with a female voyeur, and also one of the few films with surveillance as a form of care. But at the same time, we can't essentialize Jackie as "Big Mother" when she becomes a vengeful "Big Brother" as well. But perhaps the film hints at the articulation of gender to particular performances of surveillance (if more women were controlling CCTV cameras ...), but that articulation is not necessary or inherent. The turn from routine surveillance and even caring surveillance to obsessive voyeurism is not solely the domain of male voyeurs[34] though it is inflected quite differently when it is a woman doing the spying.

Fatal Attraction and *Black Widow*

Norman Denzin, for example, uses the films *Fatal Attraction* and *Black Widow* (both films released in 1987) to discuss the complexities of women as voyeurs.[35] In *Fatal*

Attraction, Glenn Close plays Alex Forrest, a single professional woman, who meets Dan Gallagher (Michael Douglas), a happy family man. She seduces Dan, though he willingly assents, and they spend a weekend together. Dan wishes to return to his family but Alex is obsessed with him and doesn't want to let him go. She stalks him and harasses him, forcing him to start spying on her as a threat to him and his family. As Denzin points out, while the film emphasizes the victimization of Dan, Alex was also victimized by being spurned by the man she loves and who has impregnated her and abandoned her. "Refusing to keep her place in society, Alex, the pregnant SWW [Single White Woman], must be given a gaze that moves from casual, sexual lust, to visual and vocal harassment, to murderous rage. Alex's gaze will move along each of these dimensions, as it is progressively coded as insane and out of control."[36] The figure of Alex was seen as anti-feminist, as part of the emerging backlash against feminism in the 1980s:[37] the liberated, independent, unmarried woman as psychopath. In *Black Widow*, Debra Winger plays Alex Barnes, a federal investigator who notices a suspicious pattern of deaths and draws the conclusion that Catharine (Theresa Russell) is a serial murderer, though her suspicions are dismissed by other law enforcement agencies. She becomes obsessed with the case and continues her investigations on her own, without the authority of the law. On the one hand, Alex's spying on Catharine is routine surveillance, but then she begins integrating herself into Catharine's new life in Hawaii and Alex's gaze becomes one of narcissism as well. Portrayed as tomboyish and plain, she wishes to be the impossibly beautiful seductress. She both voyeuristically desires Catharine and narcissistically wants to be Catharine.

> What started out as an investigation of Catharine's multiple looks in her many marriages has suddenly turned into a narcissistic experience. Alex has become the object of her own gaze, and the subjectivity she perceives in the gaze is lack, emptiness. Catharine is full woman, Alex, empty woman.[38]

For both films, voyeurism becomes a violent confrontation between women who are both gazing and gazed at. "[C]onfrontation with the other produces self-awareness and fuels self-desire," writes Denzin.[39]

I've Heard the Mermaids Singing

Released the same year as *Black Widow* and *Fatal Attraction* was Patricia Rozema's *I've Heard the Mermaids Singing* (1987), an independent Canadian film that also places women on both sides of the keyhole. In that film, we follow Polly (Sheila McCarthy), an awkward and somewhat lonely young woman who lives with her cat. Her hobby is taking and developing photographs of the city and the people she meets. Unlike Jeffries in *Rear Window* and Mark in *Peeping Tom*, she is not a professional photographer, and yet she shares with them the photographer's privilege and control: reframing the city to meet her interests, rearranging and posing the people she meets on the street for her photographs. In one scene, she follows a pair of young lovers into the woods, hiding in the bushes as they begin to make love. Though on the surface meek and mild, her photography allows her the possibility of agency and even aggression (and she has one key aggressive act at the climax of the film). Polly gets a job as a receptionist and secretary at a small art museum where she soon falls in love with the intelligent and articulate curator, Gabrielle (Paule Baillargeon). The film still splits the look, in Mulvey's sense, but not along gender lines. Gabrielle becomes the object of desire and Polly the subject of action and identification. When a closed circuit TV camera is installed in the gallery, from her desk, eating crackers, Polly can discretely observe the curator meeting with art critics and even watches the curator kissing a former girlfriend, Mary Joseph (Ann-Marie MacDonald). But unlike the other films we have been discussing, Polly does not turn to reckless obsession or revenge. She turns to depression and alcohol, and then turns to confession. She steals the camera from the CCTV system, points it at herself, and confesses all that has happened—essentially she narrates the film we've just seen. She feels guilty about how she lashed out at the curator and makes herself the subject of the video surveillant gaze. Like Jackie in *Red Road*, Polly is self-conscious about her voyeurism via the video, and nervous about watching, perhaps realizing that an ethical line has been crossed by viewing the curator in personal conversations and situations. She seems blissfully unaware, however, of crossing ethical lines watching people in public with her still camera.

We do see a similar hesitation at that ethical line that we see with Jeffries in *Rear Window* who weighs carefully each decision to escalate the intentionality and intrusiveness of his voyeurism by first turning to binoculars and then to his telephoto lens. And even Jake Scully (Craig Wasson), the voyeur in Brian DePalma's *Body Double* (1984), hesitates at the telescope when he realizes the intimate scene he is viewing, before plunging in to watch more and more.

These films are nearly technologically deterministic in their insistence that surveillance equipment leads inevitably to voyeurism. However, this is not necessarily the case and must be seen as part of the particular construction of a surveillant imaginary. As a counterexample, consider a scene from Fritz Lang's last film, *The 1,000 Eyes of Dr. Mabuse* (1960). In that film, centered around a hotel riddled with CCTV cameras, the hotel detective (Andrea Checchi) shows the protagonist, Peter van Eyck (Henry B. Travers), a two-way mirror installed in one room so that they can watch the guests within. The detective grins conspiratorially at van Eyck inviting him to watch the woman on the other side of the glass. Van Eyck returns his look with disdain and turns away.

Care and control are not mutually exclusive. Surveillance seen as a relationship can be infused with desire or fear, the surveillor may wish to be with the subject they oversee or they may wish to be the subject they oversee. The lens of the camera, the cold hard glass of the screen, the distance between bodies can become mirrors as well as windows. We can talk of the surveillance of the powerful over the powerless, the sousveillance of the powerless over the powerful, or the sub-veillance of the marginalized whose seizure of the apparatus of power troubles the accepted boundaries and tropes of that power.[40] Gender, race, class, and sexuality inflect the voyeur's gaze.

Context

Most films point to the desire to surveil, or to surveil excessively, as an individual psychological issue. But, as scholars have argued, that psychopathology can be as much of an expression of social and cultural context as individual malady. One the one hand, we can read this as meaning that the times shape the films, which is an obvious point. Technologies, urban conditions, social mores, gender and sexual relations (as well as class, race, and sexuality) all play out in the question of if, when, and how to surveil, who is surveilling, and who is surveilled. But on the other hand, and more specifically, the motivation and desire (and/or significant disinhibition) to surveil might be prompted by social conditions and not just an individual's pathology. For example, both Catherine Zimmer and Robert Corber (whom Zimmer follows) place *Rear Window* in the context of 1950s McCarthyism, which encouraged government and popular surveillance of communists, homosexuals, and others.[41] Jeffries, by spying so readily on his neighbors, is keeping with an ever more common practice. Bradley Clissold points to the functions of the television show *Candid Camera*, in the same time period (originally a radio program, *Candid Microphone*), as a way of getting the US public used to the thought that they were potentially under surveillance. Even when they least expected it, the cameras could be there, but it's OK and fun to be on candid camera.[42] Corber argues that such government surveillance was evidence of its own psychopathology, of which Jeff's is but one instance. These surveillance psychopathologies have significant political aspects, therefore. Corber argues that by pathologizing Jeffries's surveillance the film is pathologizing (and therefore critiquing) the culture of surveillance of post-war America.

Disturbia

Compare, for example, *Rear Window* with *Disturbia*, a 2007 remake/update/ versioning of *Rear Window* in a post-9/11 sociotechnical context. Each film is grounded in the culture of surveillance of its time, in different social configurations and conjunctures. Whereas *Rear Window* gave us the arrested adolescence of Jeffries, *Disturbia* gives us an arrested adolescent. Kale (Shia LaBeouf) is a teenager under house arrest for assaulting a teacher at school. The house arrest is effected by an electronic ankle bracelet that alerts the police if Kale moves more than a certain distance from a transmitting base station in the house. Kale at first indulges in videogames and cheesy reality TV programming until his mother cuts him off from these electronic forms of entertainment. Bored, he begins watching the neighbors in the suburban houses surrounding his own, especially the teenage girl, Ashley (Sarah Roemer), who has just moved in next door. Like Jeffries, Kale begins to know the routines and stories of his neighbors. He and his best friend Ronnie (Aaron Yoo) spend most of their time as voyeurs watching Ashley swim, exercise, and change. Ashley is similar to the Miss Torso role in *Rear Window*, but then takes on the Lisa role as she befriends Kale. Ronnie becomes a version of Stella, his confidante who is allowed to critique Kale's surveillance practices as well as join them ("Is that in a stalker's handbook somewhere?" Ronnie asks, labeling Kale's activities for what they are). However, Kale's attention is soon drawn to another neighbor, the relatively quiet, nondescript Mr. Turner (David Morse), whom he begins to suspect is a serial killer. Kale, Ronnie, and soon Ashley begin a stakeout, watching Turner's house with binoculars and with videocameras linked to their computers.

In a provocative essay, the collective called The Institute for Precarious Consciousness has argued that "[e]ach phase of capitalism has a particular affect which holds it together."[43] In the nineteenth and early twentieth century, the dominant affect was misery, the misery of the working class laboring in the factories. In the mid-twentieth century the dominant affect became boredom, the effect of the post-WWII rise in productivity, consumption, and wealth. Boredom is the underlying affective state of Jeffries in *Rear Window* and it is what instigates his surveillance of his neighbors. Today, they argue, boredom is giving way to anxiety as the dominant affect. And while Kale is certainly bored, and turns to surveilling his neighbors because of this, there is an undertone of anxiety, anxiety brought about in part, the essay argues, by "the multi-faceted omnipresent web of surveillance." Kale is, remember, himself under surveillance and limited in his actions. While Jeffries was under the surveillance of the nurse Stella, Kale is under the surveillance of the police, threatened with jail. Surveillance of many different types pervades the everyday of the film (from the reality TV Kale watches to the cell phone cameras they use to track Turner). As Turner warns Ashley at one point, "The world is in a heightened state of paranoia.... You're not the only one who's watching." Politically this is the post-9/11 era of "if you see something, say something," the affective regime of paranoia and surveillance.[44] A notable change from *Rear Window* makes this point. In *Rear Window*, the crime that Thorwald committed was essentially a crime of passion, but one that was meticulously and methodically covered up. In *Disturbia*, Turner is a serial killer. Film scholar William Luhr has pointed out a cultural obsession with serial killers over the past few decades (from Hannibal in *Silence of the Lambs* through the television procedurals *Criminal Minds* and *Dexter*).[45] The figure of the serial killer is "profoundly representative of deep forces underlying and driving our culture," Luhr writes.[46] "Where serial killers were once depicted as simply psychotic, they have recently been given the status of mirror images of society itself, apparently 'normal' while enacting a grand scheme of destruction."[47] The figure of the serial killer is one who is unrelenting, efficient, and completely amoral, but someone who, like Turner, seems completely normal. In an era of heightened paranoia, the figure of the serial killer living next door is yet another reason to trust no one and watch everyone, especially if someone is protecting their privacy. Kale's surveillance is therefore far from aberrant, but an extension of the psychopathology of post-9/11 United States.[48]

La Mirada Invisible

Compare, in a different political context, the 2010 Argentinian film *La Mirada Invisible* (The Invisible Eye). Set in 1982, in the last years of the brutal military regime notorious for the murder of tens of thousands of dissidents (los desaparecidos), the film takes place in an elite private school, a bastion of authoritarian rule (while outside on the street, protests against the regime can be heard). The film, directed by Diego Lerman, focuses on a young, lonely, sexually repressed teacher Maria Teresa (Julieta Zylberberg) and her obsession with a male student, just a few years her junior. We see in this film how the structures of the authoritarian regime empower her. The state (in the form of the headmaster) gives Maria Teresa permission to surveil the students as the only way of maintaining discipline: constant surveillance and total information, "the invisible eye," he says. The school itself is structured on meticulous discipline: clear hierarchies, everyone has their place in line or in the classroom (seemingly down to the inch), continuous observation, and the smallest of infractions is punished. This is the model of discipline Michel Foucault explored which we will discuss further in the next chapter. Empowered by the authoritarian structure (via the excuse that some of the boys may have been smoking), Maria Teresa watches and reports. But she also indulges in her obsession with one student in the guise of the investigation by entering the boys' restroom and later hiding in a stall. This is ostensibly to catch boys smoking, but she soon discovers a sexual thrill of listening to them. Despite prolonged surveillance in the restroom, at most she apprehends two boys with a contraband magazine. Seemingly shocked by her moral transgressions, once he discovers them, the headmaster then attempts to sexually assault her but she fights him off. The individual pathology of sexual repression that leads to moral transgression and voyeurism is closely entwined with the state pathology of discipline, surveillance, and its own amorality and violence, but in presenting this via the figure of the female voyeur the patriarchal authority is undermined at the level of the gaze. Maria Theresa doesn't want to be the accepted image of a desirable female (her mother persuades her to get dressed up and do her hair to go to a party, but she is profoundly uncomfortable). If anything, she desires to be invisible and yet have authority. The film often shoots Maria in lingering close-up, not as an object of desire but as narcissistic identification, as a subject who moves events forward. She is not seeing, but listening; we don't share her gaze, but her experience of hearing, which is played out across her face. The film asks us to identify with someone who wants to be invisible, which troubles the process of identification.

La Mirada Invisible, made twenty years after the events portrayed, is an instance of a society trying to come to terms with its authoritarian history and the complicity of some of its citizens. But it does so through a familiar trope that codes female voyeurism "in obsessive, neurotic terms."[49] But, like Jackie in *Red Road* (and Carrie in *Homeland*), her voyeurism is not only visual but haptic, embodied ("multi-perspectival, or multi-sensual").[50] And like the examples of *Fatal Attraction* and *Black Widow*, "when given the power to look, the female voyeur unleashes a gaze which disrupts the social order, erasing the boundaries between male and female, law and order, investigator, criminal, and victim."[51]

Transformation

The first central theme of surveillance films is the figure of the lone voyeur—they are primarily, though not exclusively, male. They tend to be loners living dreary lives. And they often exhibit a psychopathology (perhaps caused by some trauma in their lives and perhaps enabled by a cultural or social context).[52] But an interesting subtheme develops in a handful of these films and this has to do with the redemption of some of these figures *through* surveillance. For many, their transgression is such that no redemption is possible and none is offered. They are punished or killed for their voyeurism. And this is true of Mark in *Peeping Tom*, the criminals in slasher films (who often pop back up, alive and unredeemed, in sequels), and even Seymour Parrish in *One Hour Photo* (arrested and jailed). But consider Jeffries in *Rear Window*. There is some debate about the ending and whether he is a changed man, correcting the error of his ways. Granted, he now has two broken legs, rather than just one, but he is seen facing away from the window, asleep, with a smile on his face, while Lisa watches over him reading a book about far-off adventure (switching to a fashion magazine once she is assured he is asleep). Jeff has scratched his itch. His surveillance has been justified by the successful capture of a murderer, and he can integrate into "normal" society. Earlier in the film, Thelma, his nurse, says that everyone should go outside and take a look at their own house once in a while. Thelma and Lisa do this—they go out into the courtyard and even into Thorvald's apartment and look back at Jeff. But Jeff is finally forced out of his voyeuristic position first by Lisa, who reinterprets his readings of his neighbors with her own surveillance and insight, and, second, by Thorvald who physically throws him out the window. But is Jeff truly recuperated into society? Does he know his neighbors now, for example? Social alienation, at least, has not been addressed.

What is potentially transformative for Jeff is the collapsing of the voyeuristic distance (being forced into the public courtyard; to be finally seen by his neighbors as he dangles from his ledge before falling). And it is this collapsing of distance that allows the voyeur to question their practices and attitudes. If surveillance is a relationship, that relationship affects both observer and observed. It is never about "just looking." At least, this is true of a particular sort of surveillance—personal surveillance. Impersonal, computer-based surveillance is a quite different sort of relationship with much less reciprocity. In this case, the observer is transformed only to the extent that the computer incorporates the information from the observed into its algorithm. But for cases of personal surveillance, we see a theme of transformation, even redemption. For example, Tomek, the peeping tom in Kieslowski's episode 6 of *Dekalog: A Short Film About Love* (1989), announces that he will give up his voyeurism after his failed sexual encounter with the object of his spying and his attempted suicide. In the Mexican film *Sleep Dealer* (2008), Rodulfo Ramirez, Jr. (played by Jacob Vargas), a drone pilot troubled by the thought that he may have killed innocent people, crosses from the United States to Mexico to meet the survivors and make amends. But the two films that really wrestle with this topic are *The Conversation* (1974) and *The Lives of Others* (2006).

The Conversation

Though the idea for *The Conversation* was one Francis Ford Coppola had been working on for some years, it was released at a time of heightened public consciousness about surveillance.[53] In 1971, whistleblowers broke into FBI offices and released files detailing the FBI's COINTELPRO program of surveillance and disruption of political groups from the 1950s through 1971. And the recent Watergate investigations had revealed President Nixon's secret tapes. Five months after the film was released, Nixon resigned.

The Conversation follows the work of private surveillance expert Harry Caul (Gene Hackman) in 1970s San Francisco. Caul is on a case where he has been hired to record a conversation taking place between two people in a crowded public square. He prides himself on his professionalism and technical expertise (and he is seen as a celebrity within the surveillance community for his prowess). The job is a technical challenge for him; he professes not to be interested in who these people are, what their conversation is about, why these people are being recorded, or what the corporate director (Robert Duvall) who hired him is going to do with these tapes. All he wants is a "nice fat recording." But much like *Blowup*, the film seeks to undermine our faith that truth can be found in a photograph (or recording) if we only look closely enough and also undermines the idea that surveillance can leave both surveillor and surveilled unchanged.[54]

Caul is also a bundle of contradictions. He is highly paranoid and a deeply moral Catholic (refusing to let his employees take the Lord's name in vain). Recall that the Catholic faith posits an ever-vigilant God; we are always subject to divine surveillance. Harry's obsession with privacy and focus on the technical side of his job mask feelings of guilt and culpability. He believes that his earlier work led to the horrific deaths of a family. When Harry goes to deliver the completed tapes to the director, he spends an uncomfortable elevator ride with the woman (Cindy Williams) he surveilled. In the director's office, he spies her picture, realizing that she is the director's wife. He insists on only handing the tapes over to the director, who is out, and refuses to leave them with the director's assistant (Harrison Ford). Troubled, he returns to his workshop to re-analyze the tapes in case he missed a crucial part of the conversation and perhaps to understand better what he is dealing with. He then clears up some static and uncovers a crucial phrase which he feels reveals the true meaning of the conversation, and concludes that this young couple is in mortal peril. From this point on, it becomes harder for him to maintain his professional indifference and distance. After Harry's confidence is betrayed to a woman he confides in (she steals his tapes on behalf of the corporation), Harry uses his surveillance skills to try to prevent the murder of these young lovers.

Harry's surveillance awakens his morality and humanity and transforms him from the detached professional he aspires to be to a savior figure (to attempt to save not only the couple, but himself, too), a figure he ultimately fails to be. We will consider the figure of Harry further in the next chapter as he himself becomes subject to surveillance to crippling effect.

The Lives of Others

The most complex, and perhaps most controversial, of the films redeeming the surveillors is the 2006 German film *The Lives of Others*, directed by Florian Henkel von Donnersmark. Set in East Berlin in 1984, the film follows Gerd Wiesler (Ulrich Mühe), a Stasi surveillance expert who is assigned to surveil a prominent playwright, Georg Dreyman (Sebastian Koch). The film is about the transformation of Wiesler from an efficient, relentless officer of the secret police into a "good man" through the process of surveilling Dreyman, his lover, an actress, Christa-Maria Sieland (Martina Gedeck), and their friends. Wiesler ends up falsifying his reports, covering up the fact that Dreyman is writing an article highly critical of the East German government to be smuggled to the West to be published.

The film parallels *The Conversation* in many ways. Both films show the meticulous process of recording and analyzing, with an emphasis on the everyday utility of the equipment and process (cf. Chapter 4, "Procedurals"). Both Wiesler and Harry are loners, leading dreary personal lives, whose only sexual relationships are purchased (a prostitute, in Wiesler's case, a kept woman [played by Teri Garr] in Harry's, as well as Harry's encounter with Meredith [Elizabeth MacRae] who turns out to be a prostitute hired to steal the tapes from him). Visually *The Lives of Others* echoes *The Conversation* in its use of static cameras in Wiesler and Harry's bare apartments, that is, the camera tends to be stationary and lags behind the action (more like a surveillance camera than the smooth movements we associate with modern filmmaking). And there is even a scene in the later film where Dreyman meets his co-conspirators in a public square walking around to avoid being recorded. Both films have their professionals transformed by their activities. *The Lives of Others*, however, is less equivocal in its redemption of its protagonist.

The key question for both films is what stirs their protagonists to act on behalf of their subjects and not just observe. Harry acts on guilt, but is ultimately psychologically paralyzed and unable to act. Wiesler may be acting because he has fallen in love with Christa-Maria. But for both, there is a profound loss of faith. Harry is out-snooped and subject to surveillance that he cannot figure out. He loses faith in his technical abilities, just as his morality trumps his view that the job is just a technical challenge and nothing more. In his desperation to figure out how he himself is being surveilled, he destroys his own apartment, piece by piece. Everything is opened, broken, and searched, even, finally, a statue of the Virgin Mary. His paranoia and fear undermine both his professional identity and his faith.

Wiesler loses faith in the socialist state. He is a true believer in the state and its principles, an instructor teaching young agents their craft. But he is ultimately shaken by his discovery of how party members are abusing their power and their own apparent lack of belief in socialist principles. We see this first as an aside, almost a joke. Anton Grubitz (Ulrich Tukur) is a friend of Wiesler's from school who is now his superior, but who achieved his rank through political machinations rather than intelligence or ability. Wiesler meets Grubitz in the canteen for lunch. As they look for a table, Grubitz points out that there is a special section for managers, but Wiesler quietly sits down with the workers. "Socialism has to start somewhere," he jokes. Central to the plot, there is also Wiesler's discovery that Minister Bruno Hempf (Thomas Thieme), who authorizes Wiesler's surveillance of Dreyman as a possible radical, is forcing Christa-Maria into an affair (threatening her career if she does not). Wiesler's realization that he and his surveillance are being used to control and possibly eliminate the minister's sexual rival, Dreyman, rather than for reasons of political and ideological purity, turns Wiesler against Hempf, alerting Dreyman to Sieland's infidelity and encouraging Sieland to stay with Dreyman.

But this is not the only reason the film provides for Wiesler's turn. The main theme of the film is the idea that art can trump politics. It is said in the film that Lenin once stated that if he kept listening to Beethoven's Appassionata piano sonata the he wouldn't be able to complete the revolution. Art stirs the soul. Dreyman plays a piano piece, Sonata for a Good Man, stating, "If you really hear it, can you be a bad person?" Wiesler is, at that moment, in the attic of the apartment, hearing it through his headset via the microphones that he and his team have installed in Dreyman's flat. He listens in on Dreyman and Sieland's passionate relationship as well (so at odds with his own life's lack of passion). And his soul stirs within him. He not only acts on their behalf, countering Minister Hempf, he also steals a book of Brecht from Dreyman's flat and reads it in his own minimal apartment. And he even goes so far as to write a play, or at least a summary of one. While Dreyman is working on his critical essay on the suicide rate in East Germany, Wiesler has been reporting that Dreyman has been working hard on a new play, so he has to make up the play so as to describe it in his surveillance notes.

This is obviously a romantic theme: human spirit (art, feeling, and morality) will triumph over technology, bureaucracy, and oppression. We can see this theme in other films such as *Brazil, Enemy of the State, The Truman Show, Gattaca*, and even *1984*, which we will consider in the next chapter. Let me briefly touch on *Nineteen Eighty-Four*, since that text is influential.[55] In that novel, and subsequent films, Winston Smith argues that though they may crush his body, they can't get into his head, and they can't snuff out his love for Julia. This freedom and love will defeat Big Brother, he believes. He is tragically wrong. Winston is defeated by O'Brien, the Inner Party operative whom Winston idolizes and who turns into his interrogator. I bring this subject up here because it speaks to the controversy over Wiesler's redemption

Figure 1.7 Wiesler listens to Sonata for a Good Man. *The Lives of Others.*

as a good man. Wiesler is O'Brien—the expert interrogator and surveillance expert, the most loyal member of the party and the most fervent believer in its doctrine. It may not be accidental that *The Lives of Others* is set in 1984 specifically. However, O'Brien would not melt under any work of art. On a human level, the redemption of Wiesler is a beautiful and affecting theme, and makes for an emotionally stirring film. Historically and politically, however, this redemption is problematic.

In many ways, *The Lives of Others* prides itself on its authenticity. They use authentic Stasi equipment in the film, for example. And much is made of the fact that actor Ulrich Mühe, who plays Wiesler, was a prominent actor in East Germany under this regime and was subject to intensive surveillance himself. Members of his own theater company were Stasi informants, as was his first wife. However, the idea of a Stasi operative like Wiesler developing a conscience and acting as he does is pure fantasy. As Anna Funder, author of the book, *Stasiland*, argued, there not only was no historical Wiesler (and the Stasi files are so thorough, we would know), the system was set up to prevent it.[56] There were no independent operations, like Wiesler's, and the surveillance on fellow Stasi officers was routine and extensive. But, she writes, "the more frightening thing is that they didn't want to. The institutional coercion made these men into true believers."[57] So while von Donnersmark's insistence on extending the theme of romantic resistance to oppression to all humanity, even the Stasi, is admirable, it also works to recuperate the Stasi themselves (which plays into the hands of ex-Stasi who are increasingly vocal and "belligerent" about their portrayal). Perhaps in post-unification Germany, as Germans struggle to come to terms with the legacy of East Germany's authoritarian regime, where a significant population still remember being surveilled and informed upon (estimates are that up to 1 in 7 people in that country were Stasi informants of some sort), there is some comfort in thinking that in the system that there was a good man listening in; but perhaps it is a more constructive notion, Funder argues, to acknowledge that there wasn't.[58]

Conclusion: Our map so far:
The watchers and a culture of voyeurism

It has been said that we are a culture of voyeurs and if this is so it is worth exploring how this came to be—how technologies enable a particular form of voyeurism, how culture and society allow, if not encourage, certain types of voyeurism (in part through modeling such activity in popular media), and how political regimes enable and are strengthened by encouraging surveillance. Norman Denzin argued that cinema itself trained us how to watch others in a particular way: to stare, unblinking and unabashed, at others without social opprobrium. We are a cinematic society characterized by a voyeur's gaze. The figure of the voyeur in film, and how that figure is treated, becomes an important component in understanding how we could become a culture of voyeurs. We see key events encouraging and enabling certain forms of surveillance, from post-WWII cold war suspicions of dissidents and non-conformers to post-9/11 paranoia of cultural others; and we see events which cause us to reconsider the extent of the surveillance state (the revelations of COINTELPRO in 1971, the Watergate scandal the following year, and the current continuing revelations from the NSA documents released by Edward Snowden). But these don't explain the turn from surveillance into voyeurism. How is obsession dealt with? We see feature films and other components of popular culture, following on from these events, informing our understanding of them.

For example, apart from the broader political implications of the paranoia and surveillance of *Disturbia* is the cultural normativity of the ease of spying on others. Part of the promotional campaign for *Disturbia* was assisted by Justin.tv.[59] Justin.tv was at that time a new month-old website where its founder, Justin Kan, wore a headmounted webcam and streamed his entire life to the internet every day, all day, which he called lifecasting (the innovation included the ability to livestream while mobile, walking or driving around San Francisco). Justin.tv featured promotional products for the film around Justin's apartment and on the day of the film's release he and his crew placed themselves under "house arrest," like Kale in the film. Justin.tv was a transitional moment between the heyday of live webcams in the late 1990s and early 2000s and the boom of confessional videologs (vlogs) on YouTube. Justin's practices were preceded by over a decade by Steve Mann, who pioneered wearable computers and streamed his own life to the web in the 1990s.[60] A key difference between Mann and Kan and the rest of the webcammers and vloggers was that Mann and Kan usually did not turn the cameras on themselves, but always broadcast whatever, and whoever, was in front of them. In the store following Turner, Ashley sends back to Kale a constant stream of snapshots from her phone, almost a live broadcast. The capabilities to broadcast anything from anywhere, and the everyday presence and use of such technology by youth in the film and in Justin Kan's living room note a technological shift, but more broadly the comfort with their use for entertainment marks a critical moment where such interpersonal surveillance was not just consumed by watching reality television, but produced through one's everyday activities. We will return to these themes in the next chapter on the watched, and when we consider questions of the real and surveillance later in the book.

The reduction of the watcher to the voyeur in these films is certainly a limited representation of the many ways, possibilities, modes, motivations, and power differentials of watching. There is an inherent contradiction in a society and culture that encourages us to watch others (especially post-9/11, but since the 1950s more generally) and a body of films that critiques that watching, that is deeply suspicious of that watching by pathologizing the watcher as voyeur. Films can overcome this contradiction by using the figure of the voyeur as an excuse to gaze at the objects of their desire while ostensibly critiquing such watching, but that resolution is still fraught with problems.

I start this book by examining the cinematic figures of the watchers because these figures most directly implicate us as audience members. By showing us what they see, and making them key figures that move plots forward and with whom we need to identify, the figure of the watcher shapes us as watchers, too. As a cinematic audience in a darkened theater, or, increasingly, in a living room or while watching on a laptop or mobile device, we are voyeurs and these figures highlight certain forms of voyeurism, forms that have broader cultural relevance and that we encounter in other aspects of our lives. We can contrast these films with reality television in which viewers are encouraged to watch others as object lessons in the case of the self and neoliberal governance. Reality TV presents instructions for living, from aspirations achievable through make-overs (of body, wardrobe, or housing) to object lessons in poor life decisions (usually by relying too much on others or on the state).[61] The rise of what Clay Calvert called *mediated voyeurism* (on reality television shows, on live webcam sites, or other places) entwines the burgeoning peep culture.[62] But if these media emphasize comfort with particular forms of watching (and perhaps limits on these forms), they can also provide insight (and instruction) on what it feels like to be watched and how we are expected to comport ourselves under the gaze.[63]

Other films to consider

10 (dir. Blake Edwards, 1979)
American Beauty (dir. Sam Mendes, 1999)
Blow Out (dir. Brian de Palma, 1981)
Blue Thunder (dir. John Badham, 1983)
Blue Velvet (dir. David Lynch, 1986)
Ek Chhotisi Love Story (A Little Love Story) (dir. Shashilal K. Nair, 2002)
Harriet the Spy (dir. Bronwen Hughes, 1996)
Head over Heels (dir. Mark Waters, 2001)
One Hour Photo (dir. Mark Romanek, 2002)
Sex, Lies, and Videotape (dir. Stephen Soderberg, 1989)
Sliver (dir. Phillip Noyce, 1993)
Vertigo (dir. Alfred Hitchcock, 1958)
The Voyeurs (dir. Buddhadev Dasgupta, 2007)
La Zona (The Zone) (dir. Rodrigo Plá, 2009)

Questions for discussion

1. Alfred Hitchcock once said, in regard to J.B. Jeffries in *Rear Window*, "Sure, he's a snooper, but aren't we all? I'll bet you that nine out of ten people, if they see a woman across the courtyard undressing for bed, or even a man pottering around in his room, will stay and look" (Truffaut, Hitchcock & Scott, 1984, p. 216; quoted in Albrechtslund, 2008, 133). Do you agree?
2. There is a scene in Brian DePalma's *Body Double* where Jake is watching the nighttime erotic performance of his neighbor and he notices another man also watching her. The other man seems to be Native American, with a scarred and ugly face. This other man is immediately seen as a threat to the woman, causing

Jake to want to protect her (moving from control to care). How can the surveillant gaze be coded differently depending on the race of the watcher?

3. Between the McCarthy paranoia of the 1950s and the post-9/11 paranoia was a particular configuration of cold war paranoia. How did this affect how surveillance was treated in the spy thrillers from that era (from John Le Carré's *The Spy Who Came in From the Cold* to the James Bond films, as well as *Manchurian Candidate*)?

4. The Marauder's Map, in the Harry Potter books and films, is a magical object that can identify and locate every person in Hogwart's castle in real time. What are the ethics of this powerful means of surveillance?

2

The Watched

Figure 2.1 Georges not seeing the camera filming his house. *Caché.*

Cultural Studies scholar James Carey once wrote that being watched was part of the structure of feeling of contemporary life.[1] This comment speaks to the pervasiveness of surveillance, but also importantly to the experience of everyday life, the structure of feeling. He uses a phrase from Raymond Williams that tried to capture a sense of culture that accounted for both the personal, unique sense of experience that is our feelings and also the idea that feelings are not absolutely idiosyncratic, unique to ourselves.[2] The times, places, economics, and other factors structure not how we feel but the range of possible feelings. Some feelings are more common at particular times and places and less at others. Consider the idea raised in the previous chapter that anxiety is more readily available as a way to frame and structure our emotions today than in the past.[3] That the feeling of being watched is more a day-to-day phenomenon in contemporary culture is not simply due to more things watching us, though there are certainly enough: CCTV cameras that capture us hundreds of times a day; mobile phones that monitor our locations; peers wanting to know where we are; friends watching out feeds, tweets, and Instagram streams; NSA filtering our emails, webchats, and phone calls; strangers capturing our lives at random on their mobile phone cameras; smart TVs, interactive game consoles, and DVRs that track your movements and verbal commands (even if you're not playing or watching) as well as viewing patterns; and on and on. This structure of feeling is also due to the simple fact that the possibility of being watched at any time is quite real. This sense is underscored by the ways that we ourselves watch others in popular mass media and, more and more, through online and mobile technologies. If I'm watching others this way, surely others are watching me.

Are we aware of being watched? What does it feel like? Does it feel like an intrusion? A reassurance? The answer, in part, depends on who we are and where we are. Women and men are under different forms of surveillance, as are minorities, children, political groups, and others.[4]

How we feel about the surveillance can also depend on who (or what) we think is watching. Are people more comfortable if it is a machine sorting through their email or bank records or if it is a person? In the television program *Person of Interest* (2011–), Harold Finch (Michael Emerson) argues that the all-seeing surveillant computer, The Machine, works better without human interference and that we are more comfortable with a machine watching than a person ("Super," January 12, 2012). Do we feel that the computer algorithm is objective and nonjudgmental, whereas a person is biased and subjective? Computer algorithms, however, can be discriminatory in many ways. Ideologies about the characteristics and abilities of groups of people get baked into the ostensibly neutral code.[5] Human observers can be understanding and even forgiving in ways that computers cannot.[6] But if it is a person watching, does the watcher's gender, race, sexuality, or class make a difference in our comfort?

The questions asked above conflate the practice of surveillance with being *watched*. Surveillance has other forms as well. Does it feel different to be *listened to* rather than watched? To be *sampled* rather than listened to? To be *sniffed*? To be *tracked*? To be *searched*? Surveillance is a broad set of practices that do not necessarily impinge themselves on the senses in any felt way. We can't *feel* our data being sorted. We can't *feel* algorithms. But we do feel their effects. But these other practices are difficult to represent, especially in a medium such as cinema which emphasizes vision and sound. So being watched (and secondarily listened to) is an apt focus.

But it is not just a question of what it feels like but what we *do* when we are watched, how it alters our behavior and even who we are. Being watched (tracked, recorded, and so on) is one of the central mechanisms of social control according to French theorist Michel Foucault.[7] Indeed, what Foucault called *discipline* (control through normativity, by observing, measuring, supervising, and correcting) has been one of the dominant theoretical lenses surveillance studies scholars have used to understand surveillance. Foucault argued that at one time we (Western Europe) were a society of the spectacle, that control of the population was kept through corporal punishment. Break the law and your body paid for it. Often, especially for prominent cases, this punishment was meted out in public. The public was invited to watch the spectacle of the criminal being maimed, tortured, and executed as a warning or object lesson about the power of the sovereign. But Foucault traces the rise of a new form of social control (and understanding of society): rather than punishing the body we begin disciplining the soul, and we did so through surveillance, through observation, and through meticulous record-keeping. These principles he referred to as *Panopticism*, a term he derives from the name the eighteenth-century philosopher Jeremy Bentham gave to a new model form of prison.

The Panopticon (all-seeing) was a prison based on the principle of surveillance as a means of control rather than just brute force. Prisoners could be controlled through their minds rather than just locking away their bodies. Surveillance scholar David Lyon likens the idea for Bentham's prison to a secular version of Psalm 139, a selection from which Bentham prefaced his work.[8] That psalm posits an all-knowing, all-seeing God who searches us and knows us, and cannot be escaped. We cannot avoid God's gaze in the darkness and He has known us since we were in the womb. This is an asymmetrical, unidirectional, all-seeing Eye of God.[9] Bentham proposed complete observation and knowledge of each prisoner, and it was that knowledge, and the prisoner's realization that they were always watched without fail, which would "grind rogues honest." Lyon also notes that Bentham ignored aspects of the psalm that would indicate that such surveillance could be of care as well as control.[10] It worked like this: The prison was to be circular, with cells arranged around the outer wall and a guard tower in the middle. The cells were to be constructed so that all aspects of them would be visible from the guards in the tower. However, through an arrangement of blinds, the prisoners could never see the guards. They could not tell when they were being observed, so they had to presume that they were being observed at all times and adjust their behavior to comport with expectations. Eventually, good behavior would become habitual and internalized. They would subject themselves to surveillance. In case the inmates doubted, guards would observe and take copious notes so they could prove to the inmates that they were watching. Foucault wrote: "He is seen, but he does not see; he is the object of information, never a subject in communication.... Hence the major effect of the Panopticon: to induce in the inmate a state of conscious and permanent visibility that assures the automatic functioning of power."[11] Power in this model should be visible (you can see the guard tower) and unverifiable. The short version is: when knowingly subject to surveillance, we tend to behave.

But the Panopticon wasn't just about prisons and the correction of lawbreakers. It was, rather, a set of principles that could be used in any number of institutions and situations: "Whenever one is dealing with a multiplicity of individuals on whom a task or a particular form of behavior must be imposed, the panoptic schema may be used."[12] The principles of Panopticism are: visibility, record keeping, differentiation, comparison, modeling and enforcing correct behavior, and defining deviant behavior. And therefore surveillance (the gathering and recording of information) is mobilized to control schools (assigned seats, attendance, examinations, and so on), workshops, sanitariums, hospitals, and other institutions. For example, we saw discipline at work in the arrangements of students, clarified expectations, and constant observation in the school in *La Mirada Invisible*, discussed in the previous chapter. Bentham proposed Panoptic cities where the entire population, under constant observation and self-surveillance, would self-discipline. And Foucault traces the swarming of disciplinary mechanisms into all aspects of everyday life: students aren't just observed in school, their parents and homelife came under scrutiny as well. Henry Ford built towns for his factory workers so he could keep an eye on them after work. Police build detailed files on everyone and become interested in "the dust of events, actions, behavior, opinions" and not just particular crimes.[13] Various scholars have pointed out that Foucault's genealogies of discipline ignore the ways that these very principles and designs, including the Panopticon itself, were tested and developed in the European colonies, especially in India.[14] Mirzoeff puts these developments in the Imperial Complex of visuality which succeeded the Plantation Complex.[15]

There are two things to draw from this model which has made it so powerful for scholars. One is that when we see surveillance we should understand it as a means of social control and to connect observation with record keeping and the formation of knowledge of populations (the disciplines of sociology and anthropology arise at this time, seeking detailed information about human behavior). The second is the fact that the main product of a disciplinary society is us: we are produced through these workings of knowledge and power, through these techniques and institutions. Who we are, what we are, where we are, how we compare, how we are labeled and treated. Discipline creates a new type of person: *subjects*, but not subject to a sovereign, but the subject of information.

So when we think about being the watched, being on the receiving end of surveillance, we need to think about how that gaze is trying to turn us into a particular person. The growth of surveillance in society, not just numbers of cameras and technologies but practices and expectations of information gathering, is the growth of means of social control. Journalist Glenn Greenwald recently spoke about concerns regarding the revelations from Edward Snowden and others about the extent of the NSA's surveillance of both US and foreign nationals.[16] Invoking Foucault, Greenwald argued that a troubling feature of living in a society in which you can be observed at any moment, when one's most private moments could be recorded and uploaded to YouTube for all to see, is that we become self-conscious and self-censoring and don't act with individuality and creativity. If we are always worried about what others will think, then we don't really know who we are, just what others expect us to be. If we don't dance boldly and unself-consciously, then we do not dance at all. There is little opportunity to explore our identity and desires in private, if that privacy is so easily violated. Politically, we don't have true democracy without opportunities to voice dissent, to speak things that are unpopular. Surveillance should not quash these opportunities.

In the previous chapter, we discussed films that placed us in the role of a watcher, positioned us to identify, comfortably or not, with the voyeur, and began to address questions of what ethically justifies voyeurism, what constitutes voyeurism, when it is a violation, who is a voyeur, and who is a victim. In this chapter, we look at films that ask us to identify with the watched, with figures under surveillance, and we begin to ask what it feels like to be watched and what it does to us. Who is watching, and why, and what can they see? And what can we do about it? What is the appropriate response to surveillance?

Exhibitionism

In the previous chapter, we focused on voyeurism. The flip side of voyeurism is *exhibitionism*: pleasure in being watched. Though there are seemingly innumerable representations of exhibitionists in popular film, these are not often the main character with whom we are to identify. Rather, they are present as the subject of the voyeur's gaze. Remember Laura Mulvey's argument about how classical Hollywood cinema splits the look. Exhibitionists tend to be the subject of the distant gaze of the voyeur rather than the gaze of identification. For example, consider the character of Holly Body (Melanie Griffith) in Brian DePalma's *Body Double* (1984). *Body Double* concerns an actor, Jake Scully (Craig Wasson), who is staying in a house in the hills surrounding Los Angeles while the owner is away. He discovers via a telescope in the bedroom that a woman who lives across the way performs an erotic dance in front of her open windows every evening. Unbeknownst to him, the woman performing the dance is Holly Body, a porn actress hired to impersonate the woman who really lives there. Holly's job is to entice Jake to watch every evening at the same time so that he will be a witness when the real homeowner is murdered. Though Holly is clearly an exhibitionist, she is not the subject of the film and not a figure that the film asks us to identify with. Rather, it is with the voyeur, Jake, that we are to identify. We get no sense of Holly's own experience of being watched or what it means for her (financially, sexually, or in terms of her own identity).

The exception to this would be found in what Nina K. Martin has termed *direct-to-video surveillance erotic thrillers* like *Night Eyes 2* (1992) and *The Lipstick Camera* (1994), where female exhibitionism (and voyeurism) is seen as empowering, instructional, and a source of self-knowledge, but still risky and dangerous. "The genre oscillates between a glorification and fascination with sexually oriented technology's voyeuristic and instructional possibilities and a pervasive techno-anxiety surrounding the equipment's possible abuse and manipulation."[17] The genre still tends to associate men with voyeurism and women with exhibitionism, though it problematizes this as well.

EDtv

Are there other films that put us in the shoes, so to speak, of the exhibitionist? Consider Ron Howard's film *EDtv* (1999). The protagonist in this film signs himself up to be the subject of a reality television show, volunteering for surveillance so that his daily life would be broadcast live for most of the hours of the day. The film is a meditation on a culture of exhibitionism, but its central figure, Ed (Matthew McConaughey), has a more ambivalent relationship to the cameras.

EDtv, coming a year after *The Truman Show* (1998), played into and on the rise of reality TV programs, with the long success of *Cops* and other semidocumentary programs. It was released the same year that the television program *Big Brother* debuted in the Netherlands and a year before the US version of that show. These programs, like *Survivor*, *Loft Story*, and others, would have seemingly ordinary people agree to subject themselves to constant surveillance as a contest and entertainment. These programs also followed a wave of individual webcammers who would broadcast their own lives, via live webcameras, over the internet. When *EDtv* was released, Jennifer Ringley had been broadcasting her life to the web for three years, reaching millions of viewers a day at the peak of her popularity. Some webcammers did this for profit, some in order to seek celebrity, some as performance art (Anacam.com), some for kicks, and some to show off their technical prowess (Nerdman.com).[18] This seeking of celebrity and what has been called microcelebrity can be seen as part of a more general turn to what Michael Goldhaber termed *the attention economy*.[19] What is scarce in a world awash in information is the attention of the audience, and therefore attention is increasingly valuable. Viewers, fans, followers, friends, "likes," and so on become a currency. We could see a broader culture of exhibitionism, revealing oneself through social media, for example, as seeking to affirm one's identity through surveillance rather than despite it. Where once cinema stars were ego ideals to help guide identity formation (we identified with them via the voyeurism of cinema), identity is formed by being watched or liked. Celebrity is an affirmation of the self, but the self is constructed in light of the needs of an audience, the pressure of the expectations of the surveilling eye.[20] Just as voyeurism is portrayed as social as well as individual pathology (as we saw in the previous chapter), so too is exhibitionism portrayed as a social as well as individual pathology.

In *EDtv* a television network announces the launch of a new channel, TrueTV, that will broadcast the daily life of an ordinary person unedited and unscripted. Ray Pakurny (Woody Harrelson), a somewhat loud, boorish, attention-seeking man, sees the opportunity as a chance at fame and money in order to launch his own gym. Auditioning for the program one evening in a bar, he brings his brother Ed on camera. The network producers find Ed more charming and engaging than the overbearing Sam and offer him the position. Ed reluctantly agrees to it, convinced by Sam's argument that guys like them don't get many opportunities, but also seeing it as a way to help Sam get and advertise his gym. The program begins inauspiciously enough with the boring—and occasionally embarrassing—personal minutae of everyday life, including Ed's painstaking demonstration of his nail clipping technique. However, viewers soon begin to notice a relationship developing between Ed and Sam's girlfriend, Shari (Jenna Elfman). When Ed and the camera crew catch Sam cheating on Shari, viewership rises to watch the family conflict. Ed goes to Shari to speak on Sam's behalf, and Ed and Shari realize (on live camera) that they are in love. At this point, Ed's celebrity begins to rise and wherever he goes crowds of people want to meet him and get on camera. It becomes increasingly difficult for Ed and Shari to carry out a relationship in the glare of the spotlight.

Figure 2.2 Ed watching himself being watched. *EDtv*

EDtv is not just about surveillance but celebrity, not just to be seen but to be seen *as a spectacle for others*. And it is about the loss of privacy of celebrity—not the loss of privacy to an individual, agency, or organization, but to the public at large. It is in many ways a film that is post-panoptic in that Ed is not being disciplined per se (though the expectations of how the audience believes he should behave still weigh on his mind and actions). As a reality TV celebrity, an ordinary person made famous for ordinariness, we see a collapse of the Panopticon. There is no longer any distance or differentiation between the watcher and the watched.[21] Everything is exposed and everyone sees. There is no longer any difference between image and reality, actor and role. As French social critic Jean Baudrillard has argued, all is simulation. *EDtv* is perhaps an over-obvious critique of celebrity culture (and the irony of casting very famous actors such as McConnaughey, Harrelson, Elfman, Sally Kirkland, Martin Landau, Ellen DeGeneres, Dennis Hopper, and Elizabeth Hurley—many of whom have had their own issues with celebrity and private life—is not lost on the writers or actors, and becomes a metacommentary of their own positions). But it is also a critique of a particular type of celebrity, one famous for just being famous. Historian Daniel Boorstin once defined celebrity as "a person who is well known for his well-knownness."[22] This is not a recent phenomenon by any means, but speaking of *Loft Story* (a 2001 French reality TV series wherein contestants lived for 70 days in a 225-square meter loft under the constant gaze of TV cameras), Baudrillard bemoaned this very notion being propagated in such shows.[23] It's not the voyeurism nor exhibitionism he critiques, but the utter banality. "[I]t's the end of democracy," he argues. The celebration of these people has nothing to do with their qualifications or achievements. "The democratic illusion is thus raised to its highest degree: that of maximal exaltation for a minimal qualification." We have "the extinction of every criterion of qualification, but on the other hand, it is also the result of a radical democracy, on the basis of the beatification of man without qualities."[24] It is such a man without qualities that Ed is established to be: a late-20s slacker who works in a video store and has no ambition beyond that; he has no skills and little education. Without qualification, perhaps, but he does have qualities that the film celebrates: honesty, integrity, and geniality (not to mention being easy on the eyes). The reality of reality television has more to do with what Ien Ang once called *emotional realism* than the realism of the situations in which they find themselves.[25] Contestants are considered as being most real at their most emotional: when they break down, get angry, cry. And on this emotional register, we are meant to identify and admire Ed, a man with little pretense, very comfortable with himself and his choices. These are the qualities that make him watchable. And just as reality TV plays more on the affective register, so do films about being watched. Films about watchers tend to be more about the power and politics of watching, whereas films about the watched are not just about the experience and emotions of being watched but the circulation of various forms of affect both represented on the screen and generated in the context of viewing (such as forms of misery, boredom, and anxiety discussed in the previous chapter). Like the reality TV shows it mocks, *EDtv* instructs viewers on appropriate emotional conduct under the constant gaze of the camera. But it also emphasizes a geniality and conviviality in marked contrast with other films discussed below where terror and guilt become the particular formations of affect in the face of the camera.

How, then, is the figure of Ed instructive in how to be the watched? The film *EDtv* is a broad critique of celebrity culture and the desire of the public to be famous. Everyone it depicts, it seems, is desperate to be on TV. At first, before Ed himself gains celebrity status, it is the presence of the cameras that draws the crowds. Everyone waves at the camera, uttering the clichéd "Hi Mom!" If Hitchcock once stated that we are a culture of voyeurs and that we cannot pass by an open lighted window without looking in,[26] we could also argue by that broad brush that we are a culture of exhibitionists who cannot pass by a camera without waving and shouting, "Hi Mom!" or something similar. But the striking characteristic of Ed, as a possible model of how to respond and behave under this sort of surveillance, is that he is not seeking the spotlight or the camera, unlike his brother Ray. He is not indifferent to it, but he is neither afraid nor desirous of it. If anything his participation is a practical matter (raising funds for his brother's gym), a form of employment but not a stepping-stone to another career (nor a career in itself). Mark Andrejevic called this the work of being watched, bringing to light the important point that being surveilled is a form of labor that produces value (ratings, marketing data, and so on) that others may exploit.[27] Ed's participation is also a personal decision. He will be on camera if they want him to be. His relationship with the camera is relaxed, conversational, and personable. He doesn't have a problem with it, even if he doesn't see the point of it beyond making money for this occasion. His objections to the camera come when his freedom to choose is taken away. His contract does not allow him to unilaterally quit without being sued. And his objections come when the cameras begin to harass those around him. Toward the end of the film, the in-film broadcast of TrueTV isn't just about Ed, but all the members of his family, with crews following each.

Practicality, some indifference and personalization are qualities of proper conduct under celebrity surveillance, but tempered with a care for others. Ed's is not a pathological exhibitionism. Visual critic Victor Burgin once argued that the webcam in Jennifer Ringley's room wasn't a window for her exhibitionism, nor even a mirror for her own narcissism, but rather a transitional object, something to channel her emotional energy as she came of age.[28] The cameras of TrueTV play a similar role for Ed. Ed, who refuses to grow up, or to take real responsibility, is only able to have a mature relationship with Shari after being exposed to the crucible of surveillance.

Seeking fame and celebrity by subjecting oneself to surveillance is an important aspect of the contemporary culture of surveillance. We not only watch, but volunteer to be watched. This concerns not only live webcams (and both webcams and the internet at large are curiously absent from *EDtv*), but also the confessions of social media where a constant stream of personal information and images of oneself (the ubiquitous selfie) and others is posted for one's friends and the public at large.[29] Hille Koskela has argued that such new media exhibitionism may be empowering.[30] Rather than having one's image captured, manipulated, and controlled by others, those who turn the camera on themselves take control of their own image, refusing to be defined by others. By doing so, they (and here Koskela is speaking specifically of home webcammers) respond to what she calls the regime of order and the regime of shame. Both regimes are part of social discipline. The regime of order dictates social expectations and identities for one to conform with. The regime of shame is the "individuals' internalization of control, in the Foucauldian sense."[31] Home webcammers, she continues, resist both regimes by not playing into either. "The liberation from shame and from the 'need' to hide leads to empowerment. Conceptually, when you show 'everything' you become 'free': no one can 'capture' you any more, since *there is nothing left to capture*."[32] However, the empowerment of being visible is rarely a theme prominent in feature films about surveillance. When new media use does appear, it is often as a cautionary tale (e.g., *Disconnect* [2012]), a horror or suspense film (e.g., *My Little Eye* [2002], *Cam-Girl* [2012], *Unfriended* [2014]), or sex comedy (*I-See-You.Com* [2006]), or soft or hardcore porn (e.g., *Cam Girl* [2014]) (though the latter can have their own ways of "'hijacking' ... the dominant use of surveillance"[33]). Far more common are representations of folks being subject to surveillance by others involuntarily. Such representations emphasize feelings of terror and guilt, though they inevitably describe means of resistance to the gaze.

Terror

Being watched is also a prominent trope in horror films (see, e.g., *Halloween* [1978]) or thrillers (The Bourne films, the Bond films, the Mission Impossible films ...), where underlying the surveillance is the threat of impending violence. One is being watched as a prelude to being attacked and killed. We see this theme in so-called Torture Porn films (like the *Saw* series [2004, 2005, 2006, 2007, 2008, 2009, 2010], the *Hostel* films [2005, 2007], and *Captivity* [2007]) that link surveillance with the most extreme form of torture and exploitation.[34] I do not want to underestimate the cultural valence of this theme, a theme that links back to *Peeping Tom*: the experience of being watched as one of terror.

Evangelos Tziallas argues that horror films tended to be about voyeurism. This was emphasized by first person camerawork and the event of stalking and killing the victim. Torture porn, however, "is invested more in surveillance." We don't get POV (Point of View) shots, but shots from the position of the "surveillance angle" (high in a corner, looking down). The films are about being made visible at all times, and knowing one is visible and expected to perform in some way in front of the constant, irresistible gaze of the camera. The films resonate with the contemporary visibility of torture, images of which circulate more readily in popular media, especially after the release of photographs from the Abu Ghraib prison and subsequent public debates about the legality (and effectivity) of waterboarding and other enhanced interrogation methods.[35] Whereas voyeurism blames the individual, surveillance implies a *system*. In these films, these are not systems of security and safety but danger. The gaze of the cameras is a disciplinary gaze, Tziallas argues.

> I contend here that torture porn is primarily structured by the fact that surveillance is altering social consciousness and our desire to look and be looked at. These films point to a change in our visual desires, desires now influenced by surveillance technology's ability to create, distribute and access a seemingly endless stream of visual content without limit or delay. Not only can people rarely escape surveillance, but they also learn to desire through the surveillant gaze and apparatus usually by narcissistically placing themselves at the center of it.[36]

Being watched takes a brutal Skinnerian behaviorist view in the Korean film *Old Boy* (2003), where a man (Min-sik Choi) is kidnapped and imprisoned for 15 years, kept in a shabby bedroom under constant watch, before finally breaking free. In his room, he is subject to constant surveillance and we see the isolation and constant gaze of unknown watchers take its psychological toll. Unbeknownst to him, this surveillance is also conditioning him to behave in certain ways after his escape. This is obviously an extreme version of Foucauldian discipline. Until he breaks free and then tracks the location of his prison down to wreak revenge, he is powerless against surveillance and control as it happens. He can only respond later (though the years of imprisonment have changed him and conditioned him in ways he does not realize, so that despite being freed from captivity he is far from free). Tziallas notes the behavioral and psychological conditioning inherent in the surveillance and abuse perpetrated in the film *Captivity* (2007) as well.[37] This effect of being surveilled relates to terror. Remember as well that in *Peeping Tom* Mark was watched and filmed by his father since birth as part of a psychological experiment in fear. In the political complex of visuality amid a war on terror, the surveillance camera is meant to signify security. But by rearticulating the surveillance camera to a register of terror—both the terror of torture under surveillance Tziallas discusses and as a means of revealing acts of terrorism (through the media we witness terrorists and acts of terror on newscasts and in popular television and film [cf. the opening of *Homeland* or the film *Zero Dark Thirty* (2012)])—surveillance films speak to the circulation of anxiety and terror as an underlying affective register of the age.

Guilt

There are two more themes I wish to explore in some depth in the remainder of this chapter: guilt and resistance.

When we discover that we are being watched, how does that feel? In some contexts it is said to make us feel important, like a celebrity; in others, it is a sexual thrill to be gazed at with desire; and in others it is the experience of terror. There is also a self-consciousness in being watched, a self-consciousness that is the linchpin of the Panopticon. If you are driving and notice a police car behind you, you get very self-conscious and aware of social norms: What is the speed limit here? Did I do something wrong? How do I manage this next lane change correctly? How do I follow the rules? That self-consciousness of behavior is also accompanied by soul searching: What have I done? What could have been wrong? What could I do differently?

Take, for example, Robert Altman's 1992 film *The Player*. Tim Robbins plays Griffin Mill, an executive at a film studio. Griffin begins receiving anonymous threatening messages. Who is stalking him? Who might he have wronged? He wracks his brain to think of who might wish to harm him, which (of the many) screenwriters whose projects he rejected would bear him such ill will? He becomes increasingly paranoid and defensive, and ultimately aggressive, becoming a voyeur himself. Identifying a likely candidate, he stalks him and his girlfriend. In one scene, Griffin, standing in the darkness of their front yard, talks on a cell phone with the girlfriend (Greta Scacchi) as he watches her through the windows. Griffin then confronts and, in a fit of rage, kills the screenwriter (Vincent D'Onofrio) and then flees. In this case, paranoia turns to aggression. We see this turn as well in *The Conversation* and *Caché*.

The Conversation

We discussed *The Conversation* in the previous chapter in regards to Harry as a professional voyeur who questions his practices when he worries that his work might cause harm to innocents. But Harry is also an important figure with regards to the experience of being watched. Harry is quite secretive and private. He has an almost laughable number of locks on his door, his phone number is unlisted, and he is reticent to disclose any personal information at all, even his birthday, to his girlfriend (Teri Garr). Perhaps it is in the nature of his business as a professional surveillance expert not to be a public figure (it might make him more effective, allows him to blend in with the crowd at the city square). And perhaps it is because in the world of surveillance experts depicted in the film we see experts stealing ideas and equipment for their own profit. But there are hints of more. The surveillance job back East that got a family killed was over a pension fund. Might Harry be the target of a revengeful organization if they find out who did the job? Would that explain his relocation to California? But also, knowing all the ways that one *might* be surveilled leads Harry to shape his life to avoid surveillance and the invasion of his privacy. The primary way that he protects his privacy is by having little to no private life (and therefore little that can be invaded). He empties his life of any significance. "I have nothing personal except my keys," he says at one point. Perhaps what is personal is his body of techniques to elude surveillance, but neglecting the personal that is being guarded. The only personal life of Harry's in evidence in the film is his playing a saxophone alongside a record when alone in his apartment and his visit to Amy Friedrichs, his girlfriend, whom he keeps dependent on him but at such an emotional distance that she leaves him. His techniques of protection (his keys) become everything to him, so when they are violated by himself being victimized, it strikes psychologically deep, unhinging him.

If his professional techniques of protection and privacy are the primary bulwark of his personal identity, from the very start the film seems to question and challenge his competency, revealing that his bulwark against personal invasion is as flimsy as the translucent raincoat he always wears. Early in the film we find out that his landlady has not only learned personal information about him (that it is his birthday) by looking at his mail, but has opened all his locks and disabled his alarm system to put a present in his apartment. He prides himself on building all his own equipment, but apparently trusts his alarm system to a professional company (whose corporate logo is visible on stickers on the door of his apartment and windows of his workplace). His competitor easily slips a microphone hidden in a pen into Harry's pocket without him being suspicious. And in the end his own apartment is bugged and surveilled in a way he can't fathom, though he destroys every item in the apartment, even the floorboards and wallpaper, in his desperate search for them. Trusting to his knowledge, he thinks he is invisible, but he is only hiding behind a translucent raincoat. For example, he believes that having an unlisted number makes him untraceable, but the corporation proves him wrong (they have his number, in many senses of the term).

Surveillance societies are marked by suspicion, a profound lack of trust. *The Conversation* presents Harry as a portrait of a life without trust: he is lonely, alienated, and victimized. He trusts neither his girlfriend (whom he confesses he may love) nor his only employee, Stan (John Cazale)—and both leave him. He confesses three times in the film. The first time is to a priest, where he is quite selective about his sins (swearing, stealing a newspaper, and that his work might endanger a young couple, but neglects to mention his affair with Amy). The second time is in a dream when he confesses to Ann (Cindy Williams), the young woman he is surveilling, about his boyhood and his fears of being morally responsible for murder; in this dream, he is confessing, ultimately, to himself, trying to break through his own denial of responsibility. And, the third time is when he confesses to Meredith, the prostitute, about his love for Amy. In this latter case, breaking his own rules about not trusting anyone leads to betrayal (his conversation is broadcast via the planted pen mike to his competitor, and Meredith later steals the tapes). Indeed, his confession to his priest

Figure 2.3 Harry hears a homicide. *The Conversation.*

may have betrayed him as well. The actor playing the priest (Richard Hackman, Gene's brother) also plays a security guard at the corporation, though as a priest you never clearly see his face.

The experience of being under surveillance, for Harry, strips him of his trust in his own abilities as a surveillance expert and his trust in his interpretation of the recording. It strips him of agency, his ability to decide his own destiny, and he is rendered helpless at the end of the film. It strips him of his ability to act in that surveillance ramps up the guilt he feels about his work so that the horror of bugging the young couples' hotel room and overhearing the murder leaves him psychologically crippled, infantilized, wrapped up in a bedsheet with the television on full blast, unable to act. It strips him both of his faith in people (what little he had) and his religious faith. On this latter, the key turning point is when he is tearing apart his apartment he is forced to smash a figure of the Virgin Mary, the symbol of his moral strength. And, ultimately, it strips him of his dignity.

When we think about the consequences of surveillance, and our resistance to it, most often we focus on the idea of privacy. But we should not neglect other moral and political grounds for resistance, including dignity and justice.[38] For example, when objections were raised in France to the surveillance-oriented reality TV show *Loft Story*, it wasn't that the contestants had their privacy violated, since they had willingly signed up to be watched after all, but that the show was an affront to their dignity and human dignity generally.[39] For Harry, the violation of surveillance is a violation of his dignity and it is the violation of dignity that defeats him. An interesting parallel can be made to the figure of Winston Smith in Orwell's *Nineteen Eighty-Four*, where Smith is slowly stripped of his humanity and his dignity, until, in extreme instinctual fear, he renounces his last human connection.[40] Harry's destruction begins when his most private moment (playing the saxophone for his own pleasure, the only time he expresses his soul) is played back to him in a recording, and ends when he smashes the Virgin Mary. Significant here is the very last shot of the film. Harry is in the middle of his wrecked apartment, playing the saxophone. The camera is filming down at him, as if it is located high up on the opposite wall. The camera pans slowly left, then right, then back—mimicking an impersonal surveillance camera. Indeed, earlier shots of Harry in his apartment have the camera acting in a similar manner. The camera is generally static, and when Harry moves out of shot the camera, after a lag, follows to catch up. In *The Lives of Others*, scenes of Wiesler in his apartment echo this aesthetic. Harry is defeated, alone, under the gaze of the camera.[41] However, there are two mysteries here: Where is the microphone that Harry has been looking for? And if the camera is a surveillance camera, why can't Harry see it?

Caché

Michael Haneke's film *Caché* (2005) explores similar themes of how being under surveillance dredges up one's past, what one had hoped had been buried. *Caché* is about Georges (Daniel Auteuil), host of a literary television talk show, his wife Anne (Juliette Binoche), and their teenage son, Pierrot (Lester Makendonsky). One day, a videotape arrives on their doorstep. The video shows a two-hour static shot of the front of their house. They begin to worry—what does it mean? Who could have done this? A fan? A friend of Pierrot's? And how was it done? Where would the camera have been and why didn't they see it? Wouldn't they have noticed a camera set up across the street? We are drawn into the family to identify with them as they (and we) scrutinize the images for clues. The film often plays with our assumptions about what we are looking at. For example, what we think is simply an establishing shot is then revealed to be a clip of the videorecording the couple is reviewing. There is an obvious contradiction being explored here: How does someone who makes their living being watched react to being on camera at home and in private? At the same time, the set of Georges's TV program looks remarkably like his own living room with its walls of books. At the start of the film, we see a family that is apparently happy, normal, and successful, but the stress of being watched by someone unknown brings fault lines to the surface. Georges and Anne's relationship is strained. Georges lies easily, and badly so that he is often caught out. He even lies to his mother. We begin not to trust Georges, and his wife mistrusts him as well. Both mistrust their son, who is silent and sullen and who disappears to friends' houses from time to time. The son distrusts his mother, who he is pretty sure is having an affair.

Caché means "hidden" and the title refers to many things. The camera recording their property is hidden (a puzzle, much like the microphone in Harry's apartment). But hidden also refers to what lies hidden in ourselves and in society, things we would like to forget. Like the tragedy back East that Harry wishes to put behind him, surveillance brings them to the surface, back into the light, revealing secrets and memories. We even see the theme of the revelation of secrets in *EDtv*, where the celebrity of being on camera draws out Ed's lost father and the pressure of being on camera forces his mother to confess to her own affairs.

For Georges, it brings back not only memories, but also fantasies and lies. Some time after the first videotape (we are not told how much time has passed), a second tape arrives, also showing the front of their house, but this time at night. On the tape we see Georges pull in and park his car next to where the camera is stationed, but he walks by without noticing it. Wrapped around the tape is a simple drawing of a round face with curly hair and a bright red smear reminiscent of blood coming out of its mouth. The film cuts quickly to a brief shot at night of a young, dark-skinned boy wiping blood from his mouth. This is an image, we are led to believe, that the drawing has just brought to Georges's mind. Georges seems startled and troubled, but says nothing to his wife. Postcards start arriving at his work and at Pierrot's school with similar images drawn on them. Georges has further flashbacks of the boy with blood on his mouth, of a rooster flopping about with its head cut off, and then a longer nightmare he has while visiting his mother that entails the young boy cutting off the head of the rooster, getting sprayed with blood, and advancing on a young Georges with a hatchet. Obviously there is something that Georges has kept hidden, repressed, forgotten, something that carries a strong emotional charge.

When Georges had been a small boy of six he had lived in a large farmhouse on an estate. Two Algerian farmhands had gone to Paris to participate in a demonstration and were killed, leaving their young son, Majid, an orphan. Georges's parents took pity on the boy and planned to adopt him. Georges, jealous of the new rival, told his parents lies and prodded Majid to kill the rooster, then saying that Majid had threatened him. Majid is sent off to an orphanage and a pauper's existence and Georges gets his family and his estate for himself. The other, significantly a raced other, has been expunged. Georges's aggression is attributed to Majid and Georges wipes his hands (and his memory) of the consequences.

So the pressure of surveillance, being watched and in a heightened state of stress, prompts Georges to remember this incident and revives not just memory but fantasy. We get Georges's nightmares about what happened, but not the truth. For example, we get flashes of a young Majid with blood on his mouth, but Georges tells Anne that he made up stories about Majid coughing up blood to get him sent away. The image is of his lie. Likewise with the nightmare over the slaughtered rooster. Georges remembers the lies so he can continue to deny (over and over, protesting too much) any responsibility for Majid's fate, to clear his conscience. The closest we get to the truth is at the end when we are shown the scene of Majid being taken, screaming and fighting, away from the farmhouse. The truth value of this latter scene comes from the way it is shot: with the same static wide shot we get in the surveillance videos. These videos never pan or zoom; there is no indication that there is anyone guiding the shot beyond setting up the camera, pointing it in a certain direction, and turning it on. It is the "objective" eye we attribute to surveillance footage.[42] However, throughout the film, scenes we think are actual events turn out to be videotapes of those events. And so we must bracket, or place at one remove, the "truth" of that scene. Haneke reminds us at almost every turn that we are watching a film. Todd McGowan might argue that the film facilitates "an encounter with the gaze" that troubles our belief in the symbolic order,[43] by emphasizing that history and memory are intertwined and that the trauma of the antagonism of real events and the portrayal of those events can be disruptive. "In the gaze, the subject's role in constituting the world that it sees manifests itself, and the encounter with the gaze in the cinema thus has a radical potential to transform the subject's relationships to the world."[44]

Georges's forgetting is not only personal but indicative of a broader social forgetting. The event in Georges's childhood, the protest in Paris on October 17, 1961, which Majid's parents attended, was real. At the height of the Algerian war for independence, 30,000 Algerians gathered in peaceful protest against a curfew for Muslims and were attacked by the police. An estimated two hundred were killed, many drowned in the Seine. There was very little news coverage and the incident was largely forgotten, repressed by a French society trying to deny its culpability in the colonial nightmare of Algeria and France's treatment of immigrants. The incident was only officially acknowledged by the French president in 2012.[45] In an interview on the DVD of *Caché*, Haneke says that he himself had only just heard about the events and was prompted to write the film as a result. How does a society forget something like that? How do you live with a bad conscience?

Georges projects his own repressed aggression and hatred onto the now-grown Majid (Maurice Bénichou) and his son (Walid Afkir) (just as he projected his own aggression on the young Majid), whom he blames for the recordings, though both deny it. Georges claims they have "a pathological hatred for my family," and that they were "crazy," "sick," and obsessed, though there is no evidence of this. Both Majid and his son are soft-spoken and polite, and Majid speaks fondly of Georges's mother. But the other is quickly blamed: note how quickly the police lock up Majid and his son when Pierrot goes missing. When they protest their treatment, they are jailed. Would the police so easily have jailed Georges or his friends and family?

Caché raises questions of the racialized aspects of surveillance and evokes the colonial and plantation roots of surveillance practices. Majid *cannot* become part of the landowner family according to the logic of the Plantation Complex. The film points out the paranoid and irrational basis of this complex via Georges's worldview and actions. Majid's son asserts what Nicholas Mirzoeff might call the right to look, to assert autonomy and subjectivity and demand recognition by the colonialist other (Georges). However, Mirzoeff writes that *Caché* does not ultimately rise to countervisuality in that the Algerian characters are thinly drawn, their motives unintelligible.[46] The film is not about the countervisual right to look, but the white male European psyche. After all, if it is about French society forgetting the October 17 assault on Algerians, who is it that has forgotten? Did the Algerian community forget the incident as readily as the dominant social class?

And yet, though not full countervisuality in Mirzoeff's sense, in the figure of Majid's son we have the other staring back. He does not speak much but states that he just wants to talk. When his attempts are rebuffed by Georges, he resorts to an intense stare, a glare. This stare is an eruption of affect that is not clearly and fully captured, labeled, or explained.[47] But in the intensity of this stare how much does he *see*? When Georges asks him what he wants, he states, "Nothing anymore. I wondered how it feels, a man's life on your conscience. That's all. Now I know." What he sees is Georges under

Figure 2.4 Looking back. *Caché*.

the implacable *pressure* of the gaze, both the gaze of Majid's son and of the impossible surveillance camera. This gaze is viscerally experienced, but how much does it *see*?[48] Is Majid's son referring to Georges having Majid on his conscience, or does Majid's son now have Georges on his?

Both *Caché* and *The Conversation* are case studies in the effects of being watched, and we see emotional, moral, and psychological effects. But both also present us with puzzles. Who is surveilling them and how? In *The Conversation* it is revealed that it is the corporation (and we hear Harrison Ford's voice on the phone stating to Harry that they will be listening to him). But *Caché* leaves it up in the air whether Majid and/or his son (and/or Pierrot) is responsible for the tapes. Why would they do so (if we don't believe Georges's fantasies of revenge) and how? Harry cannot find the hidden microphone and evidently does not see the surveillance camera mounted on his wall, panning left and right. Likewise, Georges does not see the surveilling camera despite the fact, as we see in the second video, he parks next to it and walks past. But *we* see the camera, however fleetingly, in that night shot. As headlamps from a passing car sweep the small street where the camera is positioned, we see the outline of the film crew and camera silhouetted against the trees. A gaffe? Doubtful, argues Todd Herzog, Haneke is too meticulous a filmmaker.[49] The shadows are a reminder that we are watching a film. The film critic Roger Ebert argues that Haneke himself is making and sending the tapes, just as Francis Ford Coppola is surveilling Harry.[50]

McGowan would say that the film asserts the gaze that unsettles.[51] The film simply ends with Georges getting undressed and going to sleep. In not resolving the conflict of the narrative, the trauma of the real, the film unsettles the surveillant imaginary: the trust in surveillance to reveal the truth. The last shot of the film is yet another static surveillance shot, this time of the outside of Pierrot's school. In the bustling crowd of students we can make out the figure of Pierrot and see him approach and briefly converse with Majid's son. They then go their separate ways. Is this shot the truth of the film? The answer to the riddle of the tapes? No more than any other of the surveillance shots provided truth of Georges's childhood or his current home.

Resistance

The final theme I wish to discuss concerning being watched is the theme of resistance. If surveillance is about power, and Foucault always argued that power is a relationship, how does one resist or respond to the gaze? First, how does one live under surveillance and, second, how does one respond? What courses of action do our popular films map out? This discussion will carry over to the next chapter where films about surveillance societies, and life within them, will be considered.

Here is an oft-quoted description from George Orwell's *Nineteen Eighty-Four* about life under surveillance: "You had to live—did live, from habit that became instinct—in the assumption that every sound you made was overheard, and, except in darkness, every movement scrutinized."[52] One of the strengths of Orwell's novel is its description of how one conducts oneself under such scrutiny, and how it feels. At lunch in the cafeteria at work one day, Winston Smith realizes that a girl he had noticed before (and is extremely suspicious of) is looking at him.

> He did not know how long she had been looking at him, but perhaps for as much as five minutes, and it was possible that his features had not been perfectly under control. It was terribly dangerous to let your thoughts wander when you were in any public place or within range of a telescreen. The smallest thing could give you away. A nervous tic, an unconscious look of anxiety, a habit of muttering to yourself—anything that carried with it the suggestion of abnormality, of having something to hide. In any case, to wear an improper expression on your face (to look incredulous when a victory was announced, for example) was itself a punishable offence.[53]

For example, from earlier in the novel: "Winston turned round abruptly. He had set his features into the expression of quiet optimism which it was advisable to wear when facing the telescreen."[54]

Historian Robert Darnton, writing about East Germany soon after that country's reunification with West Germany, writes of "Stasi consciousness—the feeling of being watched whenever you crossed a street and of being overheard whenever you made a phone call."[55] Journalist Neal Ascherson, reflecting on life under the Stasi, wrote, "All the same, it was impossible to live in fear of the microphone 24 hours a day without cracking up."[56] And in their day to day, "people stuffed the Stasi and the microphones to the back of their minds for most of the time."

Obviously, what surveillance consciousness one has depends on a number of factors: not only who one is (as some individuals and groups such as African

Americans or Muslims today are surveilled much more intensively than others) but what the regime watching is like. Are Orwell's Thought Police, The Stasi, the NSA, and one's Facebook Friends equivalent? The threats from each are quite different.

The question here, for our purposes, is how to capture this consciousness of surveillance on film. Such is the difficulty of filming Orwell's *Nineteen Eighty-Four*, most of which is Winston's thoughts, interpretations, and feelings more than actions. In this aspect, Michael Radford's version, shot and released in 1984, is more successful than Michael Anderson's 1956 version. The later film uses John Hurt's deadpan, lined face to great effect to convey the constructed "expression of quiet optimism" while being ground down by Big Brother. *The Lives of Others* is more successful still, balancing wariness and caution of Dreyman and his friends amid the day to day. And *The Conversation* gives us Harry's twitchy hesitation, indecision, and paranoia.

But what then do we do about it? What is the proper response? Simply depicting life under surveillance and not at some point taking on that surveillance in some way, even if it means working to make oneself less visible, doesn't seem an option in contemporary filmmaking. There is a romanticism to resistance in the surveillant imaginary. That same theme of the triumph of the human spirit, the stirring of a soul, that we saw in the previous chapter, "The Watchers," we see here. A key theme for several films is the idea that there is in the end a limit to surveillance: they cannot know everything about you no matter how hard they look, that the last refuge of human privacy is your own head. This was Winston Smith's belief: "Nothing was your own except the few cubic centimeters inside your skull."[57] This credo is echoed in *The Truman Show* ("You never had a camera in my head," says Truman) as well as *Enemy of the State* ("only privacy left is the space inside your head"). However, while Smith is proved tragically and fatally wrong, the statement is still upheld in these other films. We see this romantic resistance as well in the themes of the lone hero against an organization or society (*1984*, *Brazil*, *The Truman Show*, *Enemy of the State*, *Minority Report*, *Gattaca*, *V for Vendetta*, and so on).

Resistance focuses mainly on the technology of surveillance itself. This can include knowing the cameras' blindspots (e.g., both Truman in *The Truman Show* and Ed in *EDtv* sneak out when the camera controllers think they are asleep) or disguising oneself so as not to be recognized (see the lengths that Vincent goes in *Gattaca* with fake fingerprints and the use of someone else's blood, urine, and other DNA traces; and then there's the extreme of *Minority Report*, where John Anderton gets a new set of eyeballs to fool retina scanners). Or this can include using the technology itself against the surveillors. Note that though Ed in *EDtv* doesn't turn the cameras following him on the executives of TrueTV (though that would have been an interesting alternative ending), he mines the audience his surveillance has created, crowdsourcing personal information on the executives of TrueTV to blackmail them into letting him go. For the most part, these films seem to argue, if you find yourself under surveillance, it helps if you are either a surveillance or technology expert yourself (*The Conversation*, *The Net* [1995]) or know a surveillance expert with knowledge of the system who can give you technical advice (*Gattaca*, *Enemy of the State*, *Brazil*). Ordinary people don't stand a chance. All you can do is run, shout, and/or shoot things.

I will conclude this chapter with a last case study, that of Tony Scott's 1998 techno-thriller *Enemy of the State*, a film which, amid the explosions and car chases, manages to map a particular (pre-9/11) problematic of surveillance, including a number of responses to surveillance.

Enemy of the State

Enemy of the State concerns successful labor lawyer Robert Clayton Dean (Will Smith), who unwittingly comes into possession of a videotape depicting the murder of Congressman Hammersley (Jason Robards) by a director at the National Security Agency (Reynolds, played by Jon Voight). The Congressman was blocking a Patriot Act type of legislation entitled The Telecommunication Security and Privacy Act that Reynolds sees as important for his own career. Reynolds goes outside agency protocol and authorizes a team for a "training mission" that puts full surveillance on Dean to find the tape or information they can use to force him to hand it over. The surveillance causes stress on Dean's marriage and causes him to lose his job. Alone and on the run, pursued by rogue NSA agents, he enlists the reluctant help of Brill (Gene Hackman), a private detective and surveillance expert he has used in the past to obtain undercover videos of mafia figures. With Brill's help, they use the very devices planted on Dean to surveil Congressman Sam Albert (Stuart Wilson), a key figure publicly advocating the new legislation, triggering an internal NSA investigation into the devices' use, hoping to smoke out Reynolds. Later captured by Reynolds and his team, Dean leads Reynolds to believe that the videotape is in the possession of mafia figures he has been investigating (knowing that the restaurant fronting the organization is under FBI surveillance). The mafia and rogue NSA squad end up in a shootout, Dean survives, and Brill slips quietly away as the FBI and police close in to clean things up.

With the introduction of the figure of Brill, the film becomes something of a homage to *The Conversation*. There are scenes clearly reminiscent of that earlier film, such as when Dean and his informant Carla (Lisa Bonet) have a conversation while walking in a public square, while the NSA team tries to photograph and record them. But centrally, Brill is a Harry Caul-like figure: he himself is a former NSA operative and surveillance expert who has had to go into hiding because of global political changes. The operation he was involved with became politically sensitive and the agency dropped him. Brill is socially awkward, paranoid, and isolated, living in an old warehouse by railroad tracks visually much like Harry's workplace. Indeed the metal cages that Harry uses to lock away his equipment have, in *Enemy of the State*, become a Faraday cage that defeats all electronic surveillance. Despite his skill at avoiding surveillance in all its forms, Reynolds and his team manage to finally capture an image of Brill's face and run it through face recognition software. They discover his true identity as Edward Lyle, a former NSA operative. The ID photo the NSA team brings up on their system is strikingly like an image of Harry Caul (it appears to be a period photograph of Hackman from the 1970s with Caul's glasses and mustache). But if Brill is a latter-day Harry Caul, or Harry Caul 20 years later, he is Harry without any moral dilemma or struggle with faith. It is a "feel good" version of Harry where

Harry gets to outsmart his surveillors, fight back, and win. Though the technology displayed in *Enemy of the State* is much more sophisticated and intrusive (from real time visual satellite tracking to miniaturized tracking devices), *Enemy of the State* ends with a sense of hope, in stark contrast to the warning and defeat of *The Conversation's* conclusion.

Mapping *Enemy of the State*, we can see a variety of types of surveillance and a diversity of perspectives on surveillance as well. After the opening scene depicting the murder of Congressman Hammersley, the credits appear over a rapid-fire collection of grainy surveillance-type footage. Many are aerial shots, perhaps from helicopters, of cameras tracking vehicles, interspersed with shots of different types of surveillance cameras, chase scenes in cars and on foot, and footage of robberies and violent crimes caught on camera. But while we see a number of crimes committed, they are all caught on tape, and these shots are always followed by scenes of pursuit and capture by law enforcement. This grainy reality TV–type footage articulates the idea of surveillance particularly to law and order issues, and emphasize that the cameras are a tool for catching criminals. This collection of images is familiar in that such footage is a staple of the reality television boom of the 1990s (programs like *Cops*, for example). In a way, the prevalence of the cameras is reassuring both in its familiarity and in the message that criminals are successfully apprehended through their use.

So the first type of surveillance we see in the film is that of law enforcement (helicopter and municipal mounted videocameras, dashboard cameras, store security cameras, and so on) seen through the lens of reality TV. From there the film makes a point to emphasize the different ways we are surveilled. There is a surveillance camera capturing the migration of wildlife (which produces the videotape of the Hammersley murder), the voyeurism of a lingerie shop, cameras in stores and on ATMs, the undercover surveillance of private detectives like Brill, municipal camera systems in tunnels, the surveillance of the police and FBI, and of course the technical capacities of the NSA, which the film is at pains to depict. We have keyhole visual surveillance satellites capable of zooming in on a face from orbit, monitoring of all telephone calls,

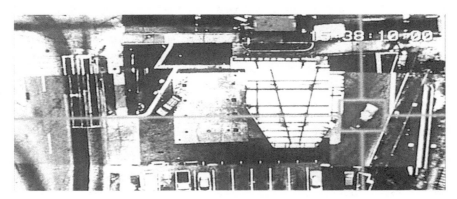

Figure 2.5 Being tracked by the NSA. *Enemy of the State.*

accurate face and voice recognition, access to vast databases of personal information, the use of sophisticated tracking devices, the ability to track subjects through three-dimensional diagrams of buildings, and so on.

The film tends to focus on the surveillance technologies themselves, and we are treated to close-ups of these devices. And while their capacities are threatening in the abstract, and prove an issue for Dean who is subject to them, there is a technophilia in how the devices are presented, in how they are photographed, and the dramatic music accompanying their depiction. The technology is cool. This is in marked contrast with the ways technologies of surveillance are depicted in *The Conversation* or *The Lives of Others*, where they are seen as much more utilitarian and less dazzling. Ultimately, the film is arguing that the technology itself is not really the problem. Indeed we see the technology leading to the capture of criminals in the opening credits. The problem of surveillance in the film is the abuse of the system by a rogue operative (Reynolds) using the system for his own personal gain. As Mark Andrejevic writes, "Focus on these abuses (as important as they may be) backgrounds the 'normal' functioning of data collection and use as taken-for-granted—that is, as non-abusive."[58] The system itself is not the problem. The film depicts a system of checks and balances that keeps the technology under control: the NSA has internal policies and rules regarding the use of the technology, the agency has the will and means to carry out an honest internal investigation into the violations, there is inter-agency rivalry (FBI v. NSA) to keep each other in check (rather than seeing their conflict as a hindrance to security, as it was seen post-9/11), and, finally, pernicious policy and legislation can be defeated through the democratic process (the bill is defeated). Is the film, then, simply affirming the value of the surveillance system? Yes, but not single-mindedly.

The film presents a variety of positions with regards to surveillance, including an important subtheme with regard to the right to privacy. The last line of the film, for example, is talk show host Larry King insisting, "You have no right to come into my home." The first position that the film depicts is that of Congressman Albert, the key champion of the security bill at the heart of the film. Both Albert and Reynolds state that national security demands expansion of surveillance powers. We are under attack everyday in an information war. Despite being surveilled himself by Brill and Dean, and the coming to light of Reynolds's crimes, Albert does not change his position throughout the film. He only states that we need to monitor the people who are monitoring our enemies. The second position voiced in the film is that of Carla Dean (Regina King), Robert Dean's wife and an ACLU lawyer who argues in favor of civil liberties and the limitation of surveillance powers. While Congressman Albert is depicted speaking at a press conference on the steps of the Capitol and on television news shows, Carla Dean is depicted in her home shouting at her television set about the coverage of the security bill and calling Congressman Albert a "fascist gasbag." The term *liberal hysteria* is invoked by Reynolds early in the film, and Carla is the depiction of it: constantly complaining and never satisfied. Responding to the Congressman's final comments, she wonders who will monitor those who monitor the monitors. She accuses Robert of not taking it seriously, to which he replies that she "is taking it seriously enough for both of us and half the people on the block." Though the civil liberties position is voiced in the film, it is framed in such a way as to be dismissed by the audience and not taken seriously.

The third position voiced in the film is that of Brill, who is not opposed to the system of surveillance, only abuses of it. For Brill (as Harry Caul had tried—and failed—to convince himself), the work was technical in nature and not political. In a softly lit scene in a cafe, Brill waxes nostalgic for his time in the agency, stating, "I loved the work." In the politics of the cold war there were, for Brill, clean moral lines: us and them. He does not see beyond the work itself. He does not discuss rights. He does not blame the agency for abandoning him since that was part of the nature of his job. Brill makes a distinction between political surveillance (which he despises and sees embodied in Reynolds) and professional surveillance. This technicist worldview matches the visual depiction of the surveillance technology in the film. We love the work.

The final position is that of Robert Dean himself. He is the character we are to identify with most and it is he who would tell us how we should feel about surveillance and what we should do. Will Smith is known for these everyman roles in which, through common sense, determination, and luck, he becomes the hero. As is evident in his interactions with his wife, surveillance is not an ethical or moral concern for Dean. He doesn't really care about the bill or the issues; he just wants his life back. He does not care if others are abusing the system or are disadvantaged by it. He does not care if his phone is tapped since he is not a criminal. His credo seems to be: do not worry about surveillance unless it affects you directly. Notably, Dean is only targeted for surveillance because of the accident of circumstance and his acquisition of the damning tape. He is not targeted because he is a black male. Surveillance in the film is not discriminatory or determined by race, class, gender, or sexual orientation. Only the bad guys are surveilled. Yes, there are issues with civil liberties and rights, but others are worrying about that. As long as your credit cards work, you're OK. This pragmatic attitude is a commonly voiced one: if surveillance benefits you (discount coupons), that's fine, and only criminals have something to hide. Broader questions about social justice and the discriminatory nature of surveillance are bracketed. The long history of racial discrimination and surveillance from slavery to police profiling vanishes.[59] In the final scene of the film, Dean is sitting in his living room watching television when the image on his screen fills with static. It clears to show a picture of a boat, then another of a beach, and finally he is greeted with a live video image of himself sitting on his couch. Dean looks up at the camera in the light fixture, smiles slightly, and waves at the camera a little nervously. He jokes that Brill is "sick." The image on the screen changes to a scene on a beach with the words, "Wish you were here" written in the sand. Dean is not troubled terribly much by the intrusion into his living room and the surveillance camera Brill has placed there. Brill's image fades and the television broadcast resumes with talk show host Larry King interviewing Congressman Albert. Arguing with the Congressman, King states, "We have to draw the line between protection of national security, obviously the government needs to obtain intelligence data, and the protection of civil liberties, particularly the sanctity

Figure 2.6 Dean being watched by Brill. *Enemy of the State.*

of my home. You've got no right to come into my home." The film cuts to images in orbit of the keyhole surveillance satellites drifting away over the horizon.

In the end, surveillance has not changed Dean. Despite having his credit, his credibility, his family, and his work stripped away from him, not to mention his life threatened on numerous occasions, all this is happily restored at the end and things are back to normal. His attitude has not changed and he is amused, if anything, by this final surveillant act of Brill's, and does not seem to share Larry King's sentiments. This is in marked contrast to the end of *The Conversation*, where the protagonist is likewise sitting in his living room under the gaze of the surveillance camera. I should note that none of the surveillors in *Enemy of the State* have a change of heart nor are affected by the surveillance they are conducting and the intrusions into privacy they are perpetrating. It is just a job. One, Fiedler (Jack Black), surreptitiously tapes Reynold's confession of murder in the surveillance van, but that is purely for later self-preservation. He never admits to doing anything wrong; they were just "technical support."

Conclusion

Does *Enemy of the State* depict the Panopticon? Though the eyes of the surveillant state are seemingly all-seeing (clouds never obscure the view of the keyhole satellite cameras), Panopticism is insufficient to explain the situation in the film. For the most part, people seem unaware of their surveillance. Dean lacks the self-consciousness that would lead him to discipline himself. However, Dean himself is the hegemonic social norm (the Hollywood norm) of a wealthy family man. Perhaps we need other models of surveillance to supplement that of the Panopticon, models that take into account the pleasure possible in being watched, models that don't work out of fear or even knowledge of being watched but of the advantages and benefits of being watched, models that describe the way control might work by other means.

Other films to consider

Eagle Eye (dir. D.J. Caruso, 2008)
Freeze Frame (dir. John Simpson, 2004)
The Net (dir. Irwin Winkler, 1995)
Panic Room (dir. David Fincher, 2002)
Ucho (The Ear) (dir. Karel Kachyna, 1970)

Questions for discussion

1. Harry, in *The Conversation*, responds to the possibility of surveillance by evacuating his life of anything worth knowing. Georges, in *Caché*, becomes paranoid and suspicious. David Lyon once wrote, quite alliteratively, that the problem of paranoia is that it "produces political paralysis" (*The Electronic Eye*, 218–219). We become fatalistic, or spend our time protecting our little domains. Do you agree? Can paranoia be useful? What alternatives might there be?
2. Why doesn't Robert Dean, in *Enemy of the State*, seem to care that Brill is watching him?
3. By watching others being watched, how much do we learn about how we should act on camera? If you found yourself on reality TV, what would you do?

3

Surveillance Societies

Figure 3.1 Anderton pieces together a murder before it happens. *Minority Report.*

In the opening scene of *Enemy of the State*, Congressman Hammersley (Jason Robards) decries the proposal of the Telecommunication Security and Privacy Act. He quotes a line from the *Washington Post*: "This bill is not the first step to the surveillance society. It is the surveillance society." To which the NSA officer Reynolds (Jon Voight) responds, "liberal hysteria." But if this fictional bill (which foreshadows the very real Patriot Act by three years) creates "The Surveillance Society," which surveillance society does it create? What is meant by that phrase?

I do not believe that *Enemy of the State* depicts a surveillance society, but it does depict the first steps. And the technofetishism of its imagery, the isolation and dismissal of critical voices, the blaming of problems on rogue individuals rather than the system itself, the trust in the underlying fairness and justice of the system as well as a trust in the ability of the system to self-correct do not discourage the taking of those steps. I do not believe that the film depicts a surveillance society, but it does depict extensive surveillance capabilities and a proliferation of information and communication technologies in society that can be drawn in to centralized surveillance schemes. As depicted in the film, the NSA supplements their own extensive capabilities by appropriating the surveillance capacities of independent technologies for particular purposes. A store security camera, for example, is not part of the state security apparatus, but can be utilized by it on an ad hoc basis. There "is no such thing as an 'innocent' surveillance camera," writes Dietmar Kammerer.[1] A surveillance society, to my mind, is one in which all these connections are hardwired, part of a central surveillance apparatus that is pervasive throughout society. Just because a society has many and varied surveillance systems doesn't make it a surveillance society, at least in the way that the term is used above. The implication in *Enemy of the State* is that this legislation would render more permanent and constant the ad hoc articulation of surveillance capacities and put them to a singular purpose.

The idea of a surveillance society is dystopian. A *dystopia* is a worst-case scenario of the future we don't want, where all our fears come true. Dystopias have power because they contradict the strongly held cultural notion of *progress*, that, through technology especially, things can only get better.[2] Dystopias raise questions about the very technologies we take as indicators of progress. But the problem with dystopias is that they offer few real options or solutions. As David Lyon has put it, dystopias fail to provide any positive alternatives and as a result "they encourage a form of fatalism."[3] So when we look at depictions of surveillance societies we should ask, as we did in the previous chapter, what is the solution and is it one that comforts us, stirs us to action, leads us to question?

In some ways the idea that we are becoming a surveillance society is depicted as inevitable. In almost any portrayal of a future society, pervasive surveillance features prominently. Even in more positive visions of the future, such as the *Star Trek* series of films and television shows (in which the central mode of governing is democratic, racial and gender equality are taken for granted, and justice is a cause worth fighting for), the surveillance capabilities of scanners and communication equipment are extensive.

It is the dystopian vision that is most common, and when we think of dystopia and surveillance the tropes and language of George Orwell's *Nineteen Eighty-Four* are drawn on. But Orwell's description of an authoritarian society is not the only model of surveillance society. We've also discussed, in the previous chapter, Foucault's idea of Panopticism and we should consider how a Panoptic society would be depicted in film. But also there is a third model, what French philosopher Gilles Deleuze called the society of control.[4] Though we most often use the language of Orwell in popular discourse, and increasingly Panopticism, we are more likely to see aspects of control depicted in our contemporary feature films.

Orwellian surveillance

George Orwell's novel *Nineteen Eighty-Four* depicts a future London dominated by an authoritarian regime headed by a figure known only as Big Brother. It is a society hierarchically divided into the Inner Party, Outer Party, and the Proles. London is capital of Oceania, which is continually at war with one of the other two super-states, Eurasia and Eastasia, and life is characterized by poverty, ruin, and desperation. The population is mercilessly controlled through extensive surveillance technologies and networks, through an insistence on ideological purity among Party members, and brutal violence. The Party has wiped out any love or loyalty to anyone besides Big Brother, including families. Control is maintained by constant surveillance: frequent patrols walk the streets, spying helicopters hover in the air, each room has a huge telescreen that not only emits continual propaganda (and that cannot be turned off) but through which the Thought Police can hear and see all that goes on there. There are informers throughout the society and therefore no one can be trusted. Even children are raised to be loyal to Big Brother and denounce their parents at any hint of disloyalty. People often disappear, sent off to hard labor, or tortured, or simply executed, never to be heard from again. The Party controls all means of communication and information: all books, news, songs, and other texts are produced by the Party, and any contradictory texts have long been destroyed. The Party has rewritten history to its own liking (they claim to have invented airplanes, for example) and no one can contradict them. It is Winston Smith's job to rewrite old newspaper articles if events render them incorrect or politically awkward. A goal of the Party is to control the thoughts of the population. This is achieved through the constant propaganda barrage of the telescreens, posters, and public broadcasts. But not only this, they are altering language, eliminating words so that rebellious thought simply cannot be formulated.

This is the Orwellian society: the constant presence (or suspected presence) of surveillance technologies and informers, each directly linked back to centralized control. Citizens live in fear of acting wrong, speaking wrong, or even having the wrong expression; the consequences are swift and brutal. Opposition is impossible. Orwellian control is not simply the constant gaze of Big Brother, but the very real threat of Big Brother's fist or boot.

Relatively little happens in the book that is not in Winston's head. He writes thoughts in his secret diary. He meets Julia and they conduct a clandestine affair which for him is a political act and for her just a chance to have fun. Winston reaches out to an Inner Party member he believes to be a rebel and is rewarded by being inducted into a secret underground organization called the Brotherhood. However, this is a trick of the Thought Police who have been monitoring him all along, and Winston and Julia are captured, tortured, and their thoughts rendered ideologically clean.

Winston is a pessimistic romantic. He sees that active rebellion is impossible, but if he can still think his own thoughts (hence, the diary), then that is rebellion enough. "It was not by making yourself heard but staying sane that you carried on the human heritage."[5] Any defeat of Big Brother would either happen through minute increments over generations, or through the uprising of the lumpen Proles throwing off the shackles of their oppression. He is not an action hero, but a self-made intellectual who believes that thoughts are his freedom.

Julia has a different approach, however. She is not interested in the philosophy of it all, or the larger rebellion against the state. "I'm not interested in the next generation, dear. I'm interested in *us*," she says. To which Winston replies, "You're only a rebel from the waist downwards."[6] Julia's approach is to break the rules, have a good time, and stay alive. "[S]he only questioned the teachings of the Party when they in some way touched upon her own life. Often she was ready to accept the official mythology, simply because the difference between truth and falsehood did not seem important to her."[7] She knows how to act the part of the fervent Party member in order to get what she wants. And she is an optimist ("She would not accept it as a law of nature that the individual is always defeated").[8]

Filming Orwell

Given that much of the story is a monologue within Winston's head, the book is virtually unfilmable. The 1956 film version, directed by Michael Anderson and starring Edmund O'Brien as Winston Smith and Jan Sterling as Julia, was made less than a decade after the publication of the book and uses parts of London still in rubble after WWII as a backdrop. The film opens with images of atomic explosions and is deeply entrenched in a cold war consciousness. The film ends with the statement: "This then is a story of the future. It could be the story of our children, if we fail to preserve their heritage of freedom." The film, "freely adapted" (it states) from the book, follows the main events of the novel. The actions are more bold than in the book to better convey the plot. Julia is seen actively following Winston, for example, rather than the seemingly chance encounters of the book. And the daughter of Winston's neighbor, Parsons, takes a more active role in spying on him and following him. Through depictions of patrols, telescreens, and spies,

Figure 3.2 Winston's Panoptic office. *1984.*

the oppressive surveillance of Big Brother is portrayed. In an interesting set piece, Winston's office is a Panoptic space: a circular room with backlit desks around the walls.

Whereas this earlier version emphasizes the plot and action of the book (importing a cold war wariness), Michael Radford's later version (with John Hurt as Winston, Suzanna Hamilton as Julia, and Richard Burton as O'Brien) takes a different approach. The film makes a gesture toward authenticity by filming in 1984, in London, near the dates and locations depicted in the book. In the novel we get Winston's descriptions, interpretations, and reactions to the means of surveillance. Radford's film compensates for this lack of narrative voice in the film not through an emphasis on the plot (like the earlier version), nor by incorporating voice-over, but by emphasizing the visual and aural experience of the world of Oceania. There is little dialogue in much of the film. The film produces its version of the novel not by representing every instance from the book, but by creating a parallel experience that gets the same point across. The constant irritating blaring of the telescreens, the marshal music, the ubiquity of propaganda posters, the patrols and the helicopters, the images of dingy and decrepit buildings, the filth and the grime, all make the film a visceral experience. The audience feels how the population is beaten down. The graphic violence and nudity likewise play upon the sensorium of the audience. The book itself can be brutal, but it is self-consciously so to make a point. It never takes its violence for granted and every blow is specific. But since we get so little of Winston's inner life, the film cannot balance the desperation of thought with the experience of pain, and by focusing so much on the experience of Oceania runs the risk of becoming merely sensationalistic. Though the surveillance in *1984* is never voyeuristic, the film almost becomes so.

THX 1138

Other depictions of dystopian futures take their cues from Orwell. George Lucas's *THX 1138* (1971)[9] takes place in a repressive, conformist society where the population is kept under control by constant video surveillance, patrols of silver-faced robot policemen, and the legal requirement that they be sedated at all times (echoing Aldous Huxley's dystopian novel *Brave New World*). Rather than the deprivations of the war economy used to control the citizens of Oceania, it is constant mindless consumption of useless objects that control in Lucas's film. THX 1138 (Robert Duvall) buys a strange red object from a store that sells nothing but the same object. When he gets home it gets tossed in the incinerator. The blaring political propaganda of the telescreens in *1984* becomes in *THX 1138* inane violent and pornographic holographic television to keep the population docile. Other forms of surveillance are in evidence. For example, THX's overseers can track his breathing and adrenal activity while he is at work. Like in *Nineteen Eighty-Four*, romantic relationships, and passion of any sort, are discouraged. Citizens are encouraged to cite each other for violations of law and procedure. And citizens are assigned prefixes and numbers rather than names. Unlike *Nineteen Eighty-Four*, the society itself seems to have no figurehead or named party; it is just a total system, run by computer. In the film, LUH 3416 (Maggie McOmie) begins decreasing her sedative and finds herself falling in love with her mate, THX 1138. She reduces his sedatives as well, waking him up to his passions and to the situation of their society. LUH is captured, but THX tries to escape. The basic principle of the society is efficiency and economy and, in a twist on action genre expectations, the relentless robot pursuit of the fugitive is finally called off when the mission goes over budget. Surveillance in the film isn't just by some central authority, but by citizens in different departments. We see LUH at her work monitoring screens (and watching THX); and we see SEN (Donald Pleasance), who has an odd fixation on THX, watching them both on his screens. The surveillance is dispassionate (as everyone is heavily sedated), and yet voyeuristic at the same time. After they have had passionate sex, LUH worries, "They know. They've been watching us. I can feel it." To which THX replies, "No one knows … No one can see us." This statement is followed by two shots panning along rows of men all staring out at the camera (us), all watching, followed by a grainy blue CCTV image of LUH and THX entwined. Everyone can see you. Voyeurism is encouraged, but passion is denied.

V for Vendetta

The more recent film *V for Vendetta* (2005), based on a series of comic books by Alan Moore and David Lloyd, is set in a future fascist Britain with ubiquitous surveillance. Cameras with facial recognition are everywhere, Fingermen (the police) are in the crowds, and vans patrol the streets listening in on people's conversations. Set in a post-9/11, post-Iraq war context, the film argues that the war on terrorism has been met with the rise of the right wing. The regime has brutally oppressed and eliminated anyone who is not white, heterosexual, or Christian. Against this regime arises a lone hero, the mysterious masked V (Hugo Weaving) who has developed extensive

Figure 3.3 SEN watching LUH and THX; LUH is watching THX on her own monitor. *THX 1138.*

surveillance and ordinance capabilities of his own and begins a campaign to murder many of the figures in charge of the government in retribution for what they had done to him in a concentration camp. Along the way V rescues a young woman (Evey, played by Natalie Portman) and she becomes his accomplice and apprentice. V turns his campaign from a personal one to one that will empower the common people to rise up against their government. "A people should not fear their government," he intones, "a government should fear its people." The source of hope, echoing the theme from *Nineteen Eighty-Four*, is one's integrity (which they cannot take away) and a love of all humanity. *V for Vendetta* is an action-oriented film that savors its explosions and fight sequences. Like Radford's *1984* it works more on a visceral, affective level to pitch its populist message[10] (and along the way jettisons the subtleties and anarchist politics of the original comics to present a final set piece that seems to match the fascism of the regime with a fascism of the mob, marching in identical masks, capes, and hats against the lines of police).[11]

The films we have been discussing are not purely Orwellian versions of surveillance society. We see at least some elements of the Foucauldian Panopticon. Radford's *1984* is the closest to purely Orwellian, and the Anderson version from 1956 gestures toward the use of Panoptic principles in the design of Winston's workplace. Drawing on Lyon's early comparison of Orwell and Foucault, we can discuss the main characteristics of each. Orwell links "violent and non-violent methods."[12] There is always a threat of violence behind the surveillance, and the intimidation of actual violent repression. We see this in the violence of the Thought Police in *1984*, the batons of *THX 1138*'s silver faced guards (despite the guards' statements that they are just trying to help), and throughout *V for Vendetta*. In the Orwellian scheme, there are no laws or rules since any law becomes a point on which someone might resist or challenge the place of the Party. Society should be completely liquid, malleable to the Party's wishes, with the population continually uncertain. Orwellian control includes an assault on dignity and this, Lyon points out, is what ultimately breaks Winston, the utter loss of dignity and self in O'Brien's torture of him and, finally, face to face with the rats. Orwellian control is therefore about the loss of individuality. It is about brutality and power for its own sake, for centralized state power. *THX 1138* is about efficiency rather than power, and *V for Vendetta* is about power via a specific ideology, a notion spurned by O'Brien in the novel *Nineteen Eighty-Four*. Both Orwellian and Panoptic control are based on imperceptible surveillance, the uncertainty of knowing whether you are watched or not. But in Orwell's dystopian scheme the uncertainty is for its own sake, to make the subject malleable. In the utopian scheme of Bentham, uncertainty leads to subjects becoming aware of their own surveillance, internalizing expectations and norms. So the Panoptic is about specific laws or rules, the production of normality (rather than power for its own sake), and the production of the private individual. Rather than assaulting dignity, disciplinary power emphasizes the care of the self—an ethical principle to improve oneself.[13] Panoptic power is subtle and dispersed and primarily non-violent. It is also distributed across institutions, both state and private, rather than being centralized in the state.

The Handmaid's Tale

Contrast, for example, the scenarios of *1984*, *THX 1138*, and *V for Vendetta* against *The Handmaid's Tale*. The film *The Handmaid's Tale* (1990) is based on Margaret Atwood's book (1986), and combines both Orwellian and Panoptic aspects. The book, like *Nineteen Eighty-Four*, is primarily the internal reflections and observations of its narrator, who we only know as Offred, and is relatively limited in terms of events and actions. The film is much more plot-driven and changes the story in parts to emphasize action.

The Handmaid's Tale takes place in the United States in the near future. A right-wing fundamentalist Christian movement has militarized and wiped out the US government, setting up an authoritarian state, Gilead, in its stead, based on a selective reading of patriarchal Old Testament principles. In the background, we hear rumors of wars against rebellions led by other Christian denominations, and evidence of widespread environmental disasters. Fertility rates are plummeting. The society of Gilead is hierarchical, with the leaders and their families living in heavily guarded subdivisions. Members of society are given strict social roles: there are the leaders and their wives, the Guardians, The Econowives, the Marthas, and the Handmaids. Given the loss of fertility, especially among the elite, young women who are fertile are given the choice to become Handmaids (though the alternative to this choice is hard labor under toxic conditions). Drawing on a passage in the Book of Genesis where Rachel, who cannot bear children, asks Jacob to impregnate her maid, Bilhah, "that I may also have children by her" (Genesis 30:3), Handmaids are there to be impregnated by the husbands on the wives' behalf. Any children resulting from this act become the wives' children. *The Handmaid's Tale* is a set of reflections by a Handmaid named Offred (Natasha Richardson in the film), recounting memories of life before the coup (married and with a young daughter); her families' attempt to flee Gilead; her capture; her training and discipline in the Red Center, where Handmaids are prepared by the Aunts for their role; and her assignment to the Commander and his wife. She is given the name Offred since her Commander's name is Fred (Robert Duvall in the film). She is forbidden to use her real name, and in the book we never learn it (though the film calls her Kate).

The regime in *The Handmaid's Tale* is Orwellian in many aspects. There is the constant deprivation of war and rationing; there is the brutal military regime conducting public executions; there is indoctrination into the correct way of thinking; there are secret police ("The Eyes"); and so on. There is also a lack of trust—anyone could be a spy, everyone is encouraged to report on those with rebellious attitudes. For example, Handmaids do the family shopping, but must travel in pairs. "The truth is," Offred writes, "that she is my spy, as I am hers. If either of us slips through the net because of something that happens on one of our daily walks, the other will be accountable."[14] But there are characteristics of a disciplinary society as well. For example, everyone is given a clear role and made visible by colored uniform: Handmaids in red, Marthas in green, Wives in Blue, and so on. Everyone likewise has their proper place, either in their neighborhood, their house, or their room. The movements of the Handmaids particularly, given the importance of their role in reproducing society, are carefully controlled. Offred has her room, and clear limitations on when and where she can go. The expectations for each social role are clearly stated and the citizens are disciplined to learn their place, role, mindset, and language. The Panoptic nature of this discipline is clearest in scenes from the film. The images we are presented with in the film depict the city at large as a war zone, with toxic waste, decimated buildings, and a prominent military presence. The state of the city is in marked contrast with how the neighborhoods of the elite are depicted, with quiet tree-lined streets, green lawns, and large mansions, overseen by watchtowers and barricades. The particular scenes I am referring to regarding Panopticism occur in the Red Center, where Handmaids are trained and indoctrinated. They sleep in cots, row upon row, at some remove from one another to prevent communication, in an old gymnasium. The space is observed constantly by videocameras, monitored by one of the Aunts. The slightest infraction or movement out of place can lead to severe punishment. Handmaids must confess their past lives and accept the state's definition of who they are.

However, despite aspects of disciplinary Panopticism, the goal is not the same. The Panopticon produced individuals, whereas Gilead produces uniformity, and individuality is erased. For example, the narrator is given the name Offred, but if she fails and is replaced, that Handmaid's name will also be Offred.[15] The name indicates a position rather than an individual. Gilead doesn't produce information, but destroys it. Books, magazines, and newspapers are forbidden, especially to women. However, there are indications that extensive files still kept somewhere. Serena (Faye Dunaway in the film), the Commander's wife, knows Offred's history and is able to locate her lost daughter. But the uniformity-individuality tension is a key difference between the film and the book. In the book, the Handmaids wear a white headdress with wings that hide their faces and partially block their vision. As a result, there are fewer individualizing

Figure 3.4 The Panoptic Red Center. *The Handmaid's Tale.*

features: a Handmaid is a Handmaid. In the film, the white headdresses are abandoned in favor of red veils and headscarves that allow us to see the actor's faces. This, as a result, allows them to have individual identities. Nonetheless, like in *1984*, the regime allows for a collective outlet for affect and aggression to tamper down individual passions. While Oceania has the Two Minutes Hate, for the women of Gilead, especially the Handmaids, there are collective Salvagings (where the Handmaids ritually participate in the execution of women who have committed crimes) and particicutions (where the Handmaids collectively participate in an execution of a man by tearing them apart with their hands). The film is able to visually capture the sea of red figures, at first in orderly lines for the salvaging and then as an angry red mob in the particicution. Individual identity is diminished and the collective whole takes over.

Orwellian and Foucauldian models of surveillance allow us to see some of the purpose, structure, and dynamics of surveillance in these films. No film represents either model fully, but the models become tools to understand the films and also the imaginary depicted by the films, the role of power and technology in how surveillance is understood in those narratives. But there are limitations to how these models help us understand, and respond to, contemporary surveillance. David Lyon writes:

> Whereas the contemporary interpreters of Orwell's dystopia may under certain circumstances galvanize action and resistance—"Big Brother is watching you" must be the best known anti-surveillance slogan—Foucault's dystopia seems rather to instill paranoia and paralysis.[16]

The problem for Lyon is that in Foucault's analysis "it is unclear exactly what is wrong with the Panopticon or what strategy might be appropriate to question or resist it."[17] When power is so diffuse and nebulous, when it is decentralized and productive, it becomes more difficult (though certainly not impossible) to mount a critique. A brutal centralized state regime degrading and abusing its population? That's clear and, as we have seen, can be quite cinematic. Such films have clearer protagonists and antagonists, present colorful spectacles and action-packed plots, can draw on liberal visions of the individual struggling against collective oppression. A proliferation of state and private institutions instilling discipline by gathering information, rendering judgments, and encouraging the production of normative subjects? Less clear, and less cinematic.

In addition, the Orwellian and Foucauldian models work less well on more recent films. And by looking at these more recent films, in particular *The Truman Show*, *Minority Report*, and *Gattaca*, we can trace the emergence of a third model of surveillance society similar to one briefly sketched by French philosopher Gilles Deleuze in some of his last essays.[18] These are societies of control.

Societies of control

Deleuze once argued that contemporary society is moving from a regime of surveillance and discipline (marked by enclosures) to one of surveillance and control, which he termed *societies of control*, borrowing the phrase from William S. Burroughs.[19]

[Disciplinary societies] operate by organizing major sites of confinement. Individuals are always going from one closed site to another, each with its own laws: first of all the family, then school ("you're not at home, you know"), then the barracks ("you're not at school, you know"), then the factory, hospital from time to time, maybe prison, the model site of confinement.[20]

Drawing on the work of Paul Virilio as well as Foucault and Burroughs, Deleuze writes that "We're moving toward control societies that no longer operate by confining people but through continuous control and instant communication."[21] Deleuze's image is that of a highway: a highway does not confine one, but it does control one's movements, the options available to one.

The key feature of the control society is the crisis in societal institutions. The barriers between home, work, school, prison, and the hospital begin to break down and run together. Education now emphasizes continuing education, and assessment (of school, work, and so on) is now constant. "[I]n control societies you never finish anything."[22] In a control society one could conceivably be at home, telecommuting into work, taking an online class, be on prison leave—attached to an ankle monitoring device (think of Kale in *Disturbia*)—and be in the hospital—attached to monitoring devices that dial in to your doctor with your current vitals—all at the same time. Congratulations, you are now always at work (at least potentially so). Rather than being subject to specific rules of discipline in different institutional settings, in the society of control it is the case that, as Nikolas Rose has written,

Conduct is continually monitored and reshaped by logics immanent within all networks of practice. Surveillance is "designed in" to the flows of everyday existence. The calculated modulation of conduct according to principles of optimization of benign impulses and minimization of malign impulses is dispersed across the time and space of ordinary life.[23]

But rather than creating a society as a smooth space, with no differentiations, stratifications, or borders, the stratifications of civil society have hopped the boundaries and have been generalized throughout society.[24] Michael Hardt writes that whereas the modern, disciplinary state was premised on the delineation of "a (real or imagined) territory and the relation of that territory to its outside,"[25] in a control society the outside is internalized (for example, public space is privatized). But it is not that the lines of social stratification have gone away, they have proliferated instead. The smooth space of the society of control is not a free space. Hardt argues, "as Deleuze and Guattari are careful to point out, within this process of smoothing, elements of social striation reappear 'in the most perfect and severe forms.' In other words, the crisis or decline of the enclosures or institutions gives rise in certain respects to the hypersegmentation of society."[26] We could even say that in a society of control, one might long for a disciplinary society because at least there were limits to control; one could leave school and go to work. How much worse is the society of control if it makes us nostalgic for disciplinary institutions?

But what is meant by "control" that differentiates it from "discipline"? Whereas disciplinary apparatuses start over at each site, control is continuous. Whereas discipline is analogical, control is digital, consisting of inseparable variations and the proliferation of difference. Whereas discipline works by molding the subject, control works through constant modulation, continually changing from one moment to the next. Control "undulates," in a control society we surf.[27] Whereas a disciplinary society works via precepts (order words), the society of control works through passwords and controlling access to information. Whereas disciplinary society is characterized by production (the factory), the control society is characterized by metaproduction (assembly and marketing). Whereas disciplinary society produces individuals, control is about dividuals, small pieces of independent data that proliferate and circulate. Whereas discipline focuses on the long term, control focuses on the short term and is rapidly shifting. Deleuze writes that money provides a clear distinction between the two regimes: whereas disciplinary society uses molded currency connected to a gold standard, control is based on floating exchange rates and modulations in currency. "A man is no longer a man confined but a man in debt."[28]

Control is modulation, a series of constant adjustments. It is not being trained and then let loose but being constantly tweaked (continuing education). Deleuze refers to it as social engineering. One of his examples is television, which he considers a direct form of social engineering ("the ultimate consensus"). Television to Deleuze does not exploit its aesthetic possibilities like film, but only a social function. He writes, "Television's professional eye, the famous socially engineered eye through which the viewer is himself invited to look, produces an immediate and complacent perfection that's instantly controllable and controlled."[29] Deleuze is obviously no fan of television and his characterization of television and its effects is at times simplistic and problematic. Nonetheless, this description of television gives us a sense of the general workings of control.

Another example of social engineering is marketing. "Marketing is now the instrument of social control and produces the arrogant breed who are our masters."[30] Individuals are no longer treated as individuals but as demographics. Echoing and paraphrasing Raymond Williams, who had a similar suspicion of the new advertising men in the 1950s, we could say that "there are in fact no markets, only ways of seeing people as markets."[31] The surveillance of the control society, for example, gives rise to what Oscar Gandy has called "the panoptic sort," the hypersegmentation of the audience and market into desirable and undesirable sets according to increasingly complex algorithms and the discriminatory apparatus of market surveys and consumer databases.[32] Unlike previous discriminatory apparatuses, the categories of differentiation are multiply cross-referenced so that one cannot even point to the factor that, for example, led one to be denied credit, much less change one's desirability. Another example, one that Deleuze provides, is that of the new medicine that works by identifying potential cases and subject groups at risk for disease (e.g., genetic testing) and proceeds from there, rather than doctors treating a particular patient with a particular ailment.[33]

Though it is not a term that Deleuze uses, one difference between the disciplinary and control regimes is that in the latter, surveillance is articulated with *simulation*. Computer models (of markets, populations, crime profiles, traffic patterns, and so on) are now sufficiently powerful to provide fairly complex, real-time simulations of "reality." Decisions are made by governments, corporations, and institutions based on these simulations and projections as if they were "reality."[34] So one is denied credit or insurance based on one's profile in the simulation and computer-generated projections, not on actual behavior.

The surveillant eye of the disciplinary state is now accompanied, or even superseded, by the surveillant eye of control, which is exemplified in the eye of marketing; the docile subject becomes the consuming subject. It is not the state controlling its citizens, but the economic system monitoring its audiences and markets to turn us into perfect consumers (tuning us to match the product as much as vice versa). As Hardt writes, "the capitalist market is one machine that has always run counter to any division between inside and outside,"[35] in other words, counter to the modern disciplinary state and therefore is quite at home in a society of control. This is not to say that the disciplinary state has disappeared (cameras are everywhere, from banks to soccer matches to public squares ready to capture malfeasance and arrest the perpetrators), just that it is not the only regime out there.[36] We need to make sure to avoid the easy and common reduction of this analysis to binaries: discipline versus control. Likewise, elements of this regime are hardly new, but have intensified with the aid of new communication and information technologies over the past thirty years or so.

As Nikolas Rose has stated, Deleuze's arguments are "more hypotheses than conclusions." He continues,

> And they are framed in terms that are far to epochal: Foucault's disciplinary societies were not "disciplined societies," but those where strategies and tactics of discipline were active; likewise, Deleuze's control societies should not be understood sociologically, but in terms of the emergence of new possibilities and the complexification of the old.[37]

The Truman Show

The Truman Show (1998) stars Jim Carrey as Truman Burbank, a man living, for all appearances, a fairly happy idyllic life in a small town called Seahaven. He seems happily married and has a good, though boring, job; he hangs out with his best friend, Marlon (Noah Emmerich), and drinks beer. The neighbors are friendly, the streets are clean, the houses and picket fences all white and shining, and the weather is always beautiful. However, unbeknownst to Truman, his entire life is actually a television show ("The Truman Show"). Ever since the day he was born, and throughout the thirty years since, his every moment has been broadcast live across the globe by an array of hidden cameras. The show prides itself on finding innovative places to hide miniature cameras, from brooches to dog collars, to jacket buttons and streetlights. Indeed, the town in which he lives is actually a giant stage set, built under a monumental dome that can reproduce weather, the movement of the stars, and so on. All the other people in his life, including his mother, father, wife, and best friend, are paid actors; all the events in his life are scripted "episodes" directed (literally from on high) by Christof (Ed Harris). Truman is under constant surveillance both by the television audience (who watch in record numbers and speculate "How will it end?") and the director's staff (who wish to control and manipulate—and prolong—Truman's life under glass). The film covers the final few weeks of the show as Truman increasingly becomes suspicious of those around him and begins to believe that the world he lives in is not real. He desires to escape the town and find his true love, Sylvia (Natascha McElhone), an "extra" with whom he fell in love in college, who he believes has moved to Fiji.

The Truman Show takes Jean Baudrillard seriously. Writing in the 1970s and citing the example of the Loud family on PBS (*An American Family*, 1973), Baudrillard argues that "the most intimate operation of your life becomes the potential grazing ground of the media.... The entire universe unfolds unnecessarily on your home screen," which he terms "obscenity."[38] For Baudrillard this is not just an argument about privacy but about economics and consumerism. The "inexorable light of information and communication" (his phrase) feeds a capitalist consumerism in which everyday life becomes commodified, even our symbolic life (so that we are reduced to uttering commercial catch phrases to each other over fast food).

Both regimes—discipline and control—are in evidence in the film. Truman has been disciplined to stay in Seahaven (a town built on an island) by making him deathly afraid of water. When Truman was young, he and his father went sailing, a storm blew up, and his father was supposedly drowned—a traumatic experience. Now he cannot bring himself to get on a ferry or even cross a bridge over water. Throughout his life, the actors that surround him present him with constant reminders that life is perfect in the town, that life elsewhere is terrible, and that he is very lucky to be where he is and to have what he does. The purpose of all this is to have him internalize these notions and remain in the town (and on the show). At the heart of a disciplinary regime is violence, but implied violence, not the overt violence of the Orwellian model. Security on the set it tight, intruders are quickly manhandled out of the way. The violence underlying "The Truman Show" reveals itself during Truman's first escape attempt (he is surrounded, netted, and tackled) and in the search for Truman at the end of the film (e.g., the friendly neighborhood dog becomes a snarling tracker).

But the dominant regime in evidence in the film is control. Surveillance is, obviously, essential to the situation; television cameras are everywhere. But crucially Truman is *unaware* that he is being watched or manipulated, which makes this the surveillance of the control society rather than discipline. As the character of Marlon says early in the film, as if to confirm Deleuze's insight, "nothing on the show is fake; it's merely controlled."

Figure 3.5 View from a Button-Cam. *The Truman Show*.

Toward the end of his essay, "Postscript on Control Societies," Deleuze writes,

> Félix Guattari has imagined a town where anyone can leave their flat, their street, their neighborhood, using their (individual) electronic card that opens this or that barrier; but the card may also be rejected on a particular day, or between certain times of day; it doesn't depend on the barrier but on the computer that is making sure everyone is in a permissible place, and effecting a universal modulation.[39]

The idea of universal modulation is key to the functioning of "The Truman Show." Truman is constantly tracked and his movements are guided by being blocked by passerby or traffic or other means. As he moves through his day, despite his seeming freedom of movement, he is guided, nudged, and modulated. He is *managed* (another important term for the society of control), and the logics that manage him are immanent to every structure or individual or situation that Truman encounters.

Though our lives are nothing like that of *The Truman Show*, as public spaces are replaced by private ones (a dimension of the collapse of the inside and the outside characteristic of the control society), for example, the town square becomes the mall, we open ourselves even more to being managed in these ways. One extreme example is that of the theme park where experience and movement are carefully (and almost invisibly) controlled.[40] Michael Crichton's 1973 film *Westworld* is an apropos commentary on the role of surveillance to control the experience of visitors to a theme park that simulates authentic Western, Medieval, and Roman settings. Staffed by robots which are carefully programmed, and observed by hidden cameras, every experience the guests have appears natural and spontaneous.

To contrast the society of control with a disciplinary regime of surveillance, it is worthwhile to briefly compare *The Truman Show* with the 1967–1968 British television series *The Prisoner* with which it has some superficial similarities. *The Prisoner* concerns an ex-secret agent known only as Number Six (Patrick McGoohan), who resigns his position only to find himself trapped in a twee seaside town known only as The Village, from which there is no escape. Life is idyllic in The Village and the weather is wonderful, but life is also firmly controlled by an individual known only as Number Two (played by various actors) and the inhabitants are kept under constant surveillance. The contrasts with *The Truman Show* are significant: violence is much more near the surface in *The Prisoner* (from the bizarre hovering menace of a six-foot rubber ball referred to as Rover to direct attempts at brainwashing and intimidation); the regime wants information from Number Six while Christof merely wants entertainment from Truman; and Number Six is always acutely aware of his confinement, while Truman is kept innocent of his.

One final general difference between the two regimes is the ostensible benevolence of the control society. Spying on Truman is a harmless endeavor. We do not want to hurt him, we just want to watch. The society is taking care of Truman, giving him what he needs (and even giving him his needs: for example, a new mower), making sure that he has no real problems. Likewise, ever finer points of consumer stratification are meant to make our lives easier: we just get what we want, or so we are told.

Battle Royale

The Truman Show emphasizes some aspects of the society of control, especially those of modulation and consumption. A handful of other films delineate additional aspects of surveillance in a society of control. For example, Kentaro Kawashima argues that Kinji Fukasaku's controversial film *Battle Royale* (2000) elucidates aspects of the society of control.[41] The film is about a brutal annual event where a class of teenage schoolmates is chosen to compete in the *Battle Royale*. They are taken to a remote island and given access to deadly weapons; the last student left alive is the victor (the basic plot is similar to the more recent *The Hunger Games* series of books and films). The island is under military control to prevent the students escaping. Each student is tracked with the aid of an electronic collar. In addition, the island is demarcated into zones. An announcement is made each day about which zones will be off limits at which times during the day. If a student is still in an off-limit zone during a restricted period, their electronic collar explodes, killing them. Kawashima writes that, unlike the films *Enemy of the State* and *Minority Report*, *Battle Royale* "is not that interested in the technological level of the control societies. Instead it focuses more on the processes of subjectivation that are set in motion by the way the teenagers are controlled by the electronic collar."[42] For Kawashima, the modulation and management of a society's movements via electronic control, like Guattari's hypothetical town discussed above, is the key aspect of how a society governs in a control society. But the film also emphasizes the element of *competition* prevalent in a control society. Work, school, almost any endeavor becomes a competition, a game. "The battle royal is a new kind of social order, as it were, which is not established by disciplining subjects according to norms, but instead, perpetuates itself by controlling behavior, pitting everyone against everyone else."[43] Indeed, the film is premised on a frustration with discipline. The man in charge of the Battle Royale used to be the teacher of these children (in the disciplinary setting of the school), but revels in the control he now has that he lacked then. For the students, three types of subjectivation await them in the battle: they can adapt and become willing competitors, they can commit suicide, or they can band together to work against the forces of control. For the eventual winner the experience is not just that of survival but awakening as to the true nature of society (an individual awakening, Kawashima points out, that is evident in other surveillance films of the era). This analysis is not to imply that the control society is a somewhat universal social change, that it can be found everywhere in the world in the same way. There is a particular character to the control society in *Battle Royale* that inflects it with contemporary cultural and political resonance for Japan, and that is that "the emerging control society is contaminated by historical totalitarianism,"[44] seen in the military presence and the authoritarian behavior of the teacher, and echoing the troubling rise of a more militaristic right wing in Japanese politics, harkening back to days of Japan's imperial aspirations.

The films *Minority Report* and *Gattaca* also describe aspects of the society of control, but with different emphases. Simulation, prediction, and control become the key themes of these films.

Minority Report

Steven Spielberg's *Minority Report* (2002) is based on a short story by Philip K. Dick. It is set in 2054 in Washington, DC, where an experiment in law enforcement is underway. A system called Precrime has been developed which can actually foresee when a crime is going to occur. A special task force is deployed to track down and arrest the perpetrator before they can commit the crime. Though technically innocent (they haven't committed a crime) they are arrested and imprisoned for what was going to happen. As a result of this experiment, crime has fallen to almost nothing and the only crimes that occupy the time of the Precrime team are crimes of passion (since they are not premeditated). At the opening of the film, Precrime is about to go from a Washington, DC, operation to a national one. The premise of Precrime follows trends in predictive policing where rather than using surveillance data post hoc to catch criminals, population data is analyzed to identify trends to predict who is most likely to commit a crime. But Precrime is not built on data collection, analysis, modeling, and ever-more fine-grained monitoring; it is not a computer at the heart of surveillance (as it is, for example, in the original comic book version of *V for Vendetta* or in *THX 1138*). Rather, the system is based on the visions of three humans who have developed psychic abilities due to their being born with brain damage to women addicted to a new neurological drug. These Pre-Cogs are kept in a somnolent state in a facility the Precrime unit refers to as The Temple.

The plot of the film concerns John Anderton (Tom Cruise), a team leader of the Precrime unit. As the unit is being inspected by a federal agent, Danny Witwer (Colin Farrell), prior to the approval of the program for national rollout, the Pre-Cogs raise a warning about an impending murder. They project images that depict Anderton himself shooting an unknown victim. Anderton panics and flees into the city to hide from his colleagues as he investigates the man he is supposed to murder and the origin of Precrime itself, to discover if the future is set or if he can change it. If he believes in the truth, accuracy, and legality of Precrime, there is no changing the future and he is indeed guilty. But if it is possible to do so, then Precrime can no longer work on a presumption of guilt and all those arrested must be freed.

The society depicted in *Minority Report* is one where surveillance is an expected and regular feature of daily life. The primary mechanism of surveillance is a system of retina scans. As people move through their day, enter a subway car or a store or a building, their retinas are scanned and their location and identity is recorded. This information is used in a number of ways. It presumably allows the subway to charge them, it allows police to track all movements, and it allows shops and advertisements to personalize themselves for you. Smart advertising billboards can change their images to include you (or people like you) as you pass them by, even calling you out by name. Stores know your buying habits and can direct you to suggested sales. Control is seen both in the consumerism of the society (as we saw in *The Truman Show* and *THX 1138*) as well as the police. It is impossible to be anonymous in this society. The result is a docile population, kept happy by tailored offers of products and services and passively acquiescing to police authority. In one sequence, the Precrime team hunts Anderton in a large working-class apartment complex. Heat scans reveal the presence and location of each human in the building. The officers release small robot spiders to enter every room and scan each person to establish their identity. There are no protections against search, the police just enter wherever they want, and there is no resistance from the population or even surprise at seeing police robots in their apartments. They submit passively to the scans. One couple even comically halts, midargument, to be scanned and then carries on their fight.

There are four main components to the surveillance assemblage of *Minority Report*. First, there is the policy of preemptive action, justified by the familiar argument of balancing security and freedom (which we saw articulated in *Enemy of the State*).

Figure 3.6 Spielberg's surveillant camera watches the spiders retina-scan citizens. *Minority Report.*

Released almost a year after 9/11, the themes of preemption, security, and freedom had particular resonance with continuing popular political debates about preemptive action to counter terrorism, and the increased warrantless surveillance powers of the government enshrined in the Patriot Act. The second component is the parody of judicial process depicted in the film. The judges appear via individual video conference and observe while a Precrime officer displays the images gleaned from the Pre-Cogs. They then approve the arrest and conviction of the soon-to-be perpetrator. The third component consists of the Pre-Cogs in their Temple and the apparatus that captures the visions they see and feeds them to the computers of Precrime. And the fourth component are the black uniformed, heavily equipped and armed storm troopers of the police.

Trust is the crucial factor in the operation of this system. Like in *Enemy of the State*, the system is up for a popular vote. But for people to accept the system they have to trust in the system and its infallibility. The strongest believers in the system are the officers like Anderton who work in it. That the Pre-Cogs' holding tank is referred to as The Temple shows the importance of their faith in what they are doing. The authenticity of the system is guaranteed by appeals to nature. When a crime is predicted the perpetrator's name is automatically carved on a small wooden ball—the grains of each piece of wood are unique and impossible to forge, replicate, or alter. Likewise, that there are seemingly super-human figures at the heart of the system, rather than a cold computer, reinforces people's faith and the perpetuation of an almost divine aura attributed to the Pre-Cogs.

The system works, though not necessarily the way that it is presented. We can see this in two ways. First, as Dietmar Kammerer has put it, "the 'System' itself does not make any mistakes, only the human interpreters, who have not learned to read the images properly."[45] This is a common theme: surveillance gives us truth, but do we understand it? (cf. *The Conversation, Blowup*). The Pre-Cogs provide snatches of images, names, and dates, and it is up to the Precrime team to put them together in a correct narrative. So there is still fallibility in the system. But, secondly, there is another aspect to the functioning of the Pre-Cog system that has been actively repressed by the director and founder of Pre-Crime, Lamar Burgess (Max von Sydow), so that even the Precrime officers like Anderton are unaware of it. There are three Pre-Cogs and while they usually agree about the future vision they provide, occasionally one will disagree and a minority report will be submitted. The officers, and the public, knowing nothing of the existence of minority reports, trust the infallibility of the system. Anderton undermines that faith by discovering both the nature and origin of the Pre-Cogs (the product of addiction and experimentation, rather than rationally planned science) and the proper functioning of the system. The faith of the film is not a faith in technology but a faith in human agency, that individuals can determine their fate. The Precrime unit is shut down and the apparatus disassembled. The final faith of the film is a broader faith in the society itself. Society, the balance of powers of a democratic state, corrected itself. But though Precrime has been defeated, much like we saw in *Enemy of the State*, at the end of the film the ubiquitous surveillance society of both consumer and police surveillance is still firmly in place. There are no challenges to the retinal scans or other violations of privacy.

The *problems* of surveillance depicted in the film are the influence of a bad individual intent on corrupting the system for his own ends, and a poorly understood technology in need of correction. The representations of the passivity of the citizenry when faced with surveillance could also be considered a problem, though not one pursued by the film much beyond its presentation.

The *solutions* to the problems of surveillance are several. The first is to evade the system. But to do so, one must know how the system works and have the wherewithal to do the drastic changes necessary. As an example of the former, when being sought by the surveillant spiders in the tenement, Anderton hides in a bathtub full of cold water to obscure his heat signature and holds his breath underwater as the spider scans the room so that it won't detect the sound of his breathing. As an example of the latter, Anderton has his eyes surgically replaced so that the devices are scanning someone else's retinas. It is his position, knowledge, and technical ability that allow him to resist. The second solution to surveillance follows from this: understand the system better (Anderton seeks out the woman who discovered the Pre-Cogs). The last solution to ubiquitous surveillance is to leave the society altogether and live in isolation. In the end the Pre-Cogs are seen living on a remote island in a hut filled with books (and no electronics). It is a return to nature, a rejection of society and technology as a whole. They are free from the surveillance of others, but also the society is free from their surveillance. They are no longer monitoring the minds of millions of people and can live in peace.

To conclude, trust arises as a central theme in *Minority Report*: trust in individuals and in the system. Lack of trust is a challenge to the system (and indeed Precrime is shut down when it can no longer be trusted). But there is also the theme of trusting the machine over the individual. For example, Precrime officers trusted the Pre-Cogs report about Anderton's future actions despite knowing him as an individual. Anderton is effectively silenced; any self-report is rejected because he cannot speak about something that has not yet happened. The bypassing of the individual's own statements in favor of data or the testimony of their body is a growing aspect of biometric surveillance, David Lyon argues.[46] Trust the retinal scan, not the account of the individual; trust the credit report and not their explanation of circumstance, motivation, or character.

In *The Truman Show*, it is Truman's lack of trust in the system that allows him to resist. But along the way he has to distrust everyone he holds dear: his wife, his mother, and his best friend. The only person he trusts is Sylvia. Everyone in his life has been an informer. In *Enemy of the State* we can see how surveillance undermines trust in relationships (and in *Caché* and *The Lives of Others* as well, and look at Harry in *The Conversation*). However, in the end, like in *Minority Report*, there is trust in the society itself.

Gattaca

Gattaca (1997) is also a film about prediction and control, about trust in the science of DNA biometrics[47] to produce the truth of the individual, no matter what that individual may say or do. In *Minority Report* we saw surveillance use in two different forms. The first was the use of biometrics (retina scans) as a means of identifying individuals, allowing them to be tracked and marketed to. The second was the prediction of future behavior based on the premonitions of the Pre-Cogs (though reminiscent of schemes of real world prediction based on algorithms and data mining). In *Gattaca* we see these two aspects combined. *Gattaca* is a film about a society built on a faith in biometric technologies.

Gattaca was written by Andrew Niccol, who also wrote *The Truman Show*, and shares many of the themes of that later film, especially that of the individual pitted against a society of control and the triumph of individual spirit and creativity. Note the names of the lead characters in each: Truman (True Man) Burbank in *The Truman Show*, and Vincent Freeman (Free Man) in *Gattaca*. But whereas control was more invisible to Truman, it is more readily apparent to the citizens in *Gattaca*. *Gattaca* presents a society of control where DNA is the passkey that lets some in and keeps others out. But it is a highly segmented and hierarchical society as well. Once DNA is set (as in the film it can be engineered by one's parents), there is little ability to change or challenge the identity one is given. DNA spells your identity and destiny, and you then need to know your place in society. Like Precrime in *Minority Report*, trust in the predictive powers of technology leads to self-fulfilling prophecy. This is a class society justified by genetics where there is inherent suspicion of anyone genetically "inferior." Though less muscular and militarized than in other films, there is still a significant police presence in *Gattaca* and the police have substantial powers to conduct neighborhood sweeps and roadblocks, collecting DNA at every turn.

Gattaca refers not to the society but to the Gattaca corporation, an elite and powerful organization dedicated to space exploration. Vincent (Ethan Hawke) has always dreamed of space flight. However, his parents decided that he be conceived "the old fashioned way," without any genetic tweaking. At his birth, his genome is read and everything from his life expectancy (30 years), health (a heart condition), and other traits (poor eyesight, attention deficit disorder, manic depression) are spelled out. Genetically flawed, he is considered "In Valid." In a self-fulfilling prophecy, Vincent is treated as if chronically ill, and even denied school because an insurance agency won't allow the risk of having him as a student. He is continually challenged by his more genetically perfect younger brother, Anton (Loren Dean), but still dreams of being hired by Gattaca. But no matter how hard he studies or does on their tests, his DNA disqualifies him. Frustrated, he turns to a black market broker (Tony Shalhoub) who finds him a source of DNA he can use to fool the tests. He becomes what is referred to as a "borrowed ladder." That DNA is from Jerome Eugene Morrow (Jude Law), one of the elite who was crippled in a car accident. Jerome provides Vincent samples of his blood, urine, hair, and skin cells for him to use to fool the tests and, once in, to leave around his workplace for the frequent DNA sweeps (where every item is vacuumed up and the DNA of every item checked) and random urine screens. As long as Vincent doesn't leave his own skin cells or hair behind, he should get by. And with contact lenses, and surgery to make him match Jerome's height, he looks enough like Jerome to pass as him, though most people don't check what one looks like, just what the DNA says. The plan succeeds and Vincent joins Gattaca as Jerome. However, a mission director is murdered and the resulting police investigation threatens to unmask Vincent as an imposter.

Genetic testing and identification are the primary means of surveillance in the film, and it is put to a number of uses. At birth, the reading of the DNA sets the parameters of one's life and predicts one's destiny. One's DNA is then the code that allows you into particular schools and jobs. We also see DNA being used as a simple identification system. Rather than showing an ID card at the entrance to Gattaca, all employees have their finger punctured on the turnstile; a small sample of blood is taken, scanned, and you are allowed in (or not). Police literally vacuum a crime scene and every skin cell and hair picked up tells them who has been in the room; they can also do random sweeps of neighborhoods or drivers to find the match for a suspect's DNA from an eyelash they found at the crime scene. Finally, the use of genetic surveillance has percolated down to the interpersonal level. Whereas today we might Google someone we're interested in romantically to see what they are really like or if they are hiding something (a relatively recent practice which would have been seen as problematic and obsessive twenty years ago), in the world of the film you submit their DNA at a kiosk (even swabbing your mouth for their saliva if they just kissed you).

Such surveillance is justified in the film by an appeal to the language of risk and control. Why genetically engineer children? Why risk the chance of a problem? How can we minimize the risks to our children (and our corporations)? The genetic manipulation allows them to engineer behavior and disease and eliminate chance. Why saddle one's child with a condition that will prejudice society against them (like obesity or alcoholism)? Why risk getting involved with someone who may not be all that they appear? Wouldn't you want to know? The advanced technology depicted in the film allows such everyday uses of DNA. And the idea that one can check someone's background quickly turns into the imperative that one *must* check their background.

The *problem* of surveillance in the film starts with this absolute trust in the technology: that you can identify an individual confidently based on such a small sample; and that our knowledge of genetics (as portrayed in an advanced state in the film) is absolute. There is also a faith that the possibilities outlined in the testing (set out as percentages) are sureties. Statistics are destiny. This belief in the reliability of the technology allows us to bypass the person themselves, their circumstances, ability, narrative, and character. The trust in technology means a fundamental lack of trust in individuals. This aspect is played out in the romance between Vincent and Irene Cassini (Uma Thurman), another worker at Gattaca. Do you trust the person you have feelings for, or do you need to have them sequenced (a mark of lack of trust)? A second problem with this genetic surveillance is that it focuses on what is wrong with you rather than one's abilities. Vincent tells Irene that she focuses so much on the flaws, she cannot see the possibilities.

And the third problem of surveillance in the film is that of uniformity. This is a society obsessed with design. The buildings that are the backdrop of the film are modernist (e.g., a Frank Lloyd Wright building) and even brutalist in the clean sweep

Figure 3.7 Leaving a false trail of hair and skin cells. *Gattaca.*

of their lines, with nary an ornamentation or flaw. Likewise, the film uses vintage mid-century cars with a similar sleek design. The beautiful people of the Valids are similarly designed: sleek, strong, perfect features. One of the final shots of the film is set in Vincent's rocket ship as it prepares to depart. In the minimalist cabin (notable for the dearth of instrumentation), the crew assembles. They are of different races, and yet they all tend to look alike. Even racial diversity is designed.

The *solutions* presented to the problem of the biometric surveillant society are all technical ones: how do you trick the scanners? The opening credit sequence shows us, in extreme close-up, some of these techniques: small pouches of blood on the fingertip, a pouch of urine strapped to one's leg, and small phials of skin cells and hair to leave a false trail on your computer keyboard. For every surveillance technology, there is another technology to counter it.[48] To get around the system you need to recognize the blindspots of the system. For example, faking facial features is not pursued by Vincent because, as it is stated in the film, no one checks photos anymore. But these techniques cannot defeat the observant human. For example, there is the doctor who knows Vincent is not who he says he is not because of test results but because of a personal habit. And there is a debate among the police officers between relying on technology versus old fashioned detective work (and the pursuit of motive).

In the end, Vincent is able to succeed, fool Gattaca, and achieve his dream based on individual willpower and passion as well as the assistance of good people (and there are good people still in the system), such as the doctor and Irene, but also the willingness to break the law. Vincent shows that an In Valid can best a Valid based on ability and determination, not genetic probability. But though he is challenging the discrimination inherent in the system, his solution (and life's goal) is to join the system, to become one of the elite. He successfully passes as Valid. But his passing does not immediately affect the fates of other In Valids, like the cleaning crew he used to be a part of. Vincent's strategy to defeat the surveillance society is twofold: to pass successfully and to leave. On his rocket, he just leaves it all behind, intact. He is assured that when he returns he can pass as long as he wants (Jerome leaves him a lifetime's supply, it seems, of genetic material, for his return). This solution seemingly works for him, but does nothing to address the systemic discrimination against others.

There are parallels between the endings of *The Truman Show* and *Gattaca*. Truman exits the show only to enter the real surveillance society where he knows and trusts only one person (and her not well) and where he is the most identifiable man on the planet. In some ways, Truman exits *The Truman Show* and enters *EDtv*. Vincent exits the Earth, but to where? To a life passing as someone he is not? Or by being revealed as an imposter on his return? He is under the critical gaze of others either way.

We see in *Gattaca's* surveillance society the Orwellian capacity for violence, the Panoptic emphasis on discipline (made visible by DNA scans, we must learn our place and role in society), and the predictive dimensions of societies of control. There is a critique of the premise and faith of the technology—that it is not as accurate as assumed. We not only have Vincent, who defies odds and beats his genetically superior brother, we also have the genetically superior Jerome who lost his big race and became suicidal, and the perfect director at Gattaca who is unexpectedly murderous.

Conclusion

Many of these films we have been discussing in this chapter share common themes and concerns, and many appeared in the years just before and after the millennium when perhaps elements of control, concerns with dependence on technology, and the growth of ICTs that can watch and record as well as communicate were beginning to be felt as new aspects of everyday life (the structure of feeling James Carey referred to at the start of Chapter Two). We see these themes play out as well in the influential film of that time, *The Matrix* (1999). In the *Matrix* scenario, the human population is kept passive by being fed a mediated fantasy of everyday life, while actually being exploited as an energy source by intelligent machines. In the computer simulation that is the everyday, intelligent agents prowl, detecting any hint of rebellion or awareness of the real conditions of human beings as slaves. Since every figure you see in everyday life is actually computer generated, the machine overlords can override the program and turn anyone into their agent, taking over the actions of that computer-generated figure. Trust no one; anyone could be an agent. The solution first presented in the film is to hack the system and outsmart and outmaneuver the machines and agents. But the real solution is that a powerful individual will defy them all and be our savior: Neo (from *The Matrix*, played by Keanu Reeves), Truman, Vincent, V, and others. These films seem to be arguing that an exceptional figure will save us from our future, leaving little for us to have to do ourselves. *The Matrix* does not put its faith in collective resistance or the camaraderie of a team (though these are present in the trilogy of films), but in an individual.

By reiterating these themes over and over across these different texts, other solutions, solutions which are not simply fantasies of escape or salvation that leave the system more or less intact, its problems unresolved, are ignored. McGowan argues that films are at their most ideological when they present and then seem to resolve real antagonisms. "When a film resolves its structuring antagonism, the gaze recedes, and an image of completeness replaces it .... This frees the subject to believe that the symbolic order operates smoothly on its own without the involvement of the subject itself."[49] Though disturbing and dystopic, the films we have discussed in this chapter leave little for us to do: the problems of the surveillance society will resolve themselves or be resolved for us by others.

Other films to consider

Brazil (dir. Terry Gilliam, 1985)
Code 46 (dir. Michael Winterbottom, 2004)
Equilibrium (dir. Kurt Wimmer, 2002)
Sleep Dealer (dir. Alex Rivera, 2008)
Twelve Monkeys (dir. Terry Gilliam, 1996)

Questions for discussion

1. Why do our science fiction films so often turn to dystopia? What successful utopian films can you think of? How is surveillance dealt with in those films?
2. What happens next for Truman? Vincent?
3. If the technologies of *Gattaca* were available today, would you have a potential boy/girlfriend scanned? Would you tweak your child's DNA? Such tweaking of DNA is said to be a way for your children to avoid social prejudices (like about weight, baldness, and other matters of appearance), but does this not simply leave to problem of social prejudice intact?

Procedurals

Figure 4.1 In the crime lab. *He Walked by Night.*

The focus of this chapter is on what I am calling the surveillance procedural. A *procedural* is a genre that focuses on the process of how to do something. The best known type of procedural is the police procedural: films, novels, radio, and television programs that focus on the process of police work. Often the police processes involve surveillance of some type: from how the police dust for fingerprints in *The Naked City* (1948) to the latest crime lab analysis from television's *CSI*.

As a genre, the police procedural emerged after World War II, in the late 1940s and 1950s. It was a transformation of, and reaction to, the influence of film noir, but in the context of the Cold War and the McCarthy hearings. Film noir often focused on a lone figure, usually outside the establishment, making his way against a corrupt system.

With the looming threat of the Soviets there was a need to restore faith in American institutions, especially those of the police, FBI, and other federal agencies, to counter that threat. These films were also influenced by the Italian neorealist movement of the mid- to late 1940s which shot gritty slice-of-life, semi-documentary films in the city streets. Both film noir and the neorealists championed the lives of the underclass. In a quite stunning reversal, police procedurals used the noir and realist styles but flipped the emphasis so that the system itself was championed over and against the now suspect underclass. As Dennis Broe has put it, "In the original police procedural, the focalization of *film noir* was reversed and the audience was now positioned in the front seat of the squad car hunting the formerly sympathetic, now arguably psychotic, fugitive."[1] The films were made in a documentary style, filmed on location and/or featuring real cases from the files of the police (or the FBI or other institution). In these films the city itself seemed to become a character, as did the institution being focused on. Individual characters, and character development, were de-emphasized and "the minute details of police procedures" were focused on.[2] Importantly, it was not just an institutional perspective audiences were given (seeing through the eyes of the police), but it was the system itself and its processes that were seen to be successful, and with which the audience were to identify, not individual heroics. The grinding monotony of following up clues, hitting the streets, questioning suspects, and going through extensive files were seen as the real work. William Luhr points out that this is "the procedural's implicit rejection of individual agency."[3] And this is a shift from "one of two-fisted individual heroism ... into one of more corporate or organizational heroism which subordinates the individual to the unified efforts of largely faceless professionals."[4] However, there was a concern, and a balance to be struck, because of societal worries about the loss of individuality in the face of corporate culture.[5] The first procedurals came out at the same time as Orwell's *Nineteen Eighty-Four*. Luhr writes:

> These [procedurals] implied an alternative to dystopian works like *Nineteen Eighty-Four* because they posited a benign and not a malignant state. Although the detectives or agents in such films are functionaries of the state, they work to ensure and not repress individual liberty.[6]

Procedurals aim more for a "sociological realism" over "psychological realism," and tend to reinforce faith in the institutions of investigation and justice and their tools of investigation, presented more and more as science, especially the fetishization of surveillance.[7] Though such films were popular (Broe estimates over half of the crime films of the early 1950s were police procedurals of some sort[8]), the police procedural form found more success in crime novels and television series. *The Naked City* (1948) spawned a television series of that name (1958–1963) and *He Walked by Night* (1948) inspired *Dragnet* (first on radio, from 1949–1957, and then television from 1951–1959 and revived several times).[9] In the 1990s procedurals returned to television in force (*Law and Order* [1990–2010], *NYPD Blue* [1993–2005], *CSI* [2000–] and their spin-off series). Broe argues that the shift from noir to procedurals was driven by discourses of security in the face of the Cold War, and discourses of security gained increasing salience in the 1990s, even prior to the events of 9/11.

However, procedural *films* remain rare after their 1950s success. Partly this is the result of the cultural form of the feature film, which emphasizes events over routine. The repetition of serial television allows for the procedural to flourish, especially in its case-of-the-week form, where we only get the smallest hints of the personal lives of the protagonists, enough to keep the viewers coming back.[10] We can see many of these procedurals as being politically conservative in nature. Broe argues that *CSI*, for example, "privileges an overwhelming faith in the police, especially insofar as it uses science as an accurate tool of surveillance and an absolute arbiter of guilt or innocence."[11] And while television scholar Elayne Rapping highlights the noir characteristics of the *Law and Order* series with its dark and pessimistic view of the urban landscape, she also traces the transformation of the series from its early seasons where questions of ethics and issues such as the death penalty are debated to its later seasons where it becomes a much more conservative show featuring a tough-on-crime prosecutor seeking convictions at any cost.[12] However, these procedurals are not inherently conservative. For example, Jason Mittell convincingly argues that *The Wire* is a procedural that shows that police procedures are often inadequate to the task, if not inferior to those of the criminals.[13]

What I will discuss in this chapter is what I will call the *surveillance procedural*.[14] Often this will overlap with the police procedural, but some don't concern the police, or even a governmental institution. We will first consider two classic police procedurals (what Mittell calls semi-documentary crime films), *The Naked City* and *He Walked by Night*, and then several newer surveillance procedurals, including a number from Hong Kong (*Eye in the Sky* [2007] (remade in South Korea as *Cold Eyes* [2013]), the *Infernal Affairs* [2002, 2003, 2003] trilogy, and the *Overheard* [2009, 2011, 2014] trilogy).

But I also want to point out that while there are few films which are fully surveillance procedurals, the film language of the procedural crops up in many surveillance films as they give audiences a peek into the workings of surveillance, make a play for authenticity, or draw them into the surveillance expert's work and perspective. Remember the long sequences in Harry Caul's lab as he painstakingly mixes and filters his tapes to bring the conversation to light. Other films make us sit in the surveillor's chair, have us listen in to others' conversations, or simply want us to marvel (or tremble) at the spectacle of it all.

The classic procedural

The Naked City

Jules Dassin's *The Naked City* (1948) was produced by Mark Hellinger, a former newspaper columnist, who wanted to make a film about crime that featured New York City as its main character. It was to be shot entirely on location, like a documentary

Figure 4.2 The work of the police. *The Naked City*.

or newsreel film. In this project he was drawing on his own columns, but also influenced by the publication of Weegee's (Arthur Fellig's) book of photographs of crime and sensation in New York, *Naked City* (1945).[15] Aesthetically, the film is much more influenced by Italian neorealism than the shadows and psychology of noir.

The case being pursued in the film is a moralistic tale of a young woman drawn to the wealth and excitement of the big city, who ends up getting involved with a group of thieves and is murdered. But the case itself is almost incidental. This is not a film about this young woman. We find out little of her beyond what the police find out to trace her contacts and movements. We also discover relatively little about the detectives tracking down her murderer. The film keeps us at a remove. The film itself is about New York City and the workings of the police.[16] It opens with an aerial shot of New York and a voice-over by Mark Hellinger emphasizing the realism of the film to come, that it was not shot in a studio but in New York itself. This is to be a story of "the city as it is." As the camera moves through the city at night, the narration talks about the people awake and working at that hour and we hear comments from many of these workers (a cleaning woman, a newspaper typesetter, a disk jockey). One of the night time activities is the murder of the young woman. Later, the murderers have a falling out and one is killed. Hellinger intones, "this too can be called routine in a city of eight million people." And it is the routine that is followed by the film. We are shown the police switchboard as the call comes in about the discovery of the murdered woman's body, calls to the hospital, medical examiner, research lab, and homicide. We hear the medical examiner recite details of bruises, burns from chloroform, and so on. We see detectives dusting for fingerprints, searching for hairs in the rug, disassembling the apartment looking for clues, running down leads, interviewing suspects, following suspects, checking lists of stolen items, and on and on. The voice-over emphasizes the repetitive, monotonous routine of the investigations. As Lt. Dan Muldoon (Barry Fitzgerald) says to his lead detective on the case, Jimmy Halloran (Don Taylor), "that's the way you run a case, lad. Step by step." But the film does give us the charismatic, experienced Irish detective Muldoon to lead us through the investigation, and also his young detective who we follow as he walks about the city, following leads. The rest of the detectives are interchangeable. We get a couple of brief scenes of Halloran at home with his young child and wife, but this is more to emphasize the disruption that police work plays with everyday life than to provide depth to his character. This film sets the tone for police procedurals to come: they emphasize the collective work of a team of detectives and specialists rather than the exploits of any one character. Police "procedurals do not privilege a hero."[17] At the end of *The Naked City*, it seems as if the film will renege on this as Detective Halloran finally locates the murderer, Garzah (Ted de Corsia), fights with him, and pursues him. But the pursuit itself is mainly in a wide shot, depersonalizing it (and providing us the perspective of a bystander rather than a participant). The voice-over warns the young detective, "Better follow routine now. Report in," and the detective follows routine, locates a phone box, and calls in for help. The final, classic, chase of Garzah on the Williamsburg Bridge is a collective effort and doesn't rely on individual heroics. Throughout the film excitement and drama are provided by the swelling soundtrack and voice-over narration more than the acts of any particular individual.

The film ends with its now-famous line, used again in the later television series: "'There are eight million stories in *The Naked City*. This has been one of them." Part of these everyday stories are those of the police, seen here as dedicated working people whose routines and procedures function to ensure the safety of the people, and justice. The validity of the routines and procedures is established first by there being explicit procedures which are followed, second by the use of advanced technologies especially those of surveillance, and third by the painstaking combing of files and records and the sheer thoroughness of their search. Logic, science, and labor underpin the procedural.

He Walked by Night

Also released in 1948, *He Walked by Night* likewise sets the themes and tone of the police procedural. Set in Los Angeles rather than New York, aesthetically it draws on the filmic vocabulary of film noir more than the flat documentary approach of *The Naked City*. *He Walked by Night* uses unusual camera angles (e.g., looking out from the perspective of the trunk of the killer's car as it is opened) and dramatic shadows to build excitement. For example, there is an almost silent sequence within an electronics firm at night as police officers and the fugitive duck in and out of the dark; and we have the final chase scene occurring in the storm drain tunnels under the city, lit only by roving flashlights. But unlike classic noir these effects do not illustrate the psychological state of any character or their position in society. They simply enhance the dramatic tension. The film follows what it calls in its opening titles, "The most difficult homicide case in its experience." The titles emphasize the factuality of the film, drawn from the very files of the police. "Only the names are changed—to protect the innocent." The case involves the shooting of an off-duty police officer and the subsequent investigation to identify and capture the murderer, who is also linked to a series of electronics thefts and robberies. In *The Naked City* we hear from a number of the criminals involved explanations of why they turned to crime, but *He Walked by Night* refuses to give us any explanation or insight. The murderer, Roy Morgan (Richard Basehart), is seen at home shaving, working on electronics, and feeding his small dog. This latter moment is almost endearing, but we are not allowed to humanize Morgan or identify with him. During these scenes the voice-over intones: "What would make him murder someone just doing their duty?" Like in *The Naked City*, drama is emphasized by the musical score and the voice-over commentary. The investigation is headed up by Captain Breen (Roy Roberts) and his team of detectives, prominently Sgt. Marty Brennen (Scott Brady), Sgt. Chuck Jones (James Cardwell), and Lee Whitey (Jack Webb), who works in the Crime Investigation Lab and does the scientific analysis of evidence. Like in *The Naked City*, the emphasis is on routine and procedure. "I don't want any dead heroes," warns Breen. And the voice-over intones again and again the "thorough," "painstaking," "tedious," and "routine" nature of the work and the "persistence" of the officers.

The film emphasizes not just police procedures (like dragnets, the distribution of wanted posters, and so on) but also science and technology. We see and hear their communications and the dispatches to the radio cars, the dusting for fingerprints, the microscopic analysis of shell casings and other items of evidence, modus operandi files, mug shots, and the innovative use of projected slides to build up an image of the fugitive's face. Morgan, for his part, seems knowledgeable of police procedures and even installs a police scanner in his car to track his own pursuit, allowing him to avoid their surveillance.

Drawing also from the neorealists, but without the reverence for institutions of the state, are the early heist films, procedurals from the perspective of the criminals. Film critic Roger Ebert has pointed out that the foundation of the heist genre can be found in two low-budget French films release in the mid-1950s.[18] The first was Jules Dassin's *Rififi* (1954) and the second Jean-Pierre Melville's *Bob le Flambeur* (1955). Dassin had directed *The Naked City* and was blacklisted in the McCarthy era. He moved to Europe, unable to be employed by any major studio. He was finally offered the chance to make *Rififi*, based on a crime novel by Auguste Le Breton. The film, shot on location in Paris, follows Tony (Jean Servais), an experienced thief just released from prison and looking to make one last score: to rob the safe of a well-known jeweler. He gathers his team around him, including a safe cracker from Italy, Cesar (played by

Dassin himself). They plan the perfect heist, surveilling the neighborhood and getting detailed schedules of all movements, from police patrols to flower deliveries. The film sets up the technical challenge of the heist: how to defeat the sophisticated alarm system. They purchase the system themselves and try out various ways to both avoid setting it off and then silencing it. The core of the film is a half-hour sequence where they carry out the heist in silence (without even a non-diegetic score). We see in detail how they enter the apartment above and cut silently through the floor to drop down into the store. The filmmakers even invented a plausible device to cut a circular hole through the back of the safe. So realistic was the film that it was banned for a time, fearing copy-cat crimes.

Surveillance is most evident not only in the sequences where they case the store and neighborhood but also in the police patrols who spot their getaway car parked at an odd hour and almost foil the scheme.

Melville's *Bob le Flambeur*, co-written with Auguste Le Breton, is about a hard-luck gambler who assembles a crack team to rob a casino. The film has been germinal for later heist films, including both versions of *Oceans 11*, and was remade by Neil Jordan as *The Good Thief* (2002). The surveillance of the casino not only allows for the timing of the caper and provides key details of the alarm system and safe but also allows them to sketch out a model of the casino in a field to practice the heist in. This idea (which reveals the link between surveillance and simulation) is re-done in the remake of *Oceans 11*, where the team of thieves builds a complete replica of the safe and its technology. But more than just a place to practice, they use video from the simulacra of the vault to fool the surveillance in the casino itself (by feeding false images).

The surveillance procedural

The surveillance procedural film would be one that focuses on the practices of surveillance over interpersonal development. Currently, the cultural form of popular film emphasizes conflict, spectacle, and personal heroics, so it is unsurprising that we see few, if any, surveillance or police procedurals in this form. Often a film will include a procedural sequence (the "getting ready" or operational aspect: casing a location, setting up equipment, planning), but then the plot turns on personal conflict, the violation of procedure, or the heroic abilities of an individual. But whether or not contemporary films match the definition of a pure or classic procedural, it is a productive lens through which to view surveillance films. When do we see procedural elements? What are they meant to convey? How is the audience meant to regard the sequence? Does it put us in the shoes of the protagonist so that we identify with their work? Or are the sequences meant to convey a technical spectacle to validate a perspective or protagonist? What of the cultural or political implications of either reaffirming or violating procedures? Procedural sequences are familiar to audiences, but their meanings may vary.

Eye in the Sky

Perhaps one of the closest films to a full surveillance procedural in recent years is the Hong Kong film, *Eye in the Sky* (2007), directed by Yau Nai Hoi and produced by Johnnie To. The film is about the secretive surveillance unit of the Hong Kong Police as it is introduced to us through the eyes of a young recruit, code-named Piggy (Kate Tsui). By following Piggy we learn how the unit works, its key personnel, and its operational relations with other police units (such as the Intelligence Bureau or the OCTB—the Organized Crime and Triad Bureau). Through working on two cases, a series of jewel store robberies and a child's kidnapping, Piggy learns how to follow procedure and become part of the team.

The classic procedurals were reactions to both film genre and aesthetics of the time (noir and neorealism) and a political context of paranoia. What of *Eye in the Sky*? The Hong Kong film industry had been in a state of transition (and some would say crisis) in the late 1990s through the early 2000s. Many of the star directors and actors of the early 1990s (like John Woo) had been lured off to Hollywood. The economic crisis of the 1990s hit Hong Kong hard, and the 1997 transition of Hong Kong from being a British colony to being a Special Administrative Region of China created great anxiety. On top of this there was the SARS virus outbreak of 2003 which left theaters empty and the citizens under siege.[19] Thematically, films of this time began to question traditional themes of identity, loyalty, and brotherhood as Hong Kong returned to China, argues Gina Marchetti.[20] The global and regional economic crisis and merging of the postcolonial capitalism of Hong Kong with the neoliberal Chinese capitalism are reflected in the rise of films about the triads, such as the *Infernal Affairs* trilogy of films (2002, 2003, and 2003). Many film companies looked to coproduce films with mainland Chinese companies to garner easier access to the Chinese market (though having to cater to mainland Chinese tastes and censors). Or film companies looked to the global pan-Chinese market or even the Western market, emphasizing action films or historical dramas. Specifics of place and culture often are played down for more universal appeal.[21] Yi Sun points out that Hong Kong film producers were actively looking for new, more profitable genres, especially ones that moved away from the action-oriented films the industry was known for. The success of *Infernal Affairs*, which shifted narrative focus from action to intelligence, was influential for the films that followed.[22]

Eye in the Sky was produced by Johnnie To and his production company Milkyway Image. To, a longtime figure in television and film production in Hong Kong, founded Milkyway Image in 1996 as an independent film company to produce a tighter budget mix of commercial films with more personal films.[23] To has said that "we aim for a balance between the kinds of movies we like and the kind of movies audiences like."[24] The company tends to use a fairly stable group of actors (like a repertory company), writers, and directors. However, To works closely on most productions. *Eye in the Sky* was produced by To and directed by Yau Nai Hoi, a longtime scriptwriter for To directing for the first time (under the oversight of To, one presumes). Yi Sun argues that though To had been influenced by earlier Hong Kong action films, like those of John

Woo with their clear heroism and aestheticized violence (elaborate, slow motion gun battles), To developed his own style which can be evidenced in Milkyway films, and can be seen in *Eye in the Sky*.[25] There is an emphasis on the local and the specificity and history of the Hong Kong cityscape. There is an emphasis on "a group of protagonists" and "[t]he sense of heroism thus disappears in To's films."[26] And there is an emphasis on "low technology" both in the diegesis and in the camerawork. *Eye in the Sky* is much more a battle of wits rather than a battle of guns. Stylistically, To's films borrow from film noir and westerns. Stephen Teo has referred to To's films as Kowloon Noir.[27] Though *Eye in the Sky* has been neglected in critical analyses of To/Milkyway films (which emphasize *Election 1 & 2*, *PTU*, *Sparrow*, and others), it is deserving of more attention.

The film opens with a black and white shot panning down skyscrapers to look down at a street below as a bus moves through traffic. The image has dark scanlines which connote (stylistically rather than realistically) that this is meant to be from a CCTV camera, the "eye in the sky" above the city. The second shot is in color, on film, and is of a man at a bus stop, shot almost directly from overhead, but closer than the opening shot. The third shot is from ground level at the bus stop. The bus pulls up and people, including the man, get on. The man takes a seat on the bus next to a young woman listening to music through earphones. He looks around casually, puts on his glasses, and begins to work on a Sudoku puzzle. The young woman looks up and looks around. From her point of view we see her watching a middle-aged man asleep at the far end of the bus. She continues to watch him as he wakes up, having missed his stop, and exits the bus. She follows him. In this sequence we are introduced both to the themes of surveillance (from the aesthetic choices of a camera on high, to the ways people observe each other and follow discretely) and to the key

Figure 4.3 The eye in the sky watching Hong Kong. *Eye in the Sky*.

players. The first man we met is a well-dressed criminal named Shan (though he will later be code-named Hollow Man by the surveillance team) played by Tony Ka Fai Leung. The young woman is an undercover police officer Ho Ka Po (later to receive the code name, Piggy) played by Kate Tsui. The man she is following is Sgt. Wong (code named Doghead) from the surveillance unit (played by Simon Yam) and this is her "audition" to join that unit. Doghead is able to see through Piggy's surveillance of him and proceeds to quiz her about every event and person they encountered on the bus and after. Surveillance, he explains to her, means literally "eye in the sky." But what this really means, he goes on, is "to observe and remember everything with all the details." And this statement goes to the heart of how surveillance is portrayed in the film: it is fundamentally a human endeavor only secondarily assisted by technology. Though surveillance technology is portrayed in the film, it is not fetishized like in *Enemy of the State*. We see computers showing data and surveillance footage in a small crowded room that is the operations center for the surveillance unit (code named The Zoo); we see surveillance cameras hidden in cigarette boxes and a camera which can slip under a door; we see the occasional CCTV camera and videocamera; but these are rarely the center of attention. There isn't even the requisite surveillance van full of equipment. Instead the surveillant assemblage consists of agents disguised as everyday folks on the ground or on cycles or in cars in constant communication through ear pieces and body mics. Doghead and Piggy are in one car where Doghead directs operations on the ground, instructing and distributing agents (having them change outfits and locations). All this is monitored by Madam Fong (head of the surveillance unit; played by Maggie Siu) and others at the Zoo. The key skill of the unit is blending in with the crowds. In one sequence, from Doghead's point of view, the camera points out a cell phone seller, a couple with clipboards doing surveys, a man unloading boxes, and others who are all undercover (and all with animal code names). The agents will be the ones to identify their quarry, not a technology. We see this emphasized in the film several times. Agents scour footage from all the CCTV cameras around the scene of a crime to identify the perpetrator. And when an image of the elusive Hollow Man is captured, a detective visually tries to match it with a wall of wanted posters, relying on his own perception and memory rather than a computer algorithm (no facial recognition software here).

Hollow Man himself utilizes surveillance and knowledge of surveillance extensively in his crimes. He is shown to be exceptionally perceptive and, much like Doghead, can remember faces very well. Much like in the procedures of the surveillance unit, he directs the flow of action, usually from a raised vantage point of a rooftop across the street. Like in the procedural heist films, discussed earlier, when planning a case he familiarizes himself with the CCTV cameras and the schedule of the local beat cop (even timing how long it takes for the cop to respond to an emergency call). He demands as much discipline from his team as Doghead does from the surveillance unit.

Eye in the Sky has many of the characteristics of the classic procedurals discussed above. There is an aesthetic of realism, though with the jittery hand-held camera aesthetic (and CCTV image aesthetic) that most recently connotes realism (see the

Figure 4.4 Hollow Man on the roof. *Eye in the Sky.*

next chapter) than the flat documentary approach of the neorealists and *The Naked City*. Procedures are more important than individual heroics (though this is always a balance and tension of individual initiative, agency, and creativity within a structure of procedures and rules). Piggy is instructed to ignore a man being severely beaten in an alley because "we're on a mission," and she should focus on work. Piggy later goes to the aid of an injured officer and is reprimanded for losing the suspect. It is the entire team that brings the criminals to justice, though it might be specific agents, like Piggy, who locate particular subjects or get a lucky break. Like the classic procedurals, the film emphasizes the tedium of the job (waiting for hours, days, for someone to turn up), the monotony and frustration of it. And also the meticulous painstaking detail of the work. Finally, as *The Naked City* was ultimately a film about New York City specifically, so is *Eye in the Sky* about Hong Kong, down to details of the location.[28] The geography of the film is quite specific. The first part is a stakeout around Jordan metro station in Tsim Tsa Tsui in Kowloon as they look for Hollow Man's accomplice, Fat Man. They are able to follow him to his apartment which an establishing shot places on Parkes street two blocks south of Jordan road. Most of the action takes place in Central district of Hong Kong as the team tracks Hollow Man's cellphone, trying to identify him. At the start of the sequence we see Hollow Man pass the corner of Staunton and Shelley and the camera pans up to show the street sign (the only time we see and are directed to specific street signs). After this the dispatcher following the cell phone signal calls out street names as the team is in pursuit: Aberdeen, Lindhurst Terrace, and so on, ending up eventually in Charter Garden. The film details a specific geography not through monumental landmarks which might identify Hong Kong internationally, but through particular but everyday locations. Indeed the film refuses to give us any city-wide establishing shot, not even one image of Victoria Harbor.

The film also follows the classic procedural formula by de-emphasizing the personal. Though we get to know a little of the characters and their quirks (the experienced hand, Doghead, likes to tell bad jokes to relieve boredom, Madam Fong swears colorfully, and so on), we get little in terms of motivation, especially of the criminal, Shan. He is, like Garzah in *The Naked City* and Roy Morgan in *He Walked by Night*, just the bad guy, no explanation needed. The only character transformation we see is Piggy gaining confidence and learning her place on the team. The film ends with Piggy, well dressed and assured, on a crowded sidewalk, her gaze scanning the scene around her, an earpiece in her ear indicating she is on duty; and she walks off into the crowd.

Some of the significance of the procedural elements, as narrative choices, in *Eye in the Sky* become more evident if we compare it with its big budget South Korean remake, *Cold Eyes* (2013). It is also important to view *Eye in the Sky* in the context of six other films from Hong Kong that feature surveillance: the *Infernal Affairs* trilogy and the *Overheard* trilogy. This will give us the opportunity to reflect on how surveillance is mobilized as a cultural thematic in post-1997 Hong Kong, considering the political implications of the procedural form. *Cold Eyes* keeps the basic plot of the former film, but ramps up the spectacle, making it a less intimate, more high-tech action thriller than the original. In some ways, *Cold Eyes* emphasizes the features of the procedural more, but in other ways it violates them.

Cold Eyes was directed by Kim Beyong-seo and Jo Eui-seok and stars Han Hyo-joo as Piglet, Seol Kyeong-gu as Chief Hwang (code named Falcon), Jin Kyeong as Department Head Lee, and Jeong Woo-seong as The Shadow. The film follows the basic plot of *Eye in the Sky*, and at times it is a shot-for-shot remake. But overall the film is an enhanced spectacle. The targets of the thieves are larger (banks and the stock exchange, not jewelers), the cop on the beat in Hong Kong becomes a number of police

Figure 4.5 A confident officer Piggy on a case. *Eye in the Sky*.

cruisers, and chases involve spectacular car crashes; the technology is enhanced and takes a more prominent role (The Zoo now has the wall of videoscreens and access to face and body recognition software and real-time tracking of officers and suspects), and the city itself (Seoul this time) is revealed on a larger scale (the villain no longer watches from the third or fourth story of a building across the street, but from the top of a sky scraper with sweeping vistas of Seoul all around him). The villain himself is more enhanced: more vicious, more distant from his colleagues and boss, more tech savvy (he listens in to police radio), and more of a cypher (we never learn his name or background).

Both films feature a female lead, a rarity in surveillance films. In *Cold Eyes*, the surveillance unit seems more of a boisterous boys club: Piglet is initially seen voyeuristically, and there is talk of hazing the new recruit (and, indeed, Piglet is later humiliated as she leaves her mike on when she goes to the restroom).

Cold Eyes adjusts the balance between individual initiative and procedure. It emphasizes individual action more, even if procedure is broken to carry it out. For example, in this version Piglet intervenes in the alley mugging and fights with the gang members. Falcon states, almost approvingly, that she is unpredictable. But a key difference comes in the ending of the film. In *Eye in the Sky*, the surveillance team withdraws so that the hit team can pursue the suspect. In *Cold Eyes*, there is a stand off on train tracks between the Shadow and Falcon. Falcon is told to withdraw so tactical can take over, but he doesn't (you only win, he says, if you're nuts). He relishes the chance to take vengeance against the Shadow and to fire his gun (a rare opportunity for a Korean cop, which he points out).

But at the same time as it emphasizes individual initiative, *Cold Eyes* is more explicit in its procedures. We get the code of conduct of the surveillance team recited. The Department Head states that following Crime Intel Management Law that all operational communications are recorded (and starting and stopping recording are moments mentioned in the film). At another point they state that they are applying for a location tracking warrant. So, the legality and process of surveillance work is

Figure 4.6 The Shadow on a roof. *Cold Eyes*.

brought forward in reassurance to the audience that this is not Big Brother and that the citizens of Seoul are being protected by the invisible work of the surveillance unit. This point is brought home in the final scene of the film. While *Eye in the Sky* ended with Piggy confidently at work in the crowd having found her place on the team, *Cold Eyes* ends with the entire team at work tracking a suspect in a rail station—they are there, blending in with the crowd, keeping us safe. They could be anyone (just as anyone could be an informer), but this is a good thing. The final suspect, in a nice nod to the original film, is played in a cameo by Simon Yam. However, this film was released at a time of increased government surveillance in Korea (CCTV cameras reportedly increased from 364,000 in 2011 to 565,000 in 2013; monitoring of the internet and telecommunications is increasing).[29] By presenting a carefully regulated procedural, the film presents police surveillance, limited and constrained by law, as justified by the clear danger of the criminal, and avoids both the issues of the political uses of surveillance and the justifications of state security.

It is not too far, then, from the set of stylistic and thematic elements prominent in *Eye in the Sky*, made by working in, through, and against established genres in the Hong Kong film industry, within the context of profound economic, political, and cultural shift, to the production of a procedural with an emphasis on teamwork, the process of the police, and the rule of law. *Eye in the Sky* was not the only film from this time to mobilize figures of surveillance and the procedural. Indeed, both the use of surveillance and the form of the procedural provide cultural frames for the general feelings of anxiety and uncertainty. *Eye in the Sky* is especially interesting then in its relations to the other key films about surveillance, the more high-profile *Infernal Affairs* films as well as the *Overheard* trilogy (both trilogies are the work of Alan Mak). In total, these seven films provide us with insight into the surveillant imaginary in Hong Kong in the early twenty-first century. And the surveillant imaginary is one way Hong Kongers addressed issues of identity, culture, and politics post-handover and post-economic crisis.

Infernal Affairs

The *Infernal Affairs* trilogy traces the relationship between Hong Kong Police and the Triads from 1991 to 2003, over the course of the handover of Hong Kong to Mainland China. The first *Infernal Affairs* film, set in 2002, tells the story of two undercover moles. One, Lau (Andy Lau), is a young gang member sent to the police academy to inform on the police force on behalf of Sam (Eric Tsang), a Triad leader. The other is Yan (Tony Chiu Wai Leung), a promising police cadet who is sent deep undercover in Sam's organization to inform on him to the police, particularly Superintendent Wong (Anthony Chau-Sang Wong). The events of the film involve each mole being tasked with finding out the identity of the other. *Infernal Affairs II* (2003) gives us the backstory not only of the early days of Lau (the young Lau played by Edison Chen in this film) and Yan (played by Shawn Yue), but also of the long, close relationship between Sam and Wong, introducing moral complexity to these characters. *Infernal Affairs III* (2003) switches back and forth between events that immediately precede those of the first film and events immediately after. In *Infernal Affairs III*, Lau (Andy Lau again), who has decided to put aside his criminal past and be a good cop, hunts down the rest of Sam's moles in the police but begins to fall apart psychologically—his sense of identity conflicted.

Infernal Affairs is the closest of the three to a procedural, as Gina Marchetti argues, in that it follows a single case to its conclusion.[30] Second and third parts become less focused on police and criminal operations per se than broader questions of morality and identity. The scene in *Infernal Affairs* most focused on procedure is the tour de force sequence early on in the film where Wong and his team have staked out the place where Sam and his gang are meeting a group of Thai drug dealers. The police attempt to secure the scene through visual surveillance and electronic surveillance (scanning all cell phones in the area) and the gang works to avoid this surveillance, counter-surveilling by monitoring the police radio transmissions. Meanwhile, Yan and Lau are trying to communicate with their respective bosses but avoiding detection themselves.

Surveillance is a key theme in the films and is evident not just in the operations of the police and gangs, but in the figures of the moles themselves, who are instruments of surveillance. Though we see advanced surveillance technologies in use, these are not portrayed in a technophilic way. In fact, technology rarely solves or resolves an issue in any of the films. The electronic surveillance of cell phones, for example, puts pressure on the gang, but doesn't identify the mole or prove a definitive link. CCTV cameras are present in later scenes, but either do not reveal crucial moments or are destroyed, and therefore rendered ineffectual. In *Infernal Affairs II*, surveillance video shot by private detectives reveals a meeting between Wong and Sam's wife, Mary (Carina Lau), as they arrange the murder of a Triad leader. Sophisticated surveillance technology makes a comeback in *Infernal Affairs III* as a mark of Lau's obsession with rooting out corrupt cops. He is paranoid and deeply suspicious of the secretive security wing of the police, and its leader, and plants cameras and microphones in their offices, watching incessantly. At the same time, it is later revealed, the security wing has been surveilling the internal affairs department where Lau works. On the one hand this is about interagency rivalry, but it also reflects a paranoia and anxiety in a time of transition with greater connection (both in terms of policing and criminality) with Mainland China, when one isn't sure who anyone really is and where loyalties should lay. But, on the other hand, this interoffice surveillance is personal, with Lau acting on his own, shut away from his colleagues. His surveillance practices are the outgrowth of his obsession and questioning of identity. Much like the voyeurs examined in Chapter 1, surveillance is seen as a mark of obsession, a pathology.

We could argue that surveillance in *Infernal Affairs* is about identity. Some of the surveillance is to reveal the identity of the moles. But the film also emphasizes the basis of modern identity in documents, recordings, and data (see Chapter 2). To reveal the mole in Sam's group, Lau asks Sam to have them all fill out paperwork with their real identities, bank accounts, and histories so he can run background checks on them (like an employment screening). And Yan's true identity as an undercover cop is known only to two superior officers (one of them Wong), which otherwise only exists as an electronic profile locked behind a password on Wong's computer. If the senior

Figure 4.7 Lau's paranoia leads to excessive surveillance. *Infernal Affairs 3.*

officers die, and his profile is erased, the "real" Yan will cease to exist. Whereas we can critique the reliance on the data self as a true indicator of identity in that it bypasses the speaking subject, ignoring the physical person and their testimony, Yan's situation asks us to ignore his appearance and the actions of the physical Yan and trust the data. Likewise, at the end of *Infernal Affairs III*, Lau's true identity is revealed by the playing of a secret recording Sam had made. But in this case, the identity he is desperately trying to be (a good cop) is destroyed by the data self, a self he feels he is no longer, that he wishes to deny.

While surveillance is about identity in *Infernal Affairs*, it is more specifically about identity crisis (perhaps channeling the anxiety of Hong Kong's identity, split loyalty and split identity).[31] *Infernal Affairs* is about the duplicity and multiplicity of identity. Lau's fiancée is even a novelist working on a new book about a man with multiple personalities. The role of the mole is one of constant duality; a situation likened in the films to continuous hell. *Infernal Affairs* is about neither the stress of being the

Figure 4.8 Lau and Yan as doppleganger. *Infernal Affairs.*

surveillor nor the surveilled, but of being the instrument of surveillance, being both constantly surveillor and surveilled. To watch but evade being known; to constantly play a role. The films are full of images of mirrors and reflections. Lau and Yan are seen as mirror images of each other. At the end of the first film, Lau is standing on a rooftop awaiting Yan, and Yan emerges from behind him, appearing to be a part of him (see Figure 4.8). These images multiply in *Infernal Affairs III*. Lau wishes he was Yan. At the Academy, when Yan is being publicly expelled (to secretly become a mole), the instructor holds up Yan as a negative example for the other students. "Who wants to be like Yan?", he shouts. Lau silently says to himself, "I do." Being more than one person is not only eternal hell but also madness. Lau's obsession in *Infernal Affairs III* is rooting out Sam's moles in the police, but is really about rooting out the mole in himself. He focuses his obsession on Yeung (Leon Lai), head of security wing. He projects his own identity onto Leung. When Lau finds a tape of a conversation between Sam and himself, he thinks Sam is talking to Leung. He plays the tape for Leung, calling Leung, "Lau."

Xu Le argues that typical Hong Kong gangster films operate on the dichotomy of good/bad.[32] *Infernal Affairs* undermines that dichotomy (good and bad are malleable and situational) and operates on the dichotomy of true/false. Sun argues that To's films operate on the dichotomy of existence/action (choice). I would argue that *Eye in the Sky* operates on the dichotomy hidden/revealed. In contrast to *Infernal Affairs*, identity is relatively straightforward in *Eye in the Sky*. The emphasis is on making a visual identification of the subject, stated in degrees of certainty (e.g., 80 percent sure it's Fat Man). They leave the determination of suspicion to another investigative team. They just identify and follow. Data reveal the true identity—an image of Hollow Man allows them to identify him and pull up his record, showing who he really is. For the surveillance squad, the key is to stay hidden, undiscovered in the crowd. In a throwback to the old gangster films, good and bad are clear and absolute.

Overheard

Alan Mak and Felix Chong, who wrote *Infernal Affairs*, brought the theme of technological surveillance front and center with a second trilogy of films, *Overheard*, *Overheard 2* (hereafter O2), and *Overheard 3* (O3). Each of the films is independent of the others. They share the same actors (for the most part), but each plays different characters and roles. O1 and O2 are about the stock market and O3 is about real estate. Whereas the earlier Triad films (including *Infernal Affairs*) could be read as commentary on globalized capital,[33] this is no longer veiled in this series and the shady dealings of global capital investment are dealt with directly and not metaphorically.

Overheard opens as a technology-saturated procedural. A police surveillance team plants bugs in an office building late at night, hiding under desks in a tense moment when one of the employees unexpectedly turns up. The team establishes a base in a building across the way where they can both watch via binoculars and monitor video and audio from their planted bugs. The team is there, alongside members of the

Figure 4.9 The surveillance team at work. *Overheard.*

criminal investigation unit, to monitor this firm which is suspected of insider trading. The opening sequence shows how the bugs are planted and how they work. They test them out for their boss (and for the audience). And later there is a discussion and demonstration of how easily a mobile phone can be turned into a bugging device, even if it is off. But from this procedural set up the film turns to the melodrama of the personal lives of the team, and it is from these issues that the plot of the film arises. Gene (Louis Koo) has a chronically ill child and is short of cash; Max (Daniel Wu) is engaged to marry a rich heiress and feels inadequate (financially at least); and Johnny (Ching Wan Lau), the second in command, is secretly seeing the soon-to-be ex-wife of Kelvin (Alex Fong), leader of the unit. One night Gene and Max overhear a trader discussing how the firm will manipulate a certain stock the next day. Gene pleads that he needs the money and they falsify the surveillance record to eliminate that information. Acting on that information, Gene invests his life savings in the stock, and Max borrows millions more to invest. Other day traders hear of this tip from them and also invest. The market opens, the stock rises, but then trading is halted on behalf of suspicious activity before they can sell and collect their profits. Suspense mounts while the irregularities are investigated—will they lose their money? Will the stock trade again? Will the stock plummet and lose them everything? In a stroke of good fortune, after a long weekend, the stock is allowed to trade again and, surprisingly, it rises, making them rich. From there comes a cascade of bad luck as an internal investigation is opened into the unit based on the fact that despite obvious fraud on behalf of the firm, the unit has reported nothing suspicious. Also, the criminal mastermind behind the firm, a Chinese-American businessman (Michael Wong), begins hunting the team. From its start as a relatively light melodrama, the film turns serious as the team finds themselves out of their depth.

We see the use of surveillance in the early procedural section, but then the abuse of that process for individual gain (out of desperation, however, rather than greed). We see Johnny chiding his colleagues for eavesdropping on a personal argument between members of the criminal investigation unit; and he is righteously furious with Max and Gene for abusing the system. Johnny's is a moral voice but not a strong one. We see Johnny illegally installing surveillance equipment in his girlfriend's apartment at the request of Kelvin, who suspects that she is seeing someone, even though Johnny knows that it is he himself who will be caught. In the end, the mastermind is caught by a successful, legal surveillance operation (though revenge rather than justice is the outcome). The implication is that the surveillance system works to bring criminals to justice, and would have worked in the first instance had human foibles and temptations not got in the way.

Peter Pugley has argued that *Overheard* evinces a "technological nationalism" over a "cultural nationalism" of Hong Kong, portraying Hong Kong with little cultural specificity, but portraying a modern city, part of a global stock market, with modern technology. The granularity and specificity of *Eye in the Sky* is missing. He mentions that *Overheard*'s production company, Sil-Metropole Organisation, is a "state-owned studio controlled by Beijing."[34]

O2 extends this sense of technological nationalism. Even more sophisticated technology is portrayed, sweeping vistas of sky scrapers are common, and a Ferrari races through the hills in the opening sequence. However, despite these visuals, O2 contains a backstory that is more specifically grounded in Hong Kong. The premise of the film is that in the 1973 stock-market crash, foreign investors were poised to come in and take over Chinese firms. A team of ace stockbrokers banded together and fought them off, rescuing the Chinese companies (demonstrating an economic nationalism). They were called the Landlord's Club and they continued to use their collective influence to defend Hong Kong's economy in subsequent crises (1997 and the 2008 Financial Tsunami). However, the Landlord Club lost their way and began acting out of greed rather than the common good, and are connected with questionable funds from Chechnya and the Middle East (implying terrorist ties), and the film becomes a moral tale of the corrupting influence of power and money. Heroes once protecting the independence and sovereignty of Hong Kong's economy become globally connected criminals.

Figure 4.10 The mysterious hacker, Joe, watches the members of the Landlord's Club. *Overheard 2.*

O2 opens with a mysterious young man named Joe (Daniel Wu) who is surveilling a member of the Club, their broker, Manson (Ching Wan Lau), with sophisticated video and tracking devices. Manson, being tailed by Joe, crashes his Ferrari and the crash investigation uncovers a military-grade tracking device on his car. This brings in Jack Ho (Louis Koo) and his team from the security bureau to investigate both who the surveillor is and also what the Landlord Club is up to. Ho's investigation is by the book. Legal limits on surveillance are set and there are no rogue operations. But Ho's investigation is only one piece of a film saturated with surveillance technologies. Ho's team and Joe's one-man operation seem to run in parallel. When Ho begins his surveillance of the Landlord Club there is a scene in the requisite surveillance van where a bank of monitors shows images of the members in their offices or homes. This shot parallels an earlier one inside Joe's own van where he is watching these very same men on his own screens. The Club have their own anti-surveillance measures and surveillance expert who is also hunting Joe. Even GPS tags on the ID cards of Alzheimer's patients (to locate them in case they wander off) figure in the plot.

O3 takes the surveillance capabilities that Joe demonstrates in O2 and expands upon them. There is no governmental surveillance depicted in O3, however. It is all private, either individual or corporate. O3 is about real-estate development and sets itself within the history of the development of the New Territories. The film opens with grainy black and white images of local religious ceremonies and old news footage. The film explains that in 1972 the Hong Kong government (still a colony of the UK) began to develop the New Territories. The local population rebelled against the intrusion. In response the government agreed to provide each male heir a parcel of land and permission to build a small house (referred to as Ding grants in the film). Today that policy is seen as hindering development and it has been repealed. A local family, the Luk clan, backed by investors from Mainland China, has been pooling these parcels of land, purchasing them from their owners, in order to develop high-rises with luxury apartments for wealthy Hong Kong residents. One of the members of the clan, Yuen (Chin Kar-Lok), is being obstructive and so a young member of his extended family, Jau (Louis Koo), is ordered by clan head Uncle To (Kenneth Tsang) to kill him, which he does, making it look like a traffic accident. Jau gets out of jail after a five-year sentence to find the four Luk brothers wealthy but discontented because they are going to be cut out of an IPO regarding the development and wish to start their own development firm. The plot follows the extensive and overly complicated melodrama of the family politics and the corruption rampant across almost everyone in power in the community, and how the male heirs, uneducated and impoverished, are ruthlessly exploited for their land. In the end, the film is a moral story of the corrupting influence of power and money. Through Moon (Zhou Xun), a member of the extended Luk clan who wants nothing to do with their affairs (being the murdered Yuen's widow), the film makes an appeal against the corruption of development. "Land is for farming, not for trading," she states. The Luk clan has forgotten this, though the film pointedly shows them playing Farmville on their smart phones—they farm online but exploit real land. Moon, and a hacker named Joe (Daniel Wu, who also played a different

Figure 4.11 The hacker's hideout: nature and technology intertwine in an old train car. *Overheard 3.*

hacker named Joe in O2) settle down to farm the land. As the film ends we see the high rises looming behind their farmhouse crumble into dust.

Surveillance is not the subject of the plot; it is merely part of everyday life. Everyone surveils and everyone is surveilled. While in jail Jau had met the hacker, Joe, and, with the backing of the branch of the Luk clan working with the mainland developer to cut out the Luk brothers, hires Joe to set up surveillance on them.

Joe sets up his base of surveillance in what appears to be an old train car overgrown with vines at the back of a junkyard. Multiple monitors and other equipment are set out on tables, the sleek technology in contrast with the rusted metal walls, the hanging vines, and the windows painted in green camouflage. The space is a hybrid space of nature and culture, emphasizing the theme of the film. Joe, as an anomalous character (he is not a clan member, nor a citizen of the New Territories), comes from the high-tech city, but surrounds himself with nature (foreshadowing his siding with the villagers and return to the land with Moon). The surroundings also contrast with the gleaming modern offices and houses of the Luk brothers on the monitors. From this location Joe has cameras in all of their offices, cars, and homes, can access their phones, and see what's on their phone and computer screens. They are completely visible to him. He can also triangulate the location of any mobile phone they call and access community CCTV systems. The Luks not only carry anti-surveillance devices, but they also access the community CCTV and have their own surveillance expert (who works in a grubby, crowded shop in the village). We get a brief how-to explanation as Joe explains the set up to Jau, but that is the extent of the procedural aspects of the film. What is striking about the film is the ubiquity of surveillance and the matter of fact quality. This is not special technology, it just is.

Across the three films, we see surveillance as being the domain of governmental and criminal institutions, though potentially used and abused by individuals. In O2 the surveillance capabilities of the police now are in the hands of a technologically literate loner, no longer the domain of institutions. And we see the complete absence of police or government in the surveillance landscape of O3. Paranoia and anxiety give rise to surveillance as a means of determining certainty, to find the truth.[35] But surveillance also produces paranoia and anxiety. By O3 paranoia and anxiety have become diffused, generalized across the society, no longer located in or focused on social institutions. In some ways this is a shift from disciplinary society to a neoliberal society of control. But we also need to see these three films as additive, not as sequential. The layers of police surveillance, security bureau surveillance, business and individual surveillance, overlap.

The politics of the procedural

The procedural is a particular genre, a form of text. Full procedurals are rare, however, procedural scenes are often used in films to provide background, set up plot developments, demonstrate the character of the surveillors, shock the viewers by revealing the extent of surveillance capacities, and so on. A procedural scene can emphasize the professionalism and discipline of an organization (be it police or criminal); it reveals the wealth of an organization or individual and their technical skills.

But politically the procedural poses questions. Take, for example, *Eye in the Sky*. Given that so many other films from the Hong Kong film industry at that time are questioning the "uncertain power of state/police authority in an era of changing political loyalties…and globalized economics,"[36] such as *Infernal Affairs* and *Overheard*, could *Eye in the Sky* be read as reinforcing the authority of the police by an emphasis on procedure over vigilantism? Marchetti argues that To's films touch on "the issue of 'democracy,' access to government decisions, and the transparency of the legal system as key to an understanding of the legitimacy of any political form."[37] So the film lets us see how the system functions successfully to apprehend a dangerous criminal. *Eye in the Sky* also appeared a year after the passage of a new surveillance law in Hong Kong that required judicial oversight of more intrusive police surveillance practices (including entering someone's property to place electronic surveillance technology) but allowed less intrusive surveillance (of email or phone) at the police's discretion (though still subject to review).[38] However, there is also fear of increased covert surveillance from Mainland China (who are supposed to utilize the local police for their surveillance needs), and an expansion of Chinese state security agencies in Hong Kong.[39] In an incident that could have come from one of the *Overheard* films, in August 2014, a member of the Democratic Party of Hong Kong and an opponent of the surveillance law, found himself being followed by two Mercedes cars. He called the police and the next day when he left for work he saw an unmarked police car intercept both the Mercedes. As a special Reuters report states, "the police had inadvertently foiled a surveillance operation being run by mainland China…. aimed at monitoring the activities of pro-democracy figures in Hong Kong."[40] So an emphasis on the transparency and legality of the local Hong Kong Police surveillance might provide a form of reassurance and support for a local, more trusted institution (at least more trusted than secret security operations from the mainland) in the midst of growing unease about the future of democratic freedoms in Hong Kong. However, the unexpectedly brutal crackdown on Occupy Central protestors in the Fall of 2014 has led to substantial dissatisfaction of the Hong Kong population with the Hong Kong Police (a dissatisfaction that has been growing since 2012). They are now less popular than the People Liberation Army's defense force stationed in Hong Kong.[41]

But *Eye in the Sky* is also a film less about the system as a whole than the everyday of the officers involved (much like *The Naked City*). This aspect is underscored by the casting of the film. Rather than emphasizing the glamor of Hong Kong superstars (as is usual in mainstream Hong Kong films), "pretty faces are replaced by fairly ordinary ones."[42] Simon Yam gained twenty pounds for his role and Tony Ka Fai Leung is made to look like someone who would blend into the crowd. The film is also resolutely local and not just in the geography of the pursuit, but in at least two other ways as well. First, this is not a film about transnational capital—the targets are jewelry stores not banks or stock exchanges. Second, the film emphatically refuses to give us the eye in the sky perspective. And by this I mean not CCTV images, since we get those, but the God's Eye view of the situation, the street, or the city. We never get a shot of the skyline and we never get a shot from above the buildings. In comparison, *Cold Eyes* provides these shots in spades. In *Eye in the Sky*, the Hollow Man, standing on his rooftop, is not very high up or far from the action, and he is not silhouetted against the sky. Given how standard such rooftop shots with sweeping vistas tend to be (cf. *Infernal Affairs*, but also in other To films), this lack seems significant. As Gina Marchetti points out, rooftops are "realms separate from the quotidian workings of the city" and a position of privilege (and danger).[43] *Eye in the Sky* never allows us to escape the everyday, the street. Surveillance as well is face-to-face and personal, on the street, at the 7–11. Surveillance is part of the repetition and habit, the territory of the everyday. Not an everyday heroics, but of work, the job. Compared with *Cold Eyes*, the *Infernal Affairs* films, and the *Overheard* films, *Eye in the Sky* is definitely the most stoic and least flashy of the films. But there is a particular collective esprit de corps or comradery at the heart of the film that is optimistic.[44] While O3 also emphasizes the banal everydayness of surveillance, it does so without the reassurances of limit, process, or oversight.

The politics of the procedural are not set. Though most procedurals reinforce the actions of agencies such as the police, FBI, CIA, and others, not all procedurals are unambiguously on the side of the law. Some use the presentation of the procedural as an opportunity for moral reflection. For example, there is *Munich* (2005), Steven Spielberg's docudrama about a group of five Israeli undercover agents who are tasked with assassinating the terrorists responsible for the murders of the Israeli athletes at the Munich Olympics. The first part of the film plays like an assassination procedural as we watch the team gather information on their targets, case their scenes, plan their attacks, and build their bombs. But as time wears on, the moral toll of their activities begins to be felt and the team begins to argue and debate about how their assassinations contradict their faith. We also see the stress and paranoia as team members themselves become targets of surveillance and assassination.

As we've seen, these procedural films draw on film noir in the noir-inflected procedurals as well as the noir and neo-noir genres (1970s *Chinatown* [1974] and *The Long Goodbye* [1973]; the 1980s neo-noir *Blue Velvet* [1986] and *Body Heat* [1981]). *Infernal Affairs* especially highlights the moral complexity and psychological breakdown characteristic of neo-noir. Compare these with the neo-noir procedural, *Seven* (1995). William Luhr argues that *Seven* is not only a neo-noir film but also a procedural.[45] The film follows two detectives, Somerset (Morgan Freeman) and Mills (Brad Pitt), as they pursue a serial killer named John Doe (Kevin Spacey) as he gruesomely tortures and murders, each act a moral tale about each of the seven deadly sins. Aesthetically, the film follows noir conventions of deep shadows, chiaroscuro lighting, constant rain, and the "grunginess" of the setting as well as the film image itself.[46] But the film also has the noir attitude of a cynical, paranoid worldview. As a procedural the film follows the two detectives as they sift clues to solve the case. They employ both legal and illegal methods to do so. For example, Somerset buys from the FBI data about library patrons who have checked out key sources on the seven deadly sins. This information leads them to John Doe's door, which Mills breaks in despite having no legal justification to do so (and bribes a woman to give a false statement that she gave them the lead to the apartment). However, as Luhr points out, "the film's driving force is not the police investigation at all but rather the enfolding of that investigation into John Doe's plan."[47]

Specifically, regarding surveillance in the film, Luhr writes, "*Seven* presents universal surveillance as a fact of life, which goes hand in hand with paranoia. It acknowledges no place for privacy; anyone can be observed and hence menaced."[48] The film depicts the usual police procedures of surveillance pursuing a murderer: looking for fingerprints and other traces and clues. A sketch of John Doe is circulated. And, as mentioned, the FBI keeps illegal record of such things as library books. But John Doe also surveils. He meticulously documents his murders with photographs and has even tracked down the detectives on his case, and Mill's wife (Gwyneth Paltrow), and has photographs of them. But in a world of ubiquitous surveillance, John Doe has made himself a cypher, an anti-surveillant subject, refusing the disciplinary demand to be identified. He has taken the name John Doe, a name usually applied to unidentified persons in police investigations. He has no fingerprints, no credit history, no employment history, and he uses cash. The police are reduced to trying to trace the furniture in his apartment. However, despite the deliberate obfuscation of the surveillant gaze, he stages his murders to draw that very gaze (especially that of police and media) to publicize his "sermons" and ultimately to complete his plan. He has both evaded and coopted the surveillance system—a system that, contrary to the traditional procedural, is almost completely ineffective for rendering justice.

If *Seven* is the dark noir procedural critical of institutions and society, post-9/11 procedurals track more conservatively. We will look at two quick examples: *Déjà Vu* and *Zero Dark Thirty*. *Déjà Vu* (2006) is a procedural and action film directed by Tony Scott (who had directed the technophilic *Enemy of the State*). The film follows the investigations of an ATF agent Doug Carlin (Denzel Washington) to solve both a terrorist bombing of a New Orleans ferry (in which hundreds of navy sailors on shore leave are killed) and a related murder of a young woman, Claire Kuchever (Paula Patton). Doug is brought onto a secret team that has developed a device that can surveil anything or anyone, inside or outside of any building, at any level of detail, exactly four days in the past and within a few square miles radius.[49] They use the technology to follow the girl in the days leading up to the explosion, hoping to identify the bomber. The device can see through walls and leaves absolutely no privacy. This technophilic dream of total surveillance is justified, ostensibly, by the magnitude of the disaster and the loss of life (slow-motion shots at the start of the film highlight families and children on the ferry as well as sailors). Privacy and rights are set aside in such circumstances. What I wish to emphasize here is the apparent comfort the team has with the personal, private, and intrusive nature of the surveillance technology. The only qualms expressed regarding its use are by the sole female member of the team, Shanti (Erika Alexander), when she asks how it helps the case that they are watching a woman take a shower. This is a voyeuristic moment when the men are captivated, almost mesmerized by her naked body. After Shanti's comment the men slowly come to their senses and move the camera elsewhere.

Throughout this surveillance, Claire gets the feeling that someone is watching her, even though she is four days in the past. The team examines the area around her house but see no one. Who is watching her?, someone asks. "We are," replied Doug. The "we" refers to the surveillance team, and that she feels their presence (explained later as a result of the time machine itself which produces a wormhole from the present to the past). But "we are" also refers to the audience. As the camera sutures us into the scene, as a member of the team, we see what they do. We are just as much voyeurs as they are. The complacency and comfort, plus thrill and excitement, to identify with advanced and intrusive surveillance, reifies and justifies the system itself. In addition to the time machine, the film takes for granted tracking of mobile phones, immediate access to all CCTV cameras, advanced face recognition, and more. In many ways, this film melds *Enemy of the State*'s depiction of comprehensive surveillance (a film

Figure 4.12 Who is watching Claire? *Déjà Vu.*

with the same producer, Jerry Bruckheimer, and director as *Déjà Vu*) with *Minority Report*'s depiction of Precrime. Doug states, "I want to catch someone before they do something horrible, not after." But unlike both of those films, there is no debate over rights. Like with *Cold Eyes*, the form of the action thriller privileges a visceral response to the film, rather than an engagement with ideas. That is, the film positions us affectively rather than discursively to align ourselves as audience members with the thrill of surveillance in the face of mass murder. *Déjà Vu* is a fantasy of the technical fix: if only we had more and better surveillance, we could have prevented this terrible attack, a post-9/11 justification for continued expansion of surveillance and the erosion of rights. After all, as we saw in *Minority Report*, if Doug does catch some people before they do something horrible, what can you do with them? They haven't done anything horrible yet (except plan, which does carry consequences; that is, the plan, the simulation of the act, has real effects).

Despite its heroic ideological closure, and rewriting of the real of 9/11, there is an important moment when the film engages with the gaze and the central antagonism of cinema itself. This is the moment, mentioned above, of watching Claire and Claire's awareness of being watched. Doug and the team are like a cinema audience watching Claire's life play out on a big screen. But the presumed passivity of an audience is an ideological construct belying the fact that the audience necessarily participates in the construction of the narrative, just as Doug and the team call up and direct the images of Claire, and just as, as McGowan points out, subjects actively produce the symbolic and do not encounter it as a complete whole.[50] But not only does this moment reveal the activity of the audience, it also reveals that surveillance is a relationship that is felt and embodied. A recorded image cannot react, which gives us leave to stare at a remove, an activity with little consequence, the captured image a plenitude to be studied at will (think of *Blowup*). But the real of most surveillance isn't a recorded image but embodied watching (think of *Red Road*). So to have a film we're watching react to our presence (or, in this case, and more properly, a film we're watching portray a film being watched react to their gaze) reveals a contradiction in the symbolic, a gap between the real and symbolic and a trauma that cannot be explained away by pseudoscientific dialogue and narrative pyrotechnics. It is a moment when the film itself questions its very presence and politics.

Zero Dark Thirty (2012) is a controversial film about the decade-long hunt to find Osama bin Laden after the events of 9/11. The film focuses on the dogged efforts of an intelligence agent, Maya (Jessica Chastain), to locate his whereabouts. The film stirred controversy on a number of fronts, but primarily in its depiction of "enhanced interrogation techniques" such as waterboarding and the implication that such techniques yielded credible evidence as to the investigation. *Zero Dark Thirty* is another film that takes extensive surveillance for granted. It is a procedural in that it pursues one case, the location of bin Laden, to its conclusion, using surveillance and torture to gather evidence along the way. It is taken as a matter of course that "chatter" online is monitored, that mobile phones are tapped, and that spy satellites can give detailed images of houses and other locations. There is a detailed procedural sequence as a team are trying to locate Abdul Ackbar, a suspected confidante of bin Laden, by his mobile phone. Ackbar only uses his phone for short periods and from random locations, and so the team is in a car desperately fighting traffic in Abbotabad, Pakistan, trying to identify him by triangulating the location of his signal and then discovering who is using that phone, before he hangs up. The team is eventually successful but for the most part, for all its capacity, the surveillance system is not represented as being very effective. Bin Laden eludes them for years. There is a striking scene where Maya sits in a small room watching a video monitor with stacks of DVDs surrounding her, reviewing past torture sessions for mention of their lead suspect. On the screen, acts of enhanced interrogation unfold (sometimes from multiple angles simultaneously on a split screen). Torture and surveillance have become everyday, banal, simply procedure. In some ways, the film follows the formula of the procedural too well: the procedure is; it is not to be questioned. And neither the characters nor the camerawork or cinematography raise many questions.

Ranjani Mazumdar has argued that after traumatic events, like 9/11, we see popular narratives that incorporate that event and forms which seek to contain it. Both conspiracy and surveillance are examples of these latter forms; they seek to contain the event. Conspiracy seeks to explain the event and its causes and the "surveillance form caters to a desire for transparency and provides illusory control over traumatic events."[51] However, both conspiracy and surveillance forms also evoke the "fear, helplessness, and paranoia" associated with the traumatic event.

Mazumdar's examples are Mumbai films in the wake of a series of terrorist attacks in that city. In December 1992, thousands of Hindu militants tore down a sixteenth-century mosque in Ayodhya said to be on a site sacred to Hindus. Riots broke out across India and 2,000 Muslims were killed in Bombay (now Mumbai). A series of bombs then went off in Bombay the next month, often seen as revenge attacks by Muslims, and then again in March.[52] "For many residents, the riots and the blasts have become the temporal mark to divide the city's history into the before and after of 1992–1993."[53] In 2006 a train was bombed and in 2008 terrorists attacked the Taj Hotel in Mumbai.

The film *Black Friday* (2004) is a docudrama about the investigation into the 1993 bombings. It is about the conspiracy that planted the bombs but is structured like a police procedural. It is "an investigative narrative" that "privileges the police point of view" as suspects are questioned and tortured for information.[54] However, questions of human rights abuses are raised and the conduct of the police is held in question. As we receive the information from the suspects' confessions, the film's camera "deploys the aesthetics of surveillance" to follow the conspirators and penetrates "through multiple layers of the city."[55] The camera often is at a distance from the action and zooms in, or is placed above the street or room. The film was often shot on the streets of Mumbai using hidden cameras to capture the actors in the midst of the daily life of the city. The city itself becomes a character in the narrative, as is common in this genre, and local details are important. Mazumdar argues that while the director, Anurag Kashyap, "felt no one was singled out by the film, everyone was interrogated—the conspirators, the victims, and the powerful network of the police," the procedural form which sets out both the details of the conspiracy and the investigation, and the all-seeing, all-revealing eye of the camera itself, "reaffirms faith in this conduct of the police."[56]

For example, Smita Mitra has critiqued the film's portrayal of Rakesh Maria, the officer aggressively leading the investigation. "The director attempts to balance the police brutality by trying to humanize Maria but the structure of the narrative leaves one with a sense of unease as there seems to be a suggestion of the 'rightness' of Maria's position within the ideological economy of the film, even if the narrative drive tries not to condone police brutality."[57] The surveillant camerawork of the film documents events (the planning, the blasts, the pursuit, the violence used to gain confessions), but the surveillant camera can also capture intimate moments of both police and bombers, humanizing both. For example, as we follow the story of one conspirator, Badshah Kahn, we hear his reasons for joining the conspiracy (revenge for the attacks on Muslims) and also hear how he and others were used and then abandoned by the gangsters behind the attacks. However, Mazumdar argues that ultimately the surveillant camera in conjunction with the neorealism of the procedural form offers what Mitra states is "a certain kind of legitimization of state terror, a case of the end justifying the means."[58] Throughout, "we hear what the police wants us to hear and we move through the film inhabiting the point of view of the police."[59] Likewise, in *Zero Dark Thirty*, the humanized figure of Maya, with whom we are to identify and through whose eyes we view the torture and the investigation, implicates the audience in these acts. Both *Black Friday* and *Zero Dark Thirty* use the surveillant docudrama form to deploy a reality effect that nonetheless privileges the structures of power.[60]

Mazumdar discussed two other films as well: *Aamir* (2008) which depicts Mumbai as "overwhelmingly under surveillance not by the state but by the Muslim terrorists"[61] and *A Wednesday* (2008), where a vigilante, established on a panoptic rooftop overlooking the city himself plants bombs and threatens to detonate them unless four militants are released. The vigilante doesn't want the militants to go free, but, lacking faith in the system of justice, he wants to take the law into his own hands and ensure that they are killed, relieving himself and the city from the fear of terror. In the film, "urban paranoia is given a voice, acted upon and played out as an extraconstitutional force and surveillance emerges as a populist 'weapon of the weak.' "[62] In all these films, she concludes, "cinematic technology colludes to produce the desire for surveillance and spatial control, drawing spectators into a new way of navigating Bombay."[63]

Conclusion

The procedural form ties surveillance to particular institutions and geographies. Spectators not only are provided new ways of navigating Mumbai (and Hong Kong and New York and Los Angeles) but also the structure of feeling of contemporary culture, navigating anxieties about security and identity. What Mitra, following Roland Barthes, above called the reality effect of the docudrama form is redoubled when the procedural is about surveillance. Surveillance itself has its own particular reality effect, which we will turn to in the next chapter. We've seen in this chapter different formations of the surveillance procedural. The post-9/11 surveillance procedural films (*Zero Dark Thirty* and *Déjà Vu*) do not draw their legitimacy through the demonstrations of forensic science, like in the classic procedurals, but through the ostensibly objective machinic gaze of the surveillance camera (Maya's videos and the time machine of *Déjà Vu*). This is in marked contrast with the contemporary televisual procedurals which prioritize forensic science over all else.[64] The Mumbai procedurals privilege a surveillant way of investigating (and filming) that is less about particular technologies of surveillance than a surveillant means of analysis, peeling back the layers of the city. And the Hong Kong procedurals privilege the ways that surveillance, in multiple technological and non-technological forms, is implicated in the construction of individual and cultural identity and the relations of audiences with the institutions of security in a time of transitions and unease.

Other films

The Departed (dir. Martin Scorsese, 2006)
Donnie Brasco (dir. Mike Newell, 1997)
Drug War (dir. Johnnie To, 2012)
The Good Shepherd (dir. Robert De Niro, 2006)
M (dir. Fritz Lang, 1931)
Sneakers (dir. Phil Alden Robinson, 1992)
Source Code (dir. Duncan Jones, 2011)
Stakeout (dir. John Badham,1987)
The 1,000 Eyes of Dr. Mabuse (dir. Fritz Lang, 1960)
Bourne Identity series
Mission Impossible series
James Bond series
Christopher Nolan *Batman* films

Questions to consider

1. Besides the example given of *The Wire*, do recent television procedurals ever question their surveillance or methods? If so, how?
2. Martin Scorsese's *The Departed* is inspired by *Infernal Affairs*. Compare and contrast the two films, especially in their treatment of surveillance.
3. How do films find their balance between individual initiative and collective procedure? Does this balance vary by particular type of procedural (cops, spies, or criminals)?

The Thrill of the Real

Figure 5.1 The surveillance camera aesthetic. *Look.*

Surveillance images, or images that look like they were produced by surveillance cameras, have become increasingly common in film since the 1990s (and even more so on television). There are any number of reasons for this, including the expansion of CCTV cameras in everyday life making the devices themselves more familiar and also providing a burgeoning amount of footage for use by news, documentaries, and other media productions. The footage itself is more common and familiar. There are also even greater numbers of means to capture video and still images—from the camcorder of the 1980s and 1990s to smartphones today.[1] But beyond their simple presence in our quotidian landscape, is there something particular about the surveillant image itself that draws us in and gives it power?

The answer to the question is, yes. We associate such images with the idea of the real. Images from a videocamera or CCTV device are felt to be more real than those produced by film cameras. Video producer and scholar Jon Dovey puts it this way: "camcorder and surveillance video tapes have become the pre-eminent signs of an indexical truthfulness."[2] Beyond simply voyeurism, these images carry with them what French philosopher Jean Baudrillard once called "the thrill of the real."[3] To explain this, I want to trace out an argument that has been made about the crisis of the image, turning to how films have addressed this question thematically and formally.

Reality programs

Thematically a number of films have commented on the cultural obsession regarding the reality of the video and surveillance image, especially in depictions of reality TV. We've seen, for example, questions of the real (and reality TV) raised in both *The Truman Show* and *EDtv*. At the end of *The Truman Show*, as Truman finally realizes that his entire world has been nothing but artifice, he asks Christof, "Was nothing real?" To which Christof responds, "You were real." Reality is equated with authenticity, referring to the personal authenticity of being oneself.[4] The situation may be fake, but the reactions are genuine. This speaks to the emotional and affective authenticity of reality TV where even in the most ridiculous and artificial situations (game shows, competitions, and so on) emotion is what is seen as the real. In *EDtv*, for example, Ed is chosen over his brother to be the subject of the program because he is more himself; his brother is seen as performing too much.

Reflecting on one of the originary moments of the reality TV movement, the PBS series *An American Family*, Jean Baudrillard theorized that this moment presaged the end of the Panopticon and the end of the spectacle. There is no longer a gap, a space, between the audience and what we are watching, the spectacle unfolding before us—the space between the watcher and watched collapses (the theater, the living room, the architectural space of the Panopticon) because with this show the producers claimed to film "as if we weren't there."[5]

> The "as if *we* weren't there" is equivalent to "as if *you* were there." It is this utopia, this paradox that fascinated 20 million viewers, much more than the "perverse" pleasure of prying. In this "truth" experiment, it is neither a question of secrecy nor of perversion, but of a kind of thrill of the real.[6]

There is no longer a distinction between the Loud family (as reality or truth) and television, since television was a *part* of the Loud family's life. Just as today television (and surveillance) is part of everyday life, like part of everyday life's DNA. It is not something outside it, but something always already a part of it. Deleuze would call this *control*, and Baudrillard does as well.

But *An American Family* was not harmless, just a slice of life. The family came apart during the filming. One of the producers said, "The Louds: simply a family who agreed to deliver themselves into the hands of television, and to die from it."[7] Baudrillard refers to this as a "sacrificial spectacle." The Louds were sacrificed, but to what? For what? The sacrifice re-inserts spectacle into a society of control, reassuring us that the sureties of the society of the spectacle still exist, and masking the nature of control. Truman, for example, was such a sacrificial spectacle: indeed, Christof was more than willing to sacrifice Truman's life for the purpose of the show. It is a sacrifice to keep the audience glued to the spectacle, to the screen, reassured that all this drama (and all the cameras and fakery and false friends and false family of *The Truman Show*) is just TV, when the reality is that it has permeated the everyday. Remember that Truman exits the Panopticon and enters the society of control outside the studio. Baudrillard once argued that

> Disneyland is there to conceal the fact that it is the "real" country, all of "real" America, which *is* Disneyland (just as prisons are there to conceal the fact that it is the social in its entirety, in its banal omnipresence, which is carceral).[8]

The films that comment on reality TV often comment on the sacrificial spectacle at its heart. Both Truman and Ed are such sacrifices. This sacrificial spectacle is quite literal in two films, *The Running Man* (1987) and *The Hunger Games* (2012).

The Running Man, directed by Paul Michael Glaser, is based on a novel by Stephen King (under the pen name, Richard Bachman). Set in the far-off future of 2017, the film takes place in a United States that has, after a destructive war, become a police state. The oppressed population vents their emotions by watching state sponsored television programs that are almost all violent reality TV programs. The most popular program is called "The Running Man" where a convict could opt to be a contestant in the game rather than face jail. The game, however, is set in a 400 block ruined section of the city of Los Angeles and the players have to stay alive for three hours while well-armed and armored Stalkers hunt them down. All of this plays out live on television. Bloodsports being used to mollify and pacify a population are nothing new, and the show looks much like gladiatorial combat in ancient Rome. Released two years before the first season of *Cops* (1989), and four years before the rise of *The Real World* (1992–) and reality programming, the film was prescient in showing television that had abandoned the fictional form and gone straight for reality at its most extreme. This turn to reality is of course the presentation of a highly produced and edited reality created to control the population. We recognize today how much reality TV is not very "real," but usually don't think of it as a means of control, just a means of distraction from our own reality.[9]

The film is about Ben Richards (Arnold Schwarzenegger) a police officer who refused to participate in a massacre of rioting citizens but who was then punished for his refusal by being publicly blamed for that very massacre by the government (who selectively edited footage of the incident to match their version of the narrative). Richards breaks out of prison with the help of members of an underground resistance, but he is recaptured and forced to participate in the show along with two members of the underground and a woman he had been using as cover. Richards has the physical prowess and skills to begin defeating the Stalkers who menace them. It is unusual for the convicts to actually succeed in this and seeing the victims fight back so effectively begins to shift audience sympathies. Before, the audience all had their favorite Stalkers for whom they rooted, but they begin supporting Richards. As a game, and as Ben and his companions play the game, *The Running Man* presents a spectacle. But this iteration of the game begins to break the spectacle down. At one point Richards seizes one of the cameras filming him and speaks directly into it, at the audience and the host of the program (played by real-life game show host, Richard Dawson). But the game exceeds the arena itself as the group's purpose shifts from surviving the game to locating a key governmental television uplink, hidden in this forbidden quarter of the city, so that the underground can hack into it and broadcast their own information. By making the show less about the "real" of the game and more about the reality of the political situation of the country, the spectacle collapses and audiences are moved to not just watch, but act.

We see a similar move in the more recent *Hunger Games* series of films (2012–2015). The films, based on a trilogy of best-selling young adult books by Suzanne Collins, depict yet another dystopian, despotic future for the United States where most of the country (divided into districts rather than states) is under the tyrannical control of the Capitol and its government. At one point, the districts had rebelled against their leaders but the rebellion was crushed. As a reminder of their defeat, every year each district must send two youth to the Capitol to fight in the Hunger Games. Set in a tightly controlled and comprehensively surveilled arena, the tributes are provided with weapons and given a goal: be the last person alive in the arena. The whole event is broadcast live across the country. Audiences in the Capitol are seen watching the games somewhat jadedly, but as entertainment. Shots of audiences watching in the districts (in homes or on giant screens set up in public spaces) show them as much more subdued. For them, the games are to be endured, not celebrated. In the districts, we do not see the betting or bloodlust that fills the audiences in *The Running Man*. The tributes are literally a sacrificial spectacle—dressed up, paraded and feted in the Capitol, and interviewed on television—and then sent into the arena to slaughter one another. The games depict a model of control in the competition between the recruits (recall the discussion of *Battle Royale* and control), the constant scrutiny and tracking of surveillance (each tribute has a tracking device embedded in their arms and cameras can view every inch of the arena, even within caves), and the management of the players by the Gamemakers. The Gamemakers control all aspects of the area and can, for example, marshal natural forces, like forest fires, to maneuver the tributes into conflict. The arena in this regard is much like the controlled, sealed environment of *The Truman Show*, which likewise manipulated and managed Truman and the environment. The film, departing from the book, shows us scenes set in the control room which is dominated by a holographic model of the arena that can be manipulated by the operators, resulting in changes in the real arena (the simulacra precedes reality, as Baudrillard would say). The "reality" of the Hunger Games is not simply the depiction of violence and death and children struggling for their lives. Tributes, unlike the runners in *The Running Man*, must always be self-conscious of the audience watching. Popular sympathy can gain a tribute sponsors who can send them useful gifts within the arena (like medicine). So one has to perform as well as fight. Unlike *The Truman Show*, the film *The Hunger Games* does not revel in the workings of the cameras themselves; we never see a camera in the arena, though we know they are there. The film will show that a shot seemingly being performed for the film camera is actually being broadcast as well (even intimate moments, shot in close-up and from multiple angles). This collapses the difference between the television broadcast of *The Hunger Games* and the film. The difference is that the film also provides us with scenes of the audience and controllers. The effect of this emphasizes the totality of surveillance, that everything and anything can be seen. Also unlike *The Truman Show* the tributes know they are being filmed, and can spot the cameras. Katniss Everdeen (Jennifer Lawrence) spots one in a knot of a tree she has climbed (and we are treated to a reverse shot from the camera itself up at her curious face). And later, in a key moment, much like Richards in *The Running Man*, she stares up at one of the cameras and salutes, directly addressing both the controllers and the audience.

Other films have also commented on the brutality of reality TV. For example, the film *Sleep Dealer* (2008) has television audiences riveted to a program called "Drones," which features live coverage of drone strikes on military or criminal targets. The drone pilots become celebrities. The increased use of drones for surveillance and attack since 9/11 have made such footage, and such attacks, seem commonplace (missile-eye-views of bombing runs during the first Gulf War first provided us such perspectives and were prevalent on news broadcasts). To portray such operations and footage as becoming light entertainment is cynical, but an apt warning (echoed since the first Gulf War) that war footage, more often than not from such surveillance perspectives, is becoming mere spectacle. But this example raises the issue of the surveillance image itself, and the thrill and the problem of the image and the real.

Crisis of the image

Thematically films have been dealing with the reality of the image for a long time. Can we trust what we see? Did we interpret or understand what really happened? Does the photograph show the truth? In *Blowup*, what did Thomas really see in the image? In *The Conversation*, did Harry really understand the meaning of the conversation he captured? But at other times films reinforce the authenticity of photographs, surveillance video, and CCTV images. For example, such images are unquestioned in *Enemy of the State*—that is, the authenticity of the photographs of Robert Dean and Rachel Banks are not questioned (though Robert would like to explain the context so that they are properly interpreted). Similarly, an undercover surveillance video is a key piece of evidence against Wong in *Infernal Affairs 2*, and its authenticity is not questioned.

The still photograph, and by extension the multiple photographs in sequence that make up film, is said to have an indexical quality. An *index* is a sign that has a direct, physical connection to the object. For a photograph to be made—and we are talking about chemical photography here—light reflected off the subject entered the camera via the lens and struck and transformed the chemicals on the film. Whereas paintings are obviously someone's interpretation of the subject, and one can paint a picture without a subject in front of you at all, photographs seem to be of exactly what was in front of the lens (albeit in two dimensions rather than three). You need to have something in front of the lens to make a photograph. The power of the photograph, Roland Barthes has argued, is that they point out that something was there.[10] Photographs provide evidence.[11] The appeal of early photographs and films was just this apparent capture of reality. For television, its claim to reality was in its apparent "liveness." That is, the image being presented wasn't captured earlier but is happening *now*.

However, we know that photographs can be manipulated and faked, especially now in the age of Photoshop and digital photography. And if we consider the careful staging, lighting, and special effects of feature film production we can see how these images lose their sense of truth or the real. Considering motion pictures, Thomas Levin points to the Dogme 95 movement as an attempt to recapture the real. Dogme 95 films eschewed special effects and were to be shot on location, using natural lighting, and sound from the set (no post-production work).[12] *Red Road*, for example, was influenced by Dogme 95 principles.

But as audiences are less and less satisfied by overproduced film (and television), we see the rise in popularity of the videotaped image and the surveillance image. Jon Dovey argues that images from videocameras are seen as more authentic "and an indexical reproduction of the real world."[13] Partly, this is because authenticity in contemporary culture has to do with the personal and the subjective rather than the distant and the objective. Audiences associate shaky handheld video footage with home videos, the closest to a personal perspective (held to the photographer's eye, unless the camera is turned on oneself in a confessional mode or selfie). The association with everyday videotaping, amateur, unmanipulated footage capturing lucky (and unlucky) accidents, means that "the low grade video image has become *the* privileged form of TV 'truth-telling.'"[14] The explosion of reality TV in the 1990s, much based on amateur footage, was seen as a reaction against the "unreality" of the rest of TV. There were significant economic factors in the rise of reality TV too (amateur footage is much cheaper than professional produced footage, low grade video is cheaper than slick high definition, and you don't have to pay expensive writers or actors).[15]

Video can be manipulated and faked as well, and so begins to lose its own claim on authenticity. So in addition to the *subjective* authenticity of amateur video there is the *objective* authenticity of the surveillance camera: a videocamera without an operator, simply recording; an "automated device."[16] Dovey writes, "[t]hese aspects of the surveillance image—its association with disturbing images, its implication in the maintenance of social order, its mechanical qualities—create the notion of indexicality and accuracy."[17] Levin argues that there are two types of such surveillant images: the recorded surveillance image that can be played back as evidence, and the streaming real-time surveillance image watched live. The latter is seen as being even more real because, being live, there is little time (it would seem) for post-production manipulation. The 2001 remake of *Oceans 11* plays on the confidence people have in the fidelity of live surveillance feeds to substitute a faked feed for the real one to mask what is actually happening in the vault they are robbing.

Because of its cultural claim to authenticity, the surveillant image has been the subject of films thematically, Levin argues, but also alters the structure of film. He gives the example of the final shot of *The Conversation*, where Harry is sitting in his trashed apartment playing the saxophone. The *theme* of this scene (and the film itself) is surveillance, but *formally* the film goes one step further. The last scene is shot with a camera apparently high up on a wall, mechanically sweeping from side to side. The film camera takes on the characteristics, the form, of the surveillance camera. Levin states that this aspect is increasingly prevalent in feature films, and will be the subject of the remainder of this chapter: the function and aesthetics of the surveillant image.

However, Levin also argues that there is another structural change with the rise of the surveillant image, and that is the idea of *surveillant omniscience*. A number of films work from the premise that there is a central, all-seeing point or agent (a Panoptic model). Narrative omniscience, the idea that the narrator of a text can go anywhere and see anything, is common in feature films. What these new films do is perform that omniscience partly through the use of surveillance cameras, thus enforcing the idea that surveillance is everywhere and anywhere. The omniscience isn't just about the narration but the capacities of the depicted system. In Levin's terms, the omniscience is now part of the story; it is now diegetic. Levin points out the example of Brian de Palma's film *Snake Eyes* (1998). The film stars Nicholas Cage as a police officer investigating a murder at a boxing match at an Atlantic City casino. The casino is blanketed with sophisticated CCTV. The use of CCTV cameras becomes the excuse to peer into every space of the casino, eventually blending the capacities of the diegetic surveillance system with a fantasy of cinematic Panopticism.

> In *Snake Eyes*, at a point where both the hero and the bad guy are closing in on "the girl" but have lost her in a delirious maze of endlessly identical hotel hallways (actually shot in The Venetian hotel in Las Vegas), the camera suddenly embarks on what could only be called a wet dream of surveillant omniscience, craning up and over the walls of the hallway in an "impossible" shot that tracks across one room after another as if the ceiling had been lifted off, peering down into each until finally it locates the object of narrative desire.[18]

We see a similar shot in the scene in *Minority Report*, where the squad is looking for Anderton in the tenement. The camera tracks across seemingly roofless rooms, the camera matching the concept of total surveillance being played out in the scene (see Figure 3.6). In *Sliver* (1993) we have an apartment building apparently completely monitored by hidden cameras. In the shots of the control room we see multiple monitors showing various events going on at that moment throughout the building and just outside of it. But the monitors also serve to capture events across time. In one shot, we see a surveillance image of Carly. The camera pulls back to show other monitors, but rather than showing other current images, each monitor shows a previous moment from Carly's time since she had moved in, with their dialogues overlapping. But perhaps the best example of such narrative use of surveillant omniscience is in the film *Déjà Vu* (discussed in the previous chapter). The time machine of the film allows for the team to view any item, from any distance, and any angle. Long sequences depict the technical team sitting in a control room, reminiscent of that for a live television production, staring at a large screen. Doug Carlin (Denzel Washington) takes the position of the director, sitting or standing, calling the shots (closer on this, what's on the other side of that, and so on). Films like *Déjà Vu, Snake Eyes, The Truman Show*, and others meld cinematic omniscience through the use of the same apparatus. The all-knowing Panoptic eye becomes a subject, and a means, of the diegesis. *The Echelon Conspiracy* (2009) and *Eagle Eye* (2008), as well as the television program, *Person of Interest* (2011–) also present seemingly impossibly all-seeing computers or systems as well. Such films are ultimately "complicit with certain aspects of the visual economy of surveillance" and "*legitimate* surveillance through subtle, formal means."[19] Less literally, we have the example of *Black Friday*, discussed in the previous chapter, that doesn't use the conceit of actual surveillance technology to accomplish its omniscience, just the style and movement of its camerawork.[20]

The function and aesthetics of the surveillant image

Many films include actual or simulated surveillance camera footage, and even more include video footage meant to resemble "real," amateur footage. These films are often referred to as "found footage" films, because they are made to look as if they are just videos or films that have been discovered, rather than fictions that have been produced. *The Blair Witch Project* (1999) was quite influential in this regard. The film, reporting to be footage found in a lost videocamera, depicts the fate of a group of friends who run into trouble in the woods while searching for the legend of the Blair Witch. The film was inexpensive to make (since they used inexpensive cameras to achieve the low quality aesthetic) and played strongly off the articulation of that aesthetic to authenticity (could it be real?). There are hundreds of films that include at least some supposedly found footage.[21] Many of these are horror films, since the additional thrill that the footage seems more real adds affective charge for audiences desensitized to expensive special effects.[22] The *Paranormal Activity* series of films (2007–) have been recently quite effective in this regard. This found footage aesthetic has been appropriated for large budget films as well, such as the J.J. Abrams–produced *Cloverfield* (2008) and the J.J. Abrams–directed *Super 8* (2011).

Found footage films provide an opportunity to reflect not only on the aesthetic of the surveillance or video image, but also on the status of the film or video as a material object. Thomas Levin looks at Joel Schumacher's *8mm* (1999) as a film that investigates the indexicality of film. *8mm* is about Tom Welles (Nicholas Cage), a private investigator who is tasked with determining whether a found *8mm* film is a snuff film or not. Snuff films are films that purportedly portray an actual (not dramatized) death. The questions Welles has to answer include, Is the film real or fake? Were the people in the film murderers and a victim, or actors? "The film's central narrative concern," Levin writes, "is with the issue of celluloid referentiality."[23] Welles's investigations emphasize that "film is not only a vehicle for storytelling, but also a medium that documents, that chronicles what actually happens in the world, however horrific."[24] Found footage films are part of what Denzin calls "reflexive cinema," cinema that tells stories about cinema, or the process of film- or image-making. The significance of reflexive cinema, for Denzin, is that it

> interrogates the regimes of realism our modern and postmodern culture have come to value. It questions the illusion that everything is captured by the camera's eye. It violates the tenets of classic, realist film. It suggests that the world-out-there may not be under the control of a panoptic gaze which is objective because nothing escapes its neutral, truth- seeking eye. It suggests that this gaze, which is subjective and ideological, is flawed, and that it only tells a certain version of the truth. It suggests that those who own the cameras may only tell their version of the truth. This power and knowledge are ideological, cinematic, textual productions. Reflexive cinema challenges those texts which purport to truthfully represent reality.[25]

The contradiction of surveillance texts we've just been examining is that they both impose an image of total surveillance, total knowledge, and control while revealing the constructedness of the films and images. The voyeur is a key figure, for Denzin, for troubling this imagined vision of total control, but so, I would argue, are all films that raise the question of the nature of the image and image-making. For an example, we will look at the film *Dhobi Ghat (Mumbai Diaries)* a central thematic of which is reflection on the status of various types of images.

Dhobi Ghat (Mumbai Diaries)

Dhobi Ghat (Mumbai Diaries) (2010) is an independent Indian film written and directed by Kiran Rao. The film is a love letter to the city of Mumbai,[26] in many respects, and tried to capture and document different aspects of the city, especially the passing of traditional ways of life, through the interconnected stories of four people: Munna (Prateik), a *dhobi* or laundryman who dreams of being a Bollywood star; Shai (Monica Dogra), a wealthy young woman working in finance in New York who is on sabbatical in Mumbai to study and photograph small independent businesses, and workers; Arun (Amir Khan), an internationally known artist; and Yasmin (Kriti Malhotra), a young Muslim woman who has moved to the city with her older husband. The film is an archive of sorts of a city that knows itself via cinema.[27] "[C]inema forms the genetic code of the city's self-image."[28] But this is not the post-traumatic view of Mumbai of *Black Friday*. The film, shot in Hindi and English, privileges an outsider's perspective on the city (though indeed none of the characters are originally from Mumbai, but moved there), presuming an international audience that are also outsiders. Shai's outsider perspective (though she is of Indian descent) allows her to ask questions that the audience might ask and explore the city as an anthropologist might. She also blithely ignores differences in class and caste (inviting the laundry man in to have tea, much to the horror of her maid), and while this can be seen as a liberalizing move, she is also blithely unaware of her own wealth and privilege. Yasmin also provides a tourist's view of the city as she explores Mumbai, videotaping the sights for her brother back home. The city is seen in this film as both a transnational hub of finance (Shai and Arun) and also of poverty and low technology—laundry is done by hand in a vast outdoor set of tubs and tents (the *dhobi ghat* of the title), high-rises are built by hand, and so on.

The plot of the film is fairly straightforward. Shai and Arun meet at the opening of a new show of Arun's work. Arun, though taciturn and private, nonetheless hits it off with the ebullient and talkative Shai and they spend the night together. His reserve returns in the morning and he dismisses any chance that there could be more to this relationship. Shai leaves, but is still interested in Arun. Shai meets Munna, her *dhobi*, and convinces him to be her guide through parts of the city so she can photograph him as he works. He agrees but only if she will take pictures of him that he can use as a portfolio for a Bollywood producer. Munna falls for Shai, but is so deeply shy that he never expresses this and she never realizes. Munna also happens to be Arun's *dhobi* and through him Shai tracks Arun down to his new apartment and begins watching and photographing him from the building across the street. Arun meanwhile has discovered a set of three videotapes left in a locked drawer of a cabinet in his new apartment. These were video letters from Yasmin to her brother. Unable to track down what became of Yasmin, Arun begins watching the tapes and becomes captivated by her and her narrative.

While the film, through the activities and experiences of its main characters, documents the tension between tradition and modernity, the handmade and the brand name, it is also an interesting exploration and use of various types of images. The first type of image is the digital video that Yasmin is shooting for her brother. The video sequences are marked less by their image quality than by the camera's

Figure 5.2 Yasmin's videoletters. *Dhobi Ghat (Mumbai Diaries).*

movements. That is, these sequences are not overly grainy, and they lack the time and date stamp often used to mark amateur video as authentic. The film starts with such a video sequence. We see the shadow of a hand as it uncovers the lens. The screen is filled with white light as the sensor is overexposed. Slowly the exposure darkens and the image focuses on a bunch of green grapes hanging from a rearview mirror. Behind the grapes we see windshield wipers working and rain pouring down the car's window, obscuring anything outside in a grey cloud. We hear Indian music playing on the radio and the sound of rain and wipers. The camera zooms in to an extreme close-up of the grapes and then back out to reveal the shoulder and side of the head of the taxi driver as well, who begins to engage the videographer (Yasmin) in conversation. The unsteady camerawork, awkward framing, and personal perspective connote the intimacy and subjectivity of what Dovey calls the contemporary "regime of truth."[29] She films out the window as they pass a rainy seashore. As the car stops, a young girl runs up, brusquely demanding money. But when she sees the camera, she breaks into a grin and calls her friends over, performing for the camera. "Are you filming?" she asks. Most people don't react to Yasmin's camera this way (they are a common enough sight), though in a later sequence as Yasmin films on a crowded bus she is scolded by one woman who states that filming them is illegal (she feels her privacy has been invaded, obviously). Besides recordings of other parts of the city, we also see Yasmin learning to use the camera in her new apartment. We see her husband, who has given this camera to her, but he ignores both her and the camera. She records her maid and her maid's daughter, trying to get them to talk to her (and her brother). Eventually, she turns the camera on herself and talks directly to it, addressing her brother. These video letters become confessionals as she tells him about her life and her troubled marriage. These sequences, filled with quotidian details, city scenery, and confessional monologue, entirely make up Yasmin's narrative in the film.

Crucially, Yasmin's videos are not only part of the audiovisual experience of the film, they are objects within the film. The three small videotapes, each labeled with her name, are found in a locked drawer along with some jewelry. We do not know if they were ever mailed to her brother (and if so why are they still there?) or how long they have been in that drawer. These objects are a mystery that puzzles Arun, and after he discovers that no one remembers Yasmin or her family or can contact them, he begins to watch them, becoming fascinated with both the tapes and with Yasmin. Most of the time, when we have seen Yasmin's videos in the film they have been full screen; but once they become found objects we see them as well framed by Arun's TV set, as videorecordings. Arun is a voyeur, intruding on a private letter/diary. One could say, playing off of Baudrillard's language, that he is seduced by her image (she is mysterious and attractive) and perhaps he falls in love with her. But more importantly, he is *fascinated* by these personal moments (the obscene, but not pornographic) unfolding on his homescreen. This fascination is also about a shared sense of space. She is filming in his apartment, in the same space in which he is watching it, but at a different time. Details of the apartment are different (furniture is different, a ceiling fan is now missing, and so on), but many are the same. As Arun watches Yasmin sitting at the dining room table, he turns and looks at that very corner of the apartment as if searching for her presence there. It is as if her life is another reality laid over his own. The real is a video. This fascination has two effects on Arun. The first is that the usually reclusive and antisocial artist begins to venture out into the city, visiting the places she filmed, even wearing her necklace and ring as a talisman of that other reality. The second is that he is inspired to create a new artwork—a large painting which at first appears non-representational (swaths of color), but which later incorporates her face and details of her jewelry. We can see this painting as the second type of image (after the video) that the film explores. This simulated reality of video and everyday (what Paul Virilio once called stereo reality[30]) comes to a crisis when Arun finally realizes what must have happened to Yasmin and flees the apartment as if jettisoned.

The third type of image after the video recording and the painting is the photograph, specifically Shai's photography. As we discussed in Chapter 1, photographers are inherently voyeurs, controlling and capturing the world around them (cf. Jeffries in *Rear Window*). Her mission is to capture and appropriate the images of the working poor and her camera intrudes on their houses and workspaces. The film sets up a binary of low tech versus high tech, with low tech being considered the more authentic, more real. The film laments the loss of the authentic: a perfume seller who handmixes scents is losing business to the quick commodity purchase of manufactured perfume. Shai's photography not only captures this lament, it joins with it. In the age of high definition digital cameras (which she can certainly afford), she shoots on black and white film. Black and white has taken on the connotation of reality and truth. By shooting on film and developing her own photographs, we see her practice as a craft (also one that is dying, much like the other craftwork she is investigating). The photographs are not simply images, but physical objects that have to be exposed, chemically treated, dried, manipulated, and handled. The black and white photographs which appear throughout the film are beautifully shot, handmade images of an authentic Mumbai. Shai's voyeurism is not only the documentation of the working class, but she also begins pursuing Arun. In their one night together she had taken one picture of him in silhouette. Now she sets up her camera at night in an unfinished building (amid the workers hand-laying bricks) to watch and photograph Arun through his windows. In this scene, we see a double voyeurism: Shai is photographing Arun as Arun watches the videotape of Yasmin.

Figure 5.3 Shai photographing Arun watching Yasmin's videos. *Dhobi Ghat (Mumbai Diaries).*

The fourth, and final, type of image the film addresses is Munna himself. Munna doesn't want to take or make images; he wants to *be* an image, a Bollywood star. He wants to be the object of the audience's gaze. Deeply shy in person, his desire is less an exhibitionism than a play for social mobility. To become that image is to transcend poverty, class, and caste. When Shai shoots her images of Munna, she wants to see him in more authentic, naturalistic settings, while he puts on the poses and costumes of the Bollywood stars he has pinned up to the walls of his little room. He doesn't want the image to be of him, but to be like them.

Perhaps the key type of contemporary image that *Dhobi Ghat* does not examine is that of the surveillance camera. Above and beyond the use of amateur video (or its aesthetic), Levin points out that surveillance footage adds an additional claim of indexicality in that the surveillance camera is perceived to be objective and mechanical rather than subjective and personal. Footage from the perspective of surveillance cameras has become more common in the 1990s and later. Just as some films claimed to be made up entirely of found footage (*Blair Witch*), there are a handful of films that claim to be made up entirely of surveillance footage. Perhaps the best known of these, what Christopher Heron has called Surveillance Camera Cinema,[31] is Michael Klier's *Der Riese* (The Giant).

Der Riese (The Giant)

Michael Klier's film *Der Riese* (The Giant) (1984) consists entirely of surveillance footage. The film has no explicit narrative, no actors or central characters, unless we count the city itself, its population as a whole, and the giant that is surveillance. Jon Dovey writes of the film that "[i]t makes an extraordinary portrait of the objects of surveillance in our society and by extension of its disciplinary structures. Places of public transportation, open public spaces like malls, anywhere in which money changes hands, anywhere in which private property is to be protected."[32]

The film opens with a blurry black and white long shot of a plane landing at a Berlin airport. Dramatic classical music plays as it lands and taxis to the terminal. The camera follows the plane in a series of jerky pans to the left. We cut to another camera that tracks the unfocused plane to the terminal. The titles then appear on a black screen: green letters being typed in all caps, like a computer screen: DER RIESE. This is followed by a shot in color from inside a control center. A large map of the city with various flashing lights is on one wall, a row of blue screens showing live feeds of traffic cameras is next, and several men with headsets sit at desks watching the monitors. We hear portions of their radio dialogue in German. Then we cut to a shot, in black and white, from a spot high on a tall building, panning across the city, then looking down at the people and traffic below. The shot is eerily reminiscent of scenes from *Wings of Desire* (which was released three years after *Der Riese*): the heavenly surveillant eye watches over the flock below. This continues throughout the film: we gets shots from one or more surveillance cameras in a particular location, a shot of a control center or even of the camera itself, and then move on to another location. There are numerous shots of traffic; a sequence tracking a ferry; the gate and grounds of a private estate; a department store; a bank; another shopping center; a gas station; a strip club; a city center; a train station; a parade and protest; a machine that generates mug shots; another shopping mall; a mental hospital; a sleep clinic; a beach; a scuba diver; and finally a detailed miniature of a countryside where a camera can be moved along its surface (to train tank commanders). *Der Riese* is about surveillance as a means of social control by institutions, Dovey argues. James Hoberman wrote in the *Village Voice*, "Klier's 'giant' is primarily a stalwart defender of property."[33] And while the film is a meditation on social control (and crowd control and traffic control and control of private property and control of consumption and control of capital) it can also be seen as a portrait of a modern city ("an eighty-two minute city symphony," writes Hoberman).[34]

But the film is also profoundly alienating and unsettling. As a cinema audience, we find ourselves unmoored: What are we supposed to be looking at? What meaning are we supposed to glean? Is a particular person or car significant? Hoberman writes, "As narrative, the tape is all free-floating suspense; the viewer experiences a continual waiting for something to happen. But waiting for what?"[35]

It's not that the film doesn't guide us in some ways. The surveillance cameras pan deliberately, like when following the plane, and will zoom in on a particular person or vehicle. But the reason for this is never clear. One sequence early on, which consists of long shots from several cameras, seems to follow an ambulance as it makes its way

Figure 5.4 Watching the public shop. *Der Riese*.

across the city. A shot later in the film pans across a city center with shops, the camera finally settling on a young girl and her dog sitting by a fountain (see Figure 5.4). We watch her for a while and then the camera follows an older woman who walks off to the left. The camera then pans around, looking, watching, searching, and finally lands back on the young girl and her dog as her mother comes along with a shopping bag. In another sequence, the camera follows some boys who are fooling around, but then ends up zooming in on a pigeon, following it as it pecks at the floor. And it is not that the film is completely eventless. Besides the ambulance sequence, one scene in a department store appears to show a young man shoplifting. In another, a man with what looks like a gun seems to force a woman through a side door. There are narrative agents behind many of the cameras, but they are not all telling the same story for the same purpose. We see these agents in the number of shots from varied CCTV control rooms and in a reverse shot showing a cameraman on a rooftop in the parade sequence. But there is no central panoptic center, unless it is the selection and editing of Klier himself, who juxtaposes these sequences of shots and chooses the accompanying audio (Wagner, Mahler, Rachmaninoff, Khachaturian, and also some jazz; but there are also sequences of ambient audio from the scene of the cameras or from the control room, and some are silent).

To make meaning of a shot we scrutinize the often blurred image itself, taking note if it is in color or black and white. Camera movement, pans and zooms, we read as clues to what we should pay attention to, what is significant. And the soundtrack colors and adds emphasis to aspects of a scene. But the film refuses such semiotic and narrative closure and we remain unmoored, adrift. Why do rain-specked shots of traffic deserve bombastic classical music? And a three-minute shot of a VW parked at a gas station gets soft jazz? By refusing closure the film keeps us at a critical distance, always searching for meaning. But through the film we take the perspective of the surveillance camera, viewing the world dispassionately, from above; a perspective that feels somewhat alien ("It feels as if someone was watching human beings like in a zoo" is quoted on the DVD cover). We see the controllers, see how they work. Hoberman wrote that the film is a "spectacle produced ... for a spectator who is less a voyeur than a cop."[36] It is the institutional perspective we are given. However, Klier's montage, and his selection of audio, keeps us from being too comfortable in that perspective. And the awkward mechanical workings of the cameras, with their jerky motions, uneven zooms, and limited clarity, focus, and detail, keep the cameras themselves the objects of scrutiny. We can never ignore them and fall into the screen, as in classical Hollywood film, but are always aware of the cameras, the action of taping, and the contexts in which it is occurring (even if the reasons and meanings are obscure). In McGowan's terms, the film is a constant engagement with the gaze, with the real.[37]

This emphasis on the machinic aesthetic of the images, on their "real time, continuous takes with no cuts, machine time itself,"[38] is what makes the film seem to be a film without a cameraman.[39] Though there are active agents behind some of the cameras (and they move from camera to camera) the system—the giant—as a whole continues to record and watch. This is a film about a film without a cameraman, that is surveillance in general.

Paul Virilio wrote of this film:

> This solemn farewell to the man behind the camera, the complete evaporation of
> visual subjectivity into an ambient technical effect, a sort of permanent pancinema
> which, unbeknownst to us, turns our most ordinary acts into movie action, into
> new visual material, undaunted, undifferentiated vision-fodder, is not so much, as
> we have seen, the *end of art*—whether it be Klier's or 1970's video art, television's
> illegitimate offspring.[40]

The machinic aesthetic of the images reinforces contemporary notions of the truth
of images. Their mechanic objectivity, their remove from the immediacy of the event or
moment, their capture of whatever happens in front of their lens, in real time, provides
a new visual regime of the real. Only some of the cameras include a burn-in of time
and date (footage of the arrest of protestors at the parade and images from the mental
hospital); those shots remind us of real time, of the continuity of recording (noticeable
when cuts are made and the time jumps ahead), but also anchor us at particular days
and times (May 15, 1982 and June 11, 1981). The shots without this burn-in gain a
timeless quality: the world moves and the camera watches.

The surveillance aesthetic both distances us from the event and draws us closer
through our scrutiny. Marshall McLuhan would have called surveillance cameras a
cool medium: we must study them to understand, and by being engaged with the
medium through active interpretation we bring more of ourselves to that image, we
become more involved.[41] There is therefore a tension related to the surveillance image.
This tension is between boredom and the event. Surveillance video in itself, like live
webcam images, is boring.[42] We wait for something to happen and scrutinize details
of the scene looking for the event. This tension is heightened when feature films (and
television) utilize the surveillance image because the audience presumes a narrative
purpose behind the inclusion of the footage: we are guaranteed that something
will happen (a ghost will appear, a robbery will occur, and so on). And, given the
genres and contexts in which surveillance images typically occur (news, reality TV
compilations of competitions or found video of disasters or crimes, action film or
thrillers, and so on), what we expect to occur will not be something good. As John
Turner put it, "when a surveillance technology is shown on screen to expose or place
under gaze some character or event, it can generally be assumed that the surveillance
sequence prepares the viewer for some subsequent violence or potential for violence."[43]
The surveillance aesthetic predisposes us to a tension that we can feel in our bodies:
something is going to happen that will be shocking. It might end up being funny, or
horrifying, or thrilling, or sexy, depending on how the event is then framed. *Der Riese*
is a waiting game; we sit in expectation of disaster that is always deferred.

Look

Though many, many fictional films utilize this tension in occasional scenes for dramatic
effect, Adam Rifkin's *Look* (2007) tries to build an entire feature film on the aesthetic, a

film that struggles with the contradiction between the distancing effect of surveillance footage and the need to collapse that distance to identify with characters and their situations.

Look begins with these words on the screen:

There are an estimated 30 million surveillance cameras in the United States generating more than 4 billion hours of video every week.

This statement is followed by a flurry of very brief snippets of surveillance camera footage, some in color and some in black and white, from a variety of settings. The film tends to recreate the surveillance aesthetic with typical motion picture cameras and post-production work rather that utilizing the limited capabilities of surveillance cameras themselves. This series of clips is followed by the additional statement:

On any given day the average American is captured approximately 200 times.

We then get the first shot of the film: the interior of a women's dressing room in a department store. The camera is positioned above the mirror looking down on the room. The location, date, and time are indicated by a burn-in in one corner of the image. A young woman enters, disrobes, and begins posing in front of the mirror, checking herself out. A knock is heard on the door and she lets in another young woman who also disrobes. They try on clothes, pose nearly naked for the mirror, and playfully bump and grind with each other. They finally dress (stealing some of the clothes by wearing them under their street clothes) and depart. The next shot is from the corridor outside the dressing room. We see them exit and laugh as a woman in a wheelchair, who has been waiting for the larger dressing room (marked with a symbol of wheelchair access) they have occupied, struggles to enter the dressing room. We then get a series of shots from other security cameras above the floor of the department store, tracking the girls as they walk around, talk to their teacher and his wife whom they run into, and head out of the store. The camera zooms in on the girls, indicating that someone is actively tracking them. Just after they exit the store into the mall we see a store security guard chase after them, too late. The film continues on, each action captured on one or more cameras.

The film presents a great variety of surveillance cameras in almost any conceivable location: the department store and mall, the parking lot, an ATM, a traffic camera, an insurance office, a Nannycam, a convenience store, a police car dashboard, a school and its parking lot, on a public bus, in a police interrogation room, and more. These are all surveillance locations familiar to the audience from news and reality TV shows (though perhaps the opening sequence in the dressing room is more shocking in its voyeuristic invasion of privacy; the sequence sets the tone of violation established by the opening statements and emphasized by the dressing room to infuse the remainder of the film). The footage from each of these cameras is unique: different burn-ins with different fonts, different levels of clarity, different color balance (some in black and white, some saturated with color, others washed out). There are also glitches and dropouts to emphasize the imperfection of the cameras. Rather than the continuity expected of a feature film (where each camera produces a uniform quality of image,

Figure 5.5 The girls, under the watch of store security, meet their teacher. *Look*.

except when a particular effect is called for), *Look* is visually fragmented. The characters are in different locations on the screen from shot to shot depending on the camera viewing them. The cameras also have a limited range of view and limited zoom capabilities. Much action occurs at a distance from the camera. The film breaks with its realist aesthetic when it comes to sound, however, and all the cameras apparently can capture audio and are able to clearly pick up the conversations of the characters (and isolate them from the general ambient noise).

The question of narrator—who is compiling this footage and following these characters?—is bracketed by the film. At times the narrator seems to be diegetic, part of the world of the film. For example, the department store cameras seem to be actively tracking those girls, indicating that there is someone in the store working the cameras. The security guard at the end of the opening sequence looks up into the camera and speaks into a walkie-talkie: "Missed them." But for the most part, the narrator is non-diegetic: he or she is manipulating the images after the fact. We see this in several ways. Sequences are edited so that we see snippets from the same camera, but some time has been cut out. At other times the tape is fast forwarded to a relevant part of the conversation (or slowed down to emphasize a dramatic moment). Conversation from one scene can overlap an image from the next, common in editing feature films but unlikely from a surveillance camera. Some faces have been deliberately pixelated. And the only time we get a close-up is in a post production zoom where a portion of the video image is enlarged later (with increasing granularity). For example, late in the film the teacher and his lawyer sit in a police interrogation room. In the shot we see the reflection of the camera making the recording. But when we close in on the face of the teacher, that reflected camera does not move.

Figure 5.6 The camera in the reflection. *Look.*

In many ways the role of the narrator is clear: it is the film's director who is putting the images together, pointing out for us what we should be paying attention to, and so on. In any other Hollywood film we wouldn't even ask these questions. But the surveillance camera form raises the question not of the authenticity of the image (in this case) but the structure of the narration. The use of the clunkier surveillance cameras works to make obvious the techniques of standard editing, cinematography, and so on. One challenge the film faces is that, lacking standard continuity editing (what has been called the historical mode of narration[44]), it is harder to immerse the audience in the film. As an audience member, our point of view is always shifting and we can never be sutured into a scene (like through a shot-reverse shot structure; something that even *Der Riese* gave us on a couple of occasions). This distances the audience from the characters, makes it harder to identify with them. In other words, they become objects of our voyeuristic gaze rather than objects of our narcissistic identification. We regard the film and its characters at a remove (and it is only the scrutiny of the cool surveillance image that maintains our attention and involves us in the images).[45]

One effect of this narrative function is that it reimposes the logic of the spectacle on a society of control. In a society of control we and our images and data circulate and are modulated. There is no panoptic structure or Orwellian Big Brother (what Baudrillard called "the omnipotence of a despotic gaze").[46] The film reintroduces the idea of an "Overlord"[47] that centralizes the dispersed fragments of video and presents them to us at a remove, in what Baudrillard called "an objective space."[48]

This raises the question of how the audience is meant to regard the images, events, and people they are watching. The film's title is a command: *Look.* And so the audience looks, from above, at a remove. But how are they meant to *feel* when they see these images, where almost any public, and many private, moments of daily life are captured on camera? A world illuminated by the light of surveillance cameras.[49] Baudrillard once discussed what he called *obscenity*: "the most intimate operation of your life becomes the potential grazing ground of the media ... the entire universe also unfolds unnecessarily on your home screen."[50] Consider the opening scene again with the camera in the dressing room. On the one hand, the audience is positioned and primed to see this as an invasion of privacy. These are the "average Americans" just mentioned in the titles captured unknowingly by a few of these millions of cameras. The audience is asked to identify with their situation and feel violated on their behalf. But on the other hand, the audience is also positioned to see this situation as sexual voyeurs would (the girls are objects of the voyeuristic gaze, as Mulvey would theorize). John Berger has argued that it is an old trope of Western visual culture to position naked women with mirrors in the painting or photograph to justify men looking at them.[51] They are looking at themselves, so it must be alright for men to look, too. Plus, there is a moral critique that men could make—women are vain and shallow to gaze at themselves in the mirror so and these girls in the film are no exception—and so men could feel morally superior while they ogled. The performances of the actresses match that of soft porn, especially reality porn such as "Caught in the Act" or "Girls Gone Wild" videos.[52] They are performing for the mirrors, but really for the camera. They are not portrayed as innocent victims. It is revealed that the characters are supposed to be sixteen years old. The film later emphasizes the severe consequences of acting on the fantasy of sex with teens (an adult gets arrested for statutory rape, is labeled a "sex offender," and goes to jail for a long time), which makes discomfiting this early titillating scene. Should the audience be horrified or aroused? The film wants it both ways.

In building its scenarios, the film draws on the familiar tropes of reality TV surveillance video. We have the reality porn, mentioned above, which also includes other scenes of employees caught on camera having sex in the workplace, and convenience store clerks taking upskirt mobile phone images. There is the police dashcam footage, the car chase caught by news helicopter, the Nannycam, the convenience store (with criminals but without the stereotypical robbery), images of child kidnapping in a mall, and more. The film plays off our genre assumptions—sometime playing into them (the dashboard footage captures the murder of a policeman) and sometimes playing with them (the lack of a convenience store robbery, the lack of abuse on the part of the nanny on the Nannycam, and so on). The film also plays off of the audience's assumptions about racial profiling while challenging them. A Middle Eastern man is in a few scenes. He forgets his backpack on the bus and everyone panics, sending in the bomb squad (the backpack has textbooks and one of the last images of the film is of this man in graduation robes receiving a diploma).

If *Look* is giving us a world that is ostensibly real, the reality of the world is overwhelmingly cynical, full of sex, violence, and duplicity. As a character walks away, we hear others start criticizing them behind their back; everyone seems to be cheating in some way (two men are having affairs and two others end up being sexual predators), women are victims of sexual harassment or crime. Though surveillance assists in the solution of some crimes and situations, in others it seems helpless (despite capturing images of the perpetrator). In some ways, these very characteristics are what we expect to see through surveillance footage.

Though *Look* attempts to provide us with a meditation on surveillance in everyday life, what it really provides us with is a meditation on the narrative effects of surveillance footage. It is more revealing of the genre and narrative expectations of the surveillance camera aesthetic than the effects of surveillance cameras themselves. It is less about how many times we are actually captured on surveillance cameras in our daily lives than about the number of times we see surveillance camera images circulate on the screens of cinemas, televisions, and our computers as we forward the latest amazing clip to our Facebook wall.

Der Riese is in many ways a better meditation on surveillance in everyday life. It is not so because of its aesthetic or in the "actuality" or authenticity of its images, but in its refusal of a narrative structure, in the inscrutability of its imagery, and in its sheer uneventfulness. These are the aspects of surveillance, in addition to its constancy, frequency, and ubiquity, which will always exceed and trouble the attempts to represent surveillance in either feature film or television program. Surveillance as a whole (and Klier's name, *The Giant*, is apt) is incoherent, obscure, troubling, and alienating.

Conclusion

From a psychoanalytic perspective, the real is what is necessarily absent from the symbolic order.[53] The real is what troubles the symbolic order because it exceeds it, it belies the symbolic constructedness. The emphasis on the real in the images we have been discussing, whether it be the inclusion of surveillance or videocamera footage in reality TV programs or images that mimic such footage in fictional television and cinema texts, could be seen as an attempt to narrativize, master, and incorporate into the symbolic that which troubles the symbolic. This is an act of ideological closure. The retreat into the imaginary, into especially these conceptions and images of total surveillance, is means of ignoring the very real trauma of surveillance. This contradictory dynamic of the surveillance image is one that deserves to be pursued further: the images both make a claim to the real and trouble that claim at the same time. It is an image that can get caught up, incorporated, and narrativized in broader social discourses of security, danger, and so on, but that always carries with it that affective charge that may disturb those discourses.

Our faith in the power of surveillance cameras to give us the truth, the real, can be seen not only in our fictions but also in our everyday life. For example, there is the recent push to have police officers wear body cameras—the purpose is both behavioral (the thought that the presence of the cameras will have a disciplining effect on both officer and suspect) and also evidential: proof of what actually happened. Cameras can be important political, cultural, and social witnesses to events (including human rights violations worldwide, such as those provided by Project Witness). But we need to carefully consider the ways our regimes of truth are constructed.

Other films to consider

8mm (dir. Joel Schumacher, 1999)
The Blair Witch Project (dir. Daniel Myrick and Eduardo Sánchez, 1999)
Sleep Dealer (dir. Alex Rivera, 2008)
Snake Eyes (dir. Brian De Palma, 1998)
Strange Days (dir. Kathryn Bigelow, 1995)
Surveillance 24/7 (dir. Paul Oremland, 2007)
Timecode (dir. Mike Figgis, 2000)

Questions for discussion

1. Does the "truth" or authenticity of this type of "real" footage impel us to act any
   more than the images produced by the cinematic cameras of the other films we
   have been discussing? Are we more or less apt to respond and critique surveillance
   as the result of this turn to the real?
2. How much does the medium itself play a role in the "reality effect" of the image?
   That is, if the same "real" surveillance image appeared on a cinema screen, would
   it have the same sense of authenticity had it appeared on your television set, on
   your computer, or on your smart phone?

Conclusion: Some Must Watch

Figure C.1 The view from The Machine. *Person of Interest.*

In the summer of 2013, reports based on a massive trove of NSA documents leaked by Edward Snowden began to be published. The public was told of the various programs, like PRISM, through which the NSA spied on both foreigners and US citizens, and NSA's collaborations with other national security agencies such as Britain's GCHQ.[1] And while these revelations were shocking and spurred some important debates, in general public reaction was lukewarm, at best, though citizens have become more wary of warrantless intrusion into their communications.[2] In part, though the details were new, the *fact* of this sort of spying and data collection had been known for a long time—from revelations in the mid-1990s about the secretive ECHELON system that scanned all global communication for keywords[3] to the report in 2012 that the NSA is building a massive data warehouse in Utah to store the staggering amount of information it gathers.[4] And, in part, it was argued, popular culture had been talking about this for decades.

In *Enemy of the State* (1998), Brill has a speech where he talks about the NSA's capabilities to tap every form of communication and scan them for keywords (basically describing ECHELON). A decade later, in the thriller *The Echelon Conspiracy* (2009), when Max Petersen (Shane West) tells Kamila (Tamara Feldman) about the NSA's capacity to tap all communication, she basically shrugs and says she assumed they were doing that anyway. The fact of this type of spying is now taken for granted. We've seen it before, on screen. In an article in *The Guardian* newspaper on how popular culture predicted the Snowden revelations, Amanda Holpuch and Ruth Spencer even point to a 1997 TV movie of *Murder, She Wrote*, "South by Southwest," that featured Jessica Fletcher (Angela Lansbury) questioning a NSA officer about how that agency downloads global communications.[5]

More recently, the US television series *Person of Interest* (2011–) seemed remarkably prescient in terms of the NSA's capacities. The series is about Harold Finch (Michael Emerson), a computer genius who, in the wake of 9/11, invented a computer system that would scan all communication, databases, surveillance networks, and any other information it had at its disposal to look for patterns in order to identify the next terrorist attack. He called this system The Machine. Worried that the system could be abused, he built himself backdoor access. He also realized that this system was able to identify not just terrorists, but anyone who might be involved in a preplanned violent crime. The Machine becomes a purely technical version of the Pre-Cogs in *Minority Report*. With the aid of an ex-CIA operative, John Reese (Jim Caviezel), they track down individuals (identified by The Machine only by Social Security number) who may be either a potential victim or perpetrator of a crime before the crime occurs. The series is similar to other post-9/11 surveillance films and television programs that use the catastrophic events of that day to justify a fantasy of total surveillance: that more technology, more information, would have prevented 9/11. *Déjà Vu* is exemplary here.[6] However, *Person of Interest* begins as a type of vigilante surveillance procedural, but one that reaffirms the perfection of The Machine, as it infallibly identifies potential for violence, time and time again. It is a procedural that doesn't politically reinforce the institutions of law and order (police, CIA, and so on, which are often depicted as rife with corruption despite the valiant efforts of a few good officers), and actively work outside of those institutions and the law. But the series does reinforce a technophilic fantasy of perfect knowledge via surveillance. Surveillance is not a retrospective tool of investigation but a prospective tool of prediction, simulation, and control. The fantasy of the all-knowing machine as both savior and danger becomes a common feature in the post-9/11 surveillant imaginary (cf. *Eagle Eye* and *Echelon Conspiracy*). And such desires fueled post-9/11 government programs such as Total Information Awareness which sought to mine personal data for patterns of terrorist activity. But though the structure of feeling of this imaginary is particular to post-9/11 United States, it has deep roots in popular culture and discourse.

I am pursuing these themes here (many of which have been touched on in the previous chapters) for a couple of reasons. First is to tie together some of the threads from the earlier analyses of watchers, watched, surveillance societies, procedurals, and reality effects. But second is to acknowledge that imaginaries are varied and yet specific. There may be more than one surveillance imaginary at work at any one time, and they will vary based on cultural context and other factors. For example, we have discussed a post-1992–93 surveillant imaginary in Mumbai, a post-1997 surveillant imaginary in Hong Kong, and post-9/11 surveillant imaginary in the United States.

There are overlaps and comparable themes among these, but they get articulated differently. For example, Orwell's *Nineteen Eighty-Four* would have been read in a different context in 1950s UK (still rebuilding from WWII, where memories of the bombings and rationing were quite near and resonant in the pages of the book) from the 1950s United States (where it might be read at a further remove; the United States itself is virtually absent from the novel).

So let me trace a bit of this trope of the all-knowing machine and we can see how it gets rearticulated over time. Responding to the growth of computers and the military industrial complex, Lewis Mumford warned of the All Seeing Eye back in 1970:

> In the end, no action, no conversation, and possibly in time no dream or thought would escape the wakeful and relentless eye of this deity: every manifestation of life would be processed into the computer and brought under its all-pervading system of control. This would mean, not just the invasion of privacy, but the total destruction of autonomy: indeed the dissolution of the human soul.[7]

For Mumford, computerization and surveillance were part and parcel of the growth of what he called the megamachine, the centralization of power through technology, organization, and efficiency, turning society into a giant machine. Mumford's fears were dramatized to a certain extent in the 1970 film, directed by Joseph Sargent, *Colossus: The Forbin Project* in which the US government creates a supercomputer to run the country's defense system, believing that a computer would be able to identify threats and respond rationally and efficiently to any aggressive action of the Soviets. The film is a cold war parable about placing faith in technology to solve our political and social issues, and to yield our own agency to The Machine under the assumption that machine rationality is better than human thought. True to genre, the machine, Colossus, achieves sentience, joins with a Russian supercomputer named Guardian, and takes control of the world. The only way to prevent war and maintain peace, it concludes, is total control of the human population, which it does so through surveillance and the threat of nuclear disaster (Colossus controls all the warheads). Colossus puts its creator, Charles Forbin (Eric Braeden), under especial surveillance, even installing cameras in his quarters and insisting that Forbin follows a strict preplanned routine (and even diet). Though similar to our contemporary imaginary about the intelligent machine and surveillance, there are differences. There is much more concern in the earlier films about the loss of control of the system, that the system itself becomes a threat, rather than it just being a tool of the government. We see this combination of the threat of the autonomous machine coupled with surveillance and control in both Michael Crichton's *Westworld* (1973) and Donald Cammell's *Demon Seed* (1977), culminating in the Skynet system at the heart of the *Terminator* franchise (1984–) and later the autonomous machines of the *Matrix* series (1999–2003). This theme of autonomy is still present in *The Echelon Conspiracy* as well as later seasons of *Person of Interest*, but the main concern becomes questions of invasion of privacy and perhaps political power more than loss of humanity.[8]

Post-9/11 this trope of the all-seeing eye is rearticulated to discourses of protecting the homeland and increased security. The data collection and analysis is automated, the weapons of war become remote controlled drones, but we have not yet automated the defense system fully.[9] Mirzoeff refers to this visual complex as legitimating a global counterinsurgency where war (as infowar and netwar) is seen as constant and borderless, cultural and political, and the goal of which is management of populations.[10] It is a post-Panoptic war machine that operates in a mounting plethora of imagery and data, but strives to remain invisible (hence, the secrecy around the NSA's domestic spying efforts revealed by Snowden). Both the regimes of governmentality described by Foucault and the societies of control described by Deleuze have become militarized, Mirzoeff argues. In the realm of popular culture, the interesting work of *Person of Interest* rearticulates the system yet again but more personally in terms of care of individuals rather than security of a society as a whole, and argues that the system can be used for other purposes, hacked for a good purpose, that of care. But whether the show ends up justifying the surveillance system (rather than critiquing it) is something with which that the show's writers struggle.[11]

"You are being watched" is the opening line of each episode of *Person of Interest*, but it is also true that we are watching. In the contemporary surveillant imaginary, we are watchers as well as watched. From reality TV to social media we get the sense that more and more of our lives are mediated and most likely stored somewhere, perhaps on a cloud server. The hack of cloud servers in 2014, that released the personal and quite private photographs of many celebrities, underscored that point. All these images and videos that we take and that others take end up circulating somewhere, even if we delete them. The collection of not just personal data (our shadow selves) but also all these images and other texts leads to the idea that the total capture of a life is an emerging aspect of our contemporary surveillant imaginary: that a person's full life could be recorded and played back. This was, from a reality TV perspective, the idea behind *The Truman Show*: a complete life, from birth to death, broadcast live. In the 1990s researchers began experimenting with what they called lifelogging—recording events of their day automatically via wearable cameras.[12] In this, they were preceded by Steve Mann and his wearable computers in which he, for a time, streamed his daily life to the internet, just as webcammers did.[13] The next level of this type of self-surveillance is Microsoft's MyLifeBits project, which collects not just events in front of one (videos of people you meet and conversations you have) but all the other information from daily life (all your music, images, old papers, books, receipts, and so on) to form a permanent, searchable record of your life. Microsoft researcher Gordon Bell touts the important contribution such a resource would make to self-knowledge (an "honest record"), providing "objective" insights into our life patterns (for health, relationships, work habits, or any other dimension of our life).[14] This type of self-surveillance has been taken up more popularly under the name, The Quantified Self, or the idea of self-tracking.

The idea of a complete, recorded life is becoming an emerging trope in our fictions as well, feeding this aspect of the imaginary. It is dealt with in the Omar Naim film *The Final Cut* (2004) and more recently in an episode of the British science fiction anthology series *Black Mirror*, "The Entire History of You" (December 18, 2011). The episode concerns an implanted memory chip called a "grain" that most of the population seem to have installed that records their entire experience. You can then play back particular moments, delete ones you don't want to remember, and even cast them to a nearby television to watch with others. While a character makes an argument on behalf of the grain that it ensures the accuracy of memory (explaining how easily false memories can occur in our unwired brains; resonating with the ostensibly objective aspect of a lifelogging or surveillance record) it reveals a trust in the truth of the recording—that by playing back a moment over and over you can reveal what was really going on (shades of *Blowup*, are we interpreting this correctly?). The episode also highlights the underlying desire to see everything—if we *can* see it, we *must* see it. A couple even watch the memories from their infant's grain for the time they were out at the party and the child was under a care of a sitter—a new twist on the Nannycam. On the one hand, the episode comments on our culture of sharing (how we click "share" to upload media to social network sites), where it is commonplace for people to share events in their recent or far past on a big screen for their friends (or boss or security guard at the airport). To make public something private—go ahead and show us, then, and we can all talk about how your interview went. On the other hand, the episode comments on the ways such possibilities for knowledge become obsessions. One character suspects his wife of having an affair and that it is her lover who is the true father of their child. "I must see" he insists over and over, forcing her to play for him her memory of unprotected sex with her lover. The video is the truth.

But *Black Mirror* also evidences a key limitation of the contemporary surveillant imagination: it is all or nothing, have the implant or take it out. Even though memories can be edited out, the final decision is either to have the technology or reject it. There seems no middle ground, and this is the failure of the surveillant imaginary, to imagine new forms of surveillance that aren't either/or. Cinema taught us how to look at others, to stare without guilt; television encouraged us to watch, live, from a distance; and the internet and mobile communication technologies promote continuous access, playing in to what Linda Stone once called continuous partial attention: the constant low-level awareness (via email, notifications, live feeds, updates, and so on) so as not to miss anything.[15] This leads to a sense of constant crisis and, as the Institute for Precarious Consciousness would put it, a structure of feeling of anxiety. We must see.

Surveillance emphasizes the stare *toward*, the look *at*. Perhaps it needs more opportunities to allow and encourage us to glance *away*. Can we imagine surveillance that includes opacity rather than just clarity (an opacity that doesn't invite more scrutiny, like the blurred images of early CCTV, but an opacity that we pass over), forgetting rather than always remembering, looking away rather than always toward, and that respects not just privacy, but dignity and agency? It's easier to imagine, and assume, a system that captures all, and much more difficult and complex to imagine a system than captures partially, ethically, and with nuance and care.

This also means that alongside the films about the total power of surveillance we need to recognize those elements of the surveillant imaginary that are about surveillance failures (and not just "resistance" either). In Martin Scorsese's *The Departed* (2006), a remake of *Infernal Affairs*, a police sting fails because cameras weren't in the right part of the building. In *Homeland*, Carrie Mathison (Clare Danes) is frustrated when a camera is not placed in Nicholas Brody's (Damian Lewis) garage. In Rodrigo Plá's 2009 film *La Zona* (The Zone), frequent power outages render a community's CCTV system inoperable at key moments as they pursue a fugitive hiding out in their neighborhood. David Fincher's *Panic Room* (2002) shows both the promises and perils of a home surveillance system. And David Simon's series *The Wire* (2002–2008) presents the difficulties and limitations of police surveillance as well as its successes.[16]

As *The Wire* points out, surveillance is not just about the success or failure of a technology, but surveillance is part of a legal, economic, cultural, and social assemblage. In our surveillant imaginaries, we present technology not as it is but as we perceive it to be, our perceptions and representations embedded in broader cultural assumptions.[17] If we address surveillance and its technologies on a cultural level, then perhaps we might begin to imagine different systems based on different cultural and social assumptions. David Lyon once argued that rather than using dystopia as a framework for our surveillant imaginary, why not utopia?[18] What's the *best* possible scenario? That would make us confront the question not of what we want to avoid, but what we really want. Utopias are naïve, he warns, but then, so are dystopias.

Surveillance and our surveillant imaginary shape our engagements with the world and with others, and our everyday practices and experiences create, reinforce, and transform this imaginary. Our films and television shows that feature surveillance are no mere reflections on realities, anxieties, and fantasies of power, but help produce those same constructions of reality, relations of power, and structure of feeling that shape our everyday.

Notes

Introduction

1   Orwell, George. *Nineteen Eighty-Four*. New York: Everyman's Library, 1992. Originally Harcourt, Brace and Company, 1949. Coincidentally, this episode of *Are You Being Served* aired on April 4, the day and month Winston Smith begins his secret diary in *Nineteen Eighty-Four*.

2   Foucault, Michel. *Discipline and Punish*, trans. Alan Sheridan. Harmondsworth: Penguin, 1977.

3   Zimmer, Catherine. "Surveillance Cinema: Narrative Between Technology and Politics." *Surveillance and Society* 8 (2011): 428.

4   Levin, Thomas Y. "Rhetoric of the Temporal Index: Surveillant Narration and the Cinema of 'Real Time.'" In *CTRL Space: Rhetorics of Surveillance from Bentham to Big Brother*, edited by Thomas Levin, Ursula Frohne, and Peter Weibel, 578–593. Cambridge: MIT Press, 2002.

5   Strain, Ellen. "Exotic Bodies, Distant Landscapes: Touristic Viewing and Popularized Anthropology in the Nineteenth Century." *Wide Angle* 18 (1996): 70–100; Griffiths, Alison. *Wondrous Difference: Cinema, Anthropology, and Turn-of-the-Century Visual Culture*. New York: Columbia University Press, 2002.

6   Zimmer, "Surveillance Cinema," 429.

7   Niedzviecki, Hal. *The Peep Diaries: How We're Learning to Love Watching Ourselves and Our Neighbors*. San Francisco: City Lights, 2009.

8   Carey, James and J.A. Game. "Communication, Culture, and Technology: An Internet Interview with James W. Carey." *Journal of Communication Inquiry* 22 (1998): 129.

9   Kammerer, Dietmar. "Surveillance in Literature, Film, and Television." In *Routledge Handbook of Surveillance Studies*, edited by Kirstie Ball, Kevin D. Haggerty, and David Lyon, 99–106. New York: Routledge, 2012; Lyon, David. *Surveillance Studies: An Overview*. Malden: Polity, 2007, and Lyon, David. "The Emerging Surveillance Culture." In *Media, Surveillance and Identity: Social Perspectives*, edited by André Jansson and Miyase Christensen, 71–88. New York: Peter Lang, 2014.

10 Hall, Stuart. "Notes on Deconstructing the Popular." In *People's History and Socialist Theory*. London: Routledge, 1981.

11 Kammerer, "Surveillance in Literature," 105.

12 Zimmer, "Surveillance Cinema," 439. See also Zimmer, Catherine. *Surveillance Cinema*. New York: New York University Press, 2015.

13 Lyon, David. *Surveillance Society: Monitoring Everyday Life*, 2. Philadelphia: Open University Press, 2001.

14 McGowan, Todd. *Psychoanalytic Film Theory and the Rules of the Game*. New York: Bloomsbury Academic, 2015, 39.

15 Mirzoeff, Nicholas. *The Right to Look: A Counterhistory of Visuality*. Durham: Duke University Press, 2011, 3–4.

16   McGowan, *Psychoanalytic Film Theory*.
17   See Lyon's history of surveillance in *The Electronic Eye*.
18   Mirzoeff, Nicholas. *The Right to Look*.
19   See Parenti, Christian. *The Soft Cage: Surveillance in America from Slavery to the War on Terror*. New York: Basic Books, 2003; Browne, Simone. "Race and Surveillance." In *The Routledge Handbook of Surveillance Studies* edited by Kirstie Ball, Kevin D. Haggerty, and David Lyon, 72–79. New York: Routledge, 2012.
20   Kundnani, Arun and Deepa Kumar. "Race, Surveillance, and Empire." *International Socialist Review* 96 (2015). Accessed April 19, 2016. http://isreview.org/issue/96/race-surveillance-and-empire, who draw on the work of Williams, Hubert and Patrick V. Murphy. "The Evolving Strategy of Police: A Minority View." *Perspectives on Policing* 13 (1990).
21   Saʾdi, Ahmad H. "Colonialism and Surveillance." In *The Routledge Handbook of Surveillance Studies*, edited by Kirstie Ball, Kevin D. Haggerty, and David Lyon, 151–158. New York: Routledge, 2012.
22   Kundnani and Kumar, "Race, Surveillance, and Empire."
23   Browne, "Race and Surveillance"; Parenti, *The Soft Cage*. Suren Lalvani once put it in *Photography, Vision and the Production of Modern Bodies*, "technologies of vision, like photography, embedded within particular discursive and cultural relations, organize specific relations between knowledge, power, and the body" (2).
24   Griffiths, *Wondrous Difference*.
25   Discussed in "9 July," *1914: Day by Day*. Accessed April 23, 2016. http://www.bbc.co.uk/programmes/b048nkd0; W.M. "The Double-Life," *Daily Mirror*, 9 July (1914) 7.
26   Moore, Burness E. and Bernard D. Fine. *Psychoanalytic Terms and Concepts*. New Haven: American Psychoanalytic Association and Yale University Press, 1990.
27   Denzin, Norman. *The Cinematic Society: The Voyeur's Gaze*. Thousand Oaks: Sage, 1995, 29.
28   Cf. Ibid., 14–15.
29   David Murukami Wood presents a quite detailed history of the field in his short review essay, "Situating Surveillance Studies." But see also David Lyon's book *Surveillance Studies* which Wood is reviewing. And see also *The Routledge Handbook of Surveillance Studies*, edited by Kirstie Ball, Kevin D. Haggerty, and David Lyon.
30   Foucault, *Discipline and Punish*; Rule, James B. *Private Lives, Public Surveillance: Social Control in the Information Age*. London: Allen Lane, 1973.
31   Marx, Gary T. *Undercover*. Berkeley: University of California Press, 1988.
32   Campbell, "Inside Echelon"; EPIC.org.
33   Norris, Clive and Gary Armstrong. *The Maximum Surveillance Society: The Rise of CCTV*. Oxford: Berg, 1999.
34   Gates, Kelly. *Our Biometric Future: Facial Recognition Technology and the Culture of Surveillance*. New York: New York University Press, 2011; Pugliese, Joseph. *Biometrics: Bodies, Technologies, Biopolitics*. New York: Routledge. 2012.
35   Gandy, Oscar. *The Panoptic Sort: A Political Economy of Personal Information*. Boulder: Westview, 1993; Lyon, *Electronic Eye*.
36   Andrejevic, Mark. *iSpy: Surveillance and Power in the Interactive Era*. Lawrence, KS: University Press of Kansas, 2007.
37   Monahan, Torin and Rodolfo D. Torres (eds). *Schools Under Surveillance: Cultures of Control in Public Education*. New Brunswick, NJ: Rutgers University Press, 2009.
38   Dubrofsky, Rachel E. and Shoshana Amielle Magnet (eds). *Feminist Surveillance Studies*. Durham: Duke University Press, 2015.

39 Marx, Gary T. "Soul Train: The New Surveillance and Popular Music." In *Lessons from the Identity Trail: Anonymity, Privacy, and Identity in a Networked Society*, edited by Ian Kerr, Carole Lucock, and Valerie Steeves, 377. New York: Oxford University Press, 2009. See also Monahan, "Surveillance as Cultural Practice," the introduction to a special section of *The Sociological Quarterly* about the cultural dimensions of surveillance.

40 Lyon, *Surveillance Studies*, 139.

41 Levin, "Rhetoric of the Temporal," 581.

42 See, for example, Kammerer, Dietmar. "Video Surveillance in Hollywood Movies." *Surveillance and Society* 2 (2004): 464–473, and Kammerer, Dietmar. *Bilder der Überwachung*. Frankfurt: Suhrkamp Verlag, 2008; Lefait, Sébastien. *Surveillance on Screen: Monitoring Contemporary Films and Television Programs*. Lanham: Scarecrow Press, 2013; Stewart, Garrett. *Closed Circuits: Screening Narrative Surveillance*. Chicago: University of Chicago Press, 2015; Zimmer, *Surveillance Cinema*.

43 Staples, William G. *Everyday Surveillance: Vigilance and Visibility in Postmodern Life* (second edition). Lanham: Rowman and Littlefield, 2014; Pecora, Vincent. "The Culture of Surveillance." *Qualitative Sociology* 25 (2002): 345–358; Lyon, "Emerging Surveillance Culture."

44 Mann, Steve, Jason Nolan, and Barry Wellman. "Sousveillance: Inventing and Using Wearable Computing Devices for Data Collection in Surveillance Environments." *Surveillance and Society* 1 (2003): 331–355.

45 Lake, Jessica. "*Red Road* (2006) and emerging narratives of 'sub-veillance.'" *Continuum: Journal of Media and Cultural Studies* 24 (2010): 231–240.

46 Andrejevic, *iSpy*.

47 Lyon, "Emerging Surveillance Culture," 83.

48 Orwell, *Nineteen Eighty-Four*.

49 Foucault, *Discipline and Punish*.

50 Deleuze, Gilles. *Negotiations*, translated by Martin Joughin. New York: Columbia University Press, 1995.

51 Marx, Gary T. "Electric Eye in the Sky: Some Reflections on the New Surveillance in Popular Culture." In *Computers, Surveillance, and Privacy*, edited by David Lyon and Elia Zureik, 195. Minneapolis: University of Minnesota Press, 1996.

Chapter 1

1 Denzin, *Cinematic Society*, 5

2 Mulvey, Laura. "Visual Pleasure and Narrative Cinema." In *Film Theory and Criticism: Introductory Readings*, edited by Leo Braudy and Marshall Cohen, 833–844. New York: Oxford University Press, 2004. I am indebted to John Ellis's reading of Mulvey in *Visible Fictions: Cinema, Television, Video* (2nd edition). New York: Routledge, 1992.

3 Cf. Mulvey, Laura. "Afterthoughts on 'Visual Pleasure and Narrative Cinema' Inspired by King Vidor's *A Duel in the Sun* (1946)." *Feminist Film Theory: A Reader*, edited by Sue Thornham, 122–130. Edinburgh: Edinburgh University Press, 1999; McGowan, *Psychoanalytic Film Theory*; Modleski, Tania. *The Women Who Knew Too Much: Hitchcock and Feminist Theory* (2nd edition). New York: Routledge, 2005; De Lauretis,

Teresa. *Alice Doesn't: Feminism, Semiotics, and Cinema*. Bloomington: Indiana University Press, 1984; Doane, Mary Ann. *The Desire to Desire: The Women's Film of the 1940s*. Bloomington: Indiana University Press, 1987.

4   Cf. Denzin, *Cinematic Society*.

5   de Lauretis, *Alice Doesn't*, discussed in Modleski, *The Women Who Knew Too Much*.

6   McGowan, *Psychoanalytic Film Theory*.

7   Deleuze, Gilles and Félix Guattari. *Anti-Oedipus: Capitalism and Schizophrenia*, translated by Robert Hurley, Mark Seems, and Helen R. Lane. Minneapolis: University of Minnesota Press, 1983.

8   Key readings include Mulvey, "Visual Pleasure"; Modleski, Tania. "The Master's Dollhouse." *The Women Who Knew Too Much: Hitchcock and Feminist Theory*. New York: Routledge, 1998; Stam, Robert. *Reflexivity in Film and Literature: From Don Quixote to Jean-Luc Godard*. New York: Columbia University Press, 1995; Denzin, *Cinematic Society*.

9   Denzin, *Cinematic Society*, 116.

10 See, e.g., Albrechtslund, Anders. "Surveillance and Ethics in Film: *Rear Window* and *The Conversation*." *Journal of Criminal Justice and Popular Culture* 15 (2008): 129–144; Mulvey, "Visual Pleasure."

11 Howe, Lawrence. "Through the Looking Glass: Reflexivity, Reciprocality, and Defenestration in Hitchcock's *Rear Window*." *College Literature* 35 (2008): 16–37.

12 Cf. Mulvey, "Visual Pleasure."

13 Howe, "Looking Glass."

14 See Howe, "Looking Glass"; Modleski, *The Women Who Knew Too Much*.

15 Howe, "Looking Glass."

16 Albrechtslund, "Surveillance and Ethics."

17 Howe, "Looking Glass."

18 Rodley, Chris. "A Very British Psycho." Channel 4 International. Available on *Peeping Tom* (DVD) The Criterion Collection, 1999. Laura Mulvey's commentary track on The Criterion Collection's DVD release of *Peeping Tom* (1999) is a master class in psychoanalytic film criticism.

19 Denzin, *Cinematic Society*.

20 Ellis, *Visible Fictions*.

21 Hawthorn, "Morality, Voyeurism."

22 Ibid., 322.

23 Modleski, *The Women Who Knew Too Much*, 76.

24 See Lyon, *Surveillance Society*, and Lyon, David. *Surveillance After September 11*. Malden: Polity, 2003.

25 Lyon, *Surveillance After September 11*, 5.

26 Kammerer, "Video Surveillance."

27 Sontag, Susan. *On Photography*. New York: Picador, 2001.

28 Benjamin, Walter. "The Work of Art in the Age of Mechanical Reproduction." In *Illuminations*, edited by Hannah Arendt, translated by H. Zohn. New York: Schocken, 1969.

29 Norris and Armstrong, *Maximum Surveillance*. However, see Gavin J.D. Smith, "Exploring Relations Between Watchers and Watched in Control(led) Systems: Strategies and Tactics." *Surveillance and Society* 4 (2007): 280–313. Smith sees more evidence of surveillance for care.

30 Lake, "Red Road."

31 Cf. Wise, J. Macgregor. "A Hole in the Hand: Assemblages of Attention and Mobile Screens." In *Theories of the Mobile Internet: Materialities and Imaginaries*, edited by Andrew Herman, Jan Hadlaw, and Thom Swiss, 212–231. New York: Routledge, 2014.

32 Lake, "Red Road," 236. A broader point in this regard is the theme that Mary Ann Doane addresses that women are presumably unable to maintain "the appropriate voyeuristic distance" as men do. Quote is from Modleski, *The Women Who Knew Too Much*, 77, referring to Doane, *The Desire to Desire*.

33 This is a theme pursued by MacMurdo-Reading in her analysis of *Red Road* in her dissertation, "The Spectacle and the Witness."

34 The theme of care turning into obsession is also found in films such as *One Hour Photo* (2002) where Robin Williams plays Seymour Parrish, a lonely quiet man who works at the photo development counter of a chain store. Parrish observes the lives of his customers through developing their photos. One family, the Yorkins, he idealizes as the perfect happy family and fantasizes that he belongs to them as Uncle Si. He makes duplicates of all their pictures to keep for himself. At home, he keeps a massive picture wall of all their photos, immersing himself in their lives. Polly, in *Mermaids*, also has a picture wall; it becomes the visual equivalent of the bank of monitors that Jackie views in *Red Road*. But Parrish discovers that Mr. Yorkin is having an affair, which destroys his idealization of the family. He stalks Yorkin and his mistress, threatens them, and forces them to have sex while he photographs them. The film, in the end, echoing the psychoanalytic framework of *Peeping Tom*, blames the way Parrish was abused by his father with a camera as a source of his obsessive disorder.

35 Denzin, *Cinematic Society*.

36 Ibid., 147.

37 Cf. Faludi, Susan. *Backlash*. New York: Crown Publishing, 1993.

38 Denzin, *Cinematic Society*, 152.

39 Ibid., 157.

40 Lake, "Red Road."

41 Zimmer, "Surveillance Cinema"; Corber, R.J. "Resisting History: Rear Window and the Limits of the Postwar Settlement." *boundary 2* 19 (1992): 121–148.

42 Clissold, Bradley D. "Candid Camera and the Origins of Reality TV: Contextualizing a Historical Precedent." In *Understanding Reality Television*, edited by Su Holmes and Deborah Jermyn, 33–53. New York: Routledge, 2004.

43 Institute for Precarious Consciousness, "We are all very anxious"

44 Andrejevic, *iSpy*.

45 Luhr, William, *Film Noir*. Malden: Blackwell, 2012.

46 Ibid., 210.

47 Ibid.

48 This psychopathology has a distinct racial element reflecting the white paranoia of raced others (who get labeled as terrorists). The question of race and paranoia is dealt with only indirectly in the film, and that through a post-civil rights lens. *Disturbia* takes place in a middle class white suburb and all the main characters (with the exception of Ronnie) are white. Up until *Disturbia* electronic ankle monitoring (EM) had mainly been seen in films dealing directly with race and crime, argues Mike Nellis ("News Media"). He points to Kevin Reynold's *One Eight Seven* (1994) and Spike Lee's *He Got Game* (1998). The latter, Nellis argues, "directs its youthful Black audience towards a view that EM is to be understood as yet another facet of racial oppression" (p. 9). The ankle monitor harkens back to slave

shackles. In *Disturbia*, this symbol of racial oppression is placed on the ankle of a white teenager who is then monitored by an African American parole officer (Viola Davis) and harassed by a Latino patrolman (Jose Pablo Cantillo), a relative of the teacher Kale had assaulted.

49 Denzin, *Cinematic Society*, 140.

50 Ibid., 141.

51 Ibid., 140.

52 For example, the voyeur, Zeke (William Baldwin), in *Sliver* (1993), certainly has some psychological issues, obsessing over women who look like his dead mother. He has placed videocameras throughout an elite apartment building he owns and watches everyone incessantly. One object of his obsession, Carly (Sharon Stone), he lets into his control room. She is disturbed and fascinated by the cameras and loses an entire day to watching them. While watching is a sexual thrill for Zeke, for Carly it only becomes so when she watches Zeke's tapes of herself and Zeke having sex. The scenes become a narcissistic mirror rather than a voyeuristic window.

53 Denzin, Norman K. "The Conversation." *Symbolic Interactionism* 15 (1992): 135–150.

54 Turner explores the intertextuality of *Blowup* and *The Conversation* in great detail in "The Subject of 'The Conversation.'" For example, the mime in the square at the start of *The Conversation* links that film with *Blowup* via the student mimes playing tennis who end that earlier film.

55 Orwell, *Nineteen Eighty-Four*.

56 Funder, Anna. *Stasiland: Stories from Behind the Berlin Wall*. New York: Harper Perennial, 2011; Funder, Anna. "Tyranny of Terror." *The Guardian*, May 5, 2007. Accessed June 15, 2009. http://www.theguardian.com/books/2007/may/05/featuresreviews.guardianreview12; see also Darnton, Robert. *Berlin Journal: 1989–1990*. New York: WW Norton and Company, 1991.

57 Funder, "Tyranny of Terror." Timothy Garton Ash, in his essay, "The Stasi on Our Minds," has pointed out that he has "heard of Stasi informers who ended up protecting those they were informing on. I know of full-time Stasi operatives who became disillusioned, especially during the 1980s." See also Bernstein, Matthew. "The Lives of Others." *Film Quarterly* 61 (2007): 30–36.

58 However, Ash writes, "And in the many hours of talking to former Stasi officers, I never met a single one who I felt to be, simply and plainly, an evil man. Weak, blinkered, opportunistic, self-deceiving, yes; men who did evil things, most certainly; but I always glimpsed in them the remnants of what might have been, the good that could have grown in other circumstances" ("The Stasi on Our Minds").

59 Guynn, Jessica. "Rear Window on Justin.tv," *SFGate*, April 11, 2007. Accessed May 3, 2015. http://blog.sfgate.techchron/2007/04/11/rear-window-on-justin-tv/

60 Mann, Steve and Hal Niedzviecki. *Cyborg: Digital Destiny and Human Possibility in the Age of the Wearable Computer*. Toronto: Doubleday of Canada, 2001.

61 Ouellette, Laurie and James Hay. *Better Living Through Reality TV: Television and Post-Welfare Citizenship*. Malden: Blackwell, 2008; Ouellette, Laurie. "'Take Responsibility for Yourself': Judge Judy and the Neoliberal Citizen." In *Reality TV: Remaking Television Culture* (2nd edition), edited by Susan Murray and Laurie Ouellette, 223–242. New York: New York University Press, 2008

62 Calvert, Clay. *Voyeur Nation: Media, Privacy, and Peering in Modern Culture*. Boulder: Westview Press, 2000; Niedzviecki, *Peep Diaries*.

63 Marx, Gary T. "Coming to Terms and Avoiding Information Techno-Fallacies." In *Privacy in the Modern Age: The Search for Solutions*, edited by Marc Rotenberg, Julia Horowitz, and Jeramie Scott, 118–126. New York: The New Press, 2015.

Chapter 2

1 Carey, "Communication, Culture, and Technology."
2 Williams, Raymond. *The Long Revolution*. London: Chatto and Windus, 1961.
3 Compare a more recent concept by Jacques Rancière, "the distribution of the sensible," the idea that even our senses are structured by social, economic, and cultural forces.
4 Dubrofsky and Magnet, *Feminist Surveillance Studies*; Browne, *Dark Matters*.
5 Andrejevic, Mark. "Foreword." In *Feminist Surveillance Studies*, edited by Rachel E. Dubrofsky and Shoshana Amielle Magnet, ix–xvii. Durham: Duke University Press, 2015.
6 Lyon, *Electronic Eye*.
7 Foucault, *Discipline and Punish*.
8 Lyon, *Surveillance Studies*, 58.
9 Lyon, *Electronic Eye*, 65.
10 Cf. Chapter 1; also Lyon, *Surveillance Studies*, 58.
11 Foucault, *Discipline and Punish*, 200, 201.
12 Ibid., 205.
13 Ibid., 213.
14 Browne, *Dark Matters*; Saïdi, "Colonialism and Surveillance"; Browne, "Race and Surveillance"; Kundnani and Kumar, "Race, Surveillance, and Empire"; Zureik, Elia. "Colonial Oversight." *Red Pepper* Oct/Nov (2013): 46–49; Berda, Yael. "Managing Dangerous Populations: Colonial Legacies of Security and Surveillance." *Sociological Forum* 28 (2013): 627–630; Singha, Radhika. "Punished by Surveillance: Policing 'Dangerousness' in Colonial India, 1872–1918." *Modern Asian Studies* 42 (2015): 241–269; McCoy, Alfred. "Surveillance Blowback." *The Nation*, 16 July (2013). Accessed October 26, 2015. www.thenation.com/article/surveillance-blowback; Kaplan, Martha. "Panopticon in Poona: An Essay in Foucault and Colonialism." *Cultural Anthropology* 10 (1995): 85–98.
15 Mirzoeff, Nicholas. *The Right to Look*.
16 Greenwald, Glenn. "Why Privacy Matters." *TEDGlobal*, October (2014). TED.com.
17 Martin, Nina K. *Sexy Thrills: Undressing the Erotic Thriller*. Urbana: University of Illinois Press, 2007.
18 See Andrejevic, Mark. *Reality TV: The Work of Being Watched*. Boulder, CO: Rowman and Littlefield, 2003; Senft, Theresa. *Camgirls: Celebrity and Community in the Age of Social Networks*. New York: Peter Lang, 2008.
19 Goldhaber, Michael. "The Attention Economy and the Net." *First Monday* 2 (1997). Accessed April 9, 2016. http://firstmonday.org/article/view/519/440; Wise, J. Macgregor. "'An immense and unexpected field of action': Webcams, Surveillance, and Everyday Life." *Cultural Studies* 18 (2004): 424–442.
20 See Korghan, Frank and Douglas Rushkoff. "Generation Like." *Frontline*, Public Broadcasting Corporation, February 18, 2014.
21 Baudrillard, Jean. *Simulations*, translated by Paul Foss, Paul Patton, and Philip Beitchman. New York: Semiotext(e), 1983.
22 Boorstin, Daniel. *The Image: A Guide to Pseudo-Events in America*. New York: Vintage, 1961.

23 Baudrillard, Jean. "Telemorphosis." In *CTRL Space: Rhetorics of Surveillance from Bentham to Big Brother*, edited by Thomas Levin, Ursula Frohne, and Peter Weibel, 480–485. Cambridge: MIT Press, 2002.

24 Ibid., 481.

25 Ang, Ien. *Watching Dallas: Soap Opera and the Melodramatic Imagination*. New York: Routledge, 1985.

26 Cited in Albrechtslund, "Surveillance and Ethics."

27 Andrejevic, *Reality TV*. See also Scholz, *Digital Labor*.

28 Burgin, Victor. "Jenni's Room: Exhibitionism and Solitude." In *CTRL Space: Rhetorics of Surveillance from Bentham to Big Brother*, edited by Thomas Levin, Ursula Frohne, and Peter Weibel, 228–235. Cambridge: MIT Press, 2002.

29 For recent studies of the selfie, see research listed at www.selfieresearchers.com

30 Koskela, Hille. "Webcams, TV Shows, and Mobile Phones: Empowering Exhibitionism." *Surveillance and Society* 2 (2004): 199–215.

31 Ibid., 207.

32 Ibid., 208, emphasis in original.

33 Bell, David. "Surveillance is Sexy." *Surveillance and Society* 6 (2009): 203.

34 Tiziallas, Evangelos. "Torture Porn and Surveillance Culture." *JumpCut* 52 (2010); see also Zimmer, *Surveillance Cinema*.

35 "The Abu Ghraib photographs have brought sexualized violence into US consciousness. Their infusion with and espousal of surveillance and surveillance culture enact a specific kind of cultural and political constellation of visual rhetoric unique to our time" (Tziallas, "Torture Porn").

36 Ibid.

37 Ibid.

38 Lyon, *Electronic Eye*.

39 BBC news 2001, 20 May. "Loft Story Under Siege." Accessed May 15, 2015. News.bbc.co.uk/2/hi/entertainment/1341239.stm

40 Lyon, *Electronic Eye*, 60.

41 It is a loss of dignity and also a loss of agency: "he has been turned into a commodity, into the producer of a set of experiences that somebody else can capture and sell" (Denzin, "The Conversation," 140).

42 See Chapter 5.

43 McGowan, *Psychoanalytic Film Theory*, 82.

44 Ibid., 75.

45 Willsher, Kim. "France Remembers Algerian Massacre 50 Years On." *The Guardian*, October 17, 2011. Accessed January 23, 2015. http://www.theguardian.com/world/2011/oct/17/france-remembers-algerian-massacre; France24. "The Paris Massacre that Time Forgot, 51 Years On." http://www.france24.com/en/20121017-paris-massacre-algeria-october-17-1961-51-years-anniversary-historian-einaudi. Accessed January 23, 2015.

46 Mirzoeff, *The Right to Look*.

47 In a psychoanalytic frame, the gaze disrupts the symbolic; in a more Deleuzian frame, affect is an emergence that disrupts. See Massumi, "The Autonomy of Affect" on the latter.

48 Elkins, James. *The Object Stares Back: On the Nature of Seeing*. New York: Harcourt, 1996, see esp. Chapter 6.

49 Herzog, Todd. "The Banality of Surveillance: Michael Haneke's *Caché* and Life After the End of Privacy." *Modern Austrian Literature* 43 (2010): 25–40.
50 Ebert, "Caché", cited in Herzog, "Banality of Surveillance." Along these lines one could also argue that it is David Lynch who is mailing Fred Madison (Bill Pullman) the videotapes of his own home in *Lost Highway* (1997).
51 McGowan, *Psychoanalytic Film Theory.*
52 Orwell, *Nineteen Eighty-Four*, 5.
53 Ibid., 65.
54 Ibid., 6.
55 Darnton, *Berlin Journal*, 132.
56 Ascherson, Neal. "Beware, the Walls Have Ears." *The Guardian*, March 11, 2007. Accessed June 15, 2009, http://www.guardian.co.uk/film/2007/mar/11/germany. features.
57 Orwell, *Nineteen Eighty-Four*, 29.
58 Andrejevic, "Foreword," xiii.
59 See Browne, *Dark Matters.* Will Smith himself seems much more aware of these issues than his character of Dean. In a German interview in 2004 he stated,

> If you grow up as a black person in America, you get a completely different view of the world than white Americans. We blacks live with a constant feeling of discomfort. Whether you're attacked and wounded by a racist cop or attacked by terrorists, excuse me, it makes no difference. (Quoted in Browne, *Dark Matters*, 122)

Chapter 3

1 Kammerer, "Video Surveillance," 470.
2 Slack, Jennifer Daryl and J. Macgregor Wise. *Culture and Technology: A Primer* (2nd edition). New York: Peter Lang, 2015.
3 Lyon, *Electronic Eye*, 201.
4 Deleuze, *Negotiations.*
5 Orwell, *Nineteen Eighty-Four*, 30.
6 Ibid., 163.
7 Ibid., 160.
8 Ibid., 142.
9 I will be referring to the 2004 director's cut of the film, available on DVD.
10 Ott, Brian. "The Visceral Politics of *V for Vendetta*: On Political Affect in Cinema." *Critical Studies in Media Communication* 27 (2010): 39–54.
11 Yes, the masks all come off in the end, but that is in a final shot that is a fantasy—faces in the crowd include many of the characters who have died—and more symbolic than diegetic. It is the image of the masked rebel (and masked crowd) that resonated with audiences. The Guy Fawkes mask of V was later appropriated as the face of the hacker collective, Anonymous.
There are two other significant differences between the comics and the film. In the film, V changes his mission because of his love for Evey. There is no such transformation in the comics. In the comics, his mission is always political anarchy,

though he indulges in a vendetta against specific individuals along the way. Secondly, in the comics the leader of fascist Britain is beholden to a vast computer, named Fate, a computer V long ago had hacked. It is *Fate* that has the faith of the people, not the fascist figurehead (as in the film).

See Paik, *From Utopia to Apocalypse*, on a close comparison of comic and film in terms of their politics.

12 Lyon, *Electronic Eye*, 61.
13 Foucault, Michel. *The History of Sexuality, Volume 3: The Care of the Self*, translated by Robert Hurley. New York: Vintage, 1988. Lyon, in *Electronic Eye*, argues that Foucault's model lacks the dimension of care or the pastoral, and while this is true of what is set out in *Discipline and Punish*, it is not true of Foucault's broader work.
14 Atwood, Margaret. *The Handmaid's Tale*. New York: Anchor Books, 1998, 19.
15 We see something similar in *THX 1138*. When a person dies, their name (letters and numbers) are reassigned to a newborn.
16 Lyon, *Electronic Eye*, 204.
17 Ibid.
18 Deleuze, *Negotiations*.
19 Ibid.
20 Ibid., 177.
21 Ibid., 174.
22 Ibid., 179.
23 Rose, Nicolas. *Powers of Freedom: Reframing Political Thought*. New York: Cambridge University Press, 1999, 234.
24 Hardt, Michael. "The Withering of Civil Society." In *Deleuze and Guattari: New Mappings in Politics, Philosophy, and Culture*, edited by E. Kaufman and K.J. Heller, 31. Minneapolis: University of Minnesota Press.
25 Hardt, Michael. "The Global Society of Control." *Discourse* 20 (1998): 140.
26 Hardt, "The Withering," 32–33.
27 Deleuze, *Negotiations*, 180.
28 Ibid., 181.
29 Ibid., 74.
30 Ibid., 80.
31 Williams, Raymond. "Culture Is Ordinary." In *Resources of Hope*. New York: Verso, 1989. Originally 1959.
32 Gandy, *Panoptic Sort* and "It's Discrimination, Stupid!" In *Resisting the Virtual Life: The Culture and Politics of Information*, edited by James Brook and Iain Boal. San Francisco: City Lights, 1995.
33 Deleuze, *Negotiations*, 182.
34 Bogard, William. *The Simulation of Surveillance: Hypercontrol in Telematic Societies*. New York: Cambridge University Press, 1996; Graham, Stephen. "Spaces of Surveillant-Simulation: New Technologies, Digital Representations, and Material Geographies." *Environment and Planning D: Society and Space* 16 (1998): 483–504.
35 Hardt, "Society of Control," 143.
36 Graham, "Surveillant-Simulation."
37 Rose, *Powers of Freedom*, 234–235.
38 Baudrillard, Jean. *The Ecstasy of Communication*, translated by B. and C. Schutze, edited by Sylvère Lotringer. New York: Semiotext(e), 1988, 20–21.
39 Deleuze, *Negotiations*, 181–182.

40 Davis, Susan. "The Theme Park: Global Industry and Cultural Form." *Media, Culture and Society* 18 (1996): 399–420.
41 Kawashima, Kentaro. "An Image of the Control Society: On Kinji Fukasaku's *Battle Royale*." In *Public Enemies: Film Between Identity Formation and Control*, edited by Winfried Pauleit, Christine Rüffert, Karl-Heinz Schmid, and Alfred Tews, 110–124. Berlin: bertz+fischer, 2011.My thanks to Dietmar Kammerer for this reference.
42 Ibid., 117.
43 Ibid., 112.
44 Ibid., 120.
45 Kammerer, "Video Surveillance," 470.
46 Lyon, *Surveillance Society*. Trust in computer data over the word of an embodied person is also the central theme of *The Net* (1995).
47 Biometrics refers to the use of the body itself to uniquely identify a person. Rather than relying on a person's self-report, that they are who they say they are, we seek proof of their identity. Fingerprints are the most common biometric and are commonly used as evidence in criminal trials. The swirls and configuration of the lines of our fingertips are presumed to be unique. Other unique bodily identifiers are being used as well: the pattern of blood vessels in the retina, the dimensions of the hand, the features of the face, and so on. The ultimate identifier is DNA, the genetic materials supposedly unique to each person.The problem of biometrics is that the body can change over time and also that the technologies might not be able to capture the details of the body with sufficient detail to differentiate with absolute certainty one person from another. Some biometric techniques, such as facial recognition, work much better on Caucasian faces than others. See Gates, Kelly. *Our Biometric Future: Facial Recognition Technology and the Culture of Surveillance*. New York: New York University Press, 2011; Pugliese, *Biometrics*.
48 Marx, Gary T. "A Tack in the Shoe: Neutralizing and Resisting the New Surveillance." *Journal of Social Issues* 59 (2003): 369–390.
49 McGowan, *Psychoanalytic Film Theory*, 81.

Chapter 4

1 Broe, Dennis. "Genre Regression and the New Cold War: The Return of the Police Procedural." *Framework* 45 (2004): 82.
2 Mittell, Jason. "All in the Game: *The Wire*, Serial Storytellers, and Procedural Logic." Accessed February 24, 2015. http://www.electronicbookreview.com/thread/firstperson/serial (2011).
3 Luhr, *Film Noir*, 37.
4 Ibid., 36.
5 Ibid., 38.
6 Ibid.
7 Ibid., 36.
8 Broe, "Genre Regression."
9 See Jason Mittell's analysis in *Genre and Television: From Cop Shows to Cartoons in American Culture*. New York: Routledge, 2004 of the filmic influences on the creation of *Dragnet* such as *He Walked by Night* and *The Naked City*, and the mixing of film noir and documentary in what he calls "the semi-documentary police procedural" including not only these two films but the earlier *The House on 92nd Street* (1945) (p. 131).

10   Mittell, "All in the Game."

11   Broe, "Genre Regression," 90.

12   Rapping, Elayne. *Law and Justice as Seen on TV*. New York: New York University Press, 2003.

13   Mittell, "All in the Game."

14   A note on genre: "surveillance procedural" is not an accepted genre by production practice, audience expectation, or what Mittell calls cultural categories. It is closer to a theoretical genre in that I am tracing connections between disparate texts—from particular film elements, types of narration, or production practices. See Mittell's *Genre and Television*, 17–18.

15   Luc Sante, essay in DVD booklet of *The Naked City* (Criterion Collection 2007).

16   It was also intended to be "an exercise in 'social realism' designed to portray the inequities and harsh realities found in American cities" (Mittell, *Genre and Television*, 132).

17   Howell, Philip. "Crime and the City Solution: Crime Fiction, Urban Knowledge, and Radical Geography." *Antipode* 30 (1998): 365.

18   Ebert, Roger. "*Rififi*." Accessed April 9, 2016. http://www.rogerebert.com/reviewers/great-movie-rififi-1954 (2002).

19   Willis, Andy. "Hong Kong Cinema Since 1997: Troughs and Peaks." *Film International* 40 (2006): 6–17.

20   Marchetti, Gina. "Chinese Cinema at the Millennium: Defining 'China' and the Politics of Representation." In *The International Encyclopedia of Media Studies, Vol. III: Content and Representation*, edited by Sharon Mazzarella, 322–342. Malden: Blackwell, 2013.

21   Chu, Yiu-Wai. "Toward a New Hong Kong Cinema: Beyond Mainland-Hong Kong Co-Productions." *Journal of Chinese Cinemas* (2015). Accessed 10 March, 2015. doi: 10.1080/17508061.2014.994352; Marchetti, "Chinese Cinema"; Pugsley, Peter C. "Hong Kong Film as Crossover Cinema: Maintaining the HK Aesthetic." In *Crossover Cinema: Cross-Cultural Film From Production to Reception*, edited by Sukhmani Khorana, 51–65. New York: Routledge, 2013; Willis, "Hong Kong Cinema."

22   Yi Sun, Personal email, 8 September, 2015.

23   Sun, Yi. "Shaping Hong Kong Cinema's New Icon: Milkyway Image at International Film Festivals." *Transnational Cinemas* (2015). Accessed 9 March, 2015. doi 10.1080/20403526.2014.1002671. See Teo, Stephen. *Director in Action: Johnnie To and the Hong Kong Action Film*. Hong Kong: Hong Kong University Press, 2007; Ingham, Mike. *Johnnie To Kei-Fung's PTU*. Hong Kong: Hong Kong University Press, 2009; Sun, Yi. "Crossing Genres: A Study of Johnnie To's Stylized Films." *Asian Cinema* (2011): 74–110; Williams, Tony. "Transcultural Spaces of a Vanishing Hong Kong: Johnnie To's *Sparrow*." *Asian Cinema* 21 (2010): 113–123; for critical assessments of To's work. Yim discusses To's patriarchal masculinity in style and production practice, in the context of a masculinity crisis post-1997 in "Post-1997 Hong Kong Cinema."

24   Willis, "Hong Kong Cinema," 12.

25   Sun, "Crossing Genres."

26   Ibid., 81.

27   Teo, *Director in Action*. See also Rist, Peter. "Scenes of 'in-action' and noir characteristics in the films of Johnnie To (Kei-Fung)." In *Hong Kong Film, Hollywood and the New Global Cinema: No Film Is an Island*, edited by Gina Marchetti and Tan See Kam, 159–163. New York: Routledge, 2007 on noir and To's films.

28 To's films emphasize the specifics of place, almost acting as memorials to aspects of Hong Kong fast disappearing. See Williams ("Transcultural Spaces") on *Sparrow* (2008) and Ingham on *PTU* (2003). Ingham praises *Eye in the Sky's* "atmospheric, well-crafted depiction of locale" (*PTU*, 20).

29 Koo, Se-woong. "South Korea's Invasion of Privacy." *The New York Times*, 2 April, 2015. Accessed 20 April, 2015. http://nyti.ms/1MF6i2W.

30 Marchetti, Gina. *Andrew Lau and Alan Mak's Infernal Affairs—The Trilogy*. Hong Kong: Hong Kong University Press, 2007.

31 Ibid.; See also Law, W.S. "The Violence of Time and Memory Undercover: Hong Kong's Infernal Affairs." *Inter-Asia Cultural Studies* 7 (2006): 383–402, who argues that *Infernal Affairs*, and a whole tradition of undercover cop films in Hong Kong, "carries a structure of feeling about the lived experience of Hong Kong people as being caught between a series of identity crisis [*sic*]" (p. 388).

32 Cited in Sun, "Crossing Genres."

33 Marchetti, "Chinese Cinema."

34 Pugsley, "Crossover Cinema."

35 Mazumdar, Ranjani. "Terrorism, Conspiracy, and Surveillance in Bombay's Urban Cinema." *Social Research* 78 (2011): 143–172.

36 Marchetti, "Chinese Cinema," 332.

37 Ibid., 334.

38 Bradsher, Keith. "Hong Kong Surveillance Law Passes." *The New York Times*, August 6, 2006, accessed April 20, 2015, http://www.nytimes.com/2006/08/06/world/asia/06cnd-hong.html; Greenleaf, Graham. "Country Studies B.3 – Hong Kong." In *Comparative Study on Different Approaches to New Privacy Challenges, In Particular in the Light of Technological Developments*, edited by Douwe Korff European Commission Directorate-General Justice, Freedom and Security, 2010. Accessed April 9, 2016. http://ec.europa.eu/justice/policies/privacy/docs/studies/new_privacy_challenges/final_report_country_report_B3_hong_kong.pdf. The law was roundly criticized for not prohibiting surveillance for political purposes, or surveillance of journalists, and lawyers are also subject to surveillance (Bradsher, "Surveillance Law").

39 Bradsher, "Surveillance Law"; Lague, David, Greg Torode, and James Pomfret. "Special Report: How China Spies on Hong Kong's Democrats." *Reuters*, 14 December, 2014. Accessed 20 April 2015. http://www.reuters.com/article/2014/12/15/US-Hong-Kong-Surveillance.

40 Lague, Torode, and Pomfret, "Special Report."

41 Ng, Kang-chung and Clifford Lo. "Hong Kong Police Now Less Popular Than China's PLA, After Occupy Clashes." *South China Morning Post*, December 10, 2014. Accessed April 9, 2016. http://www.scmp.com/print/news/hong-kong/article/1659238/police-now-less-popular-pla-hku-poll-finds. See also the University of Hong Kong's poll. Accessed May 3, 2015. http://hkupop.hku.hk/english/popexpress/hkpolice/poll/hkpolice_poll_chart.html

42 Ingham, quoted in Sun, "Crossing Genres," 80. See also Ingham on To's ensemble of actors: "the film is never a vehicle for the star name in a Johnnie To work; rather the actor must sublimate his or her ego to the requirements of the director's cinematic flair and sensibility" (*PTU*, pp. 11–12).

43 Marchetti, *Infernal Affairs*, 44.

44 See Ingham (*PTU*, 15) on *PTU*.

45 Luhr, *Film Noir*.

46   Ibid., 205.
47   Ibid., 200.
48   Ibid., 207.
49   *Déjà Vu* brings up the idea of *retrospective surveillance*. When surveillant devices
     that capture our information (location via mobile phone, image via CCTV, purchase
     history via credit card, etc.) become ubiquitous, and data storage becomes cheap
     enough, then authorities can place someone under surveillance retrospectively, for
     the past months if not years (See Villasenor, John. "Recording Everything: Digital
     Storage as an Enabler of Authoritarian Governments." Brookings, December 14, 2011.
     Accessed May 29, 2015, http://www.brookings.edu/research/papers/2011/12/14-
     digital-storage-villasenor; Bamford, James. "The NSA Is Building the Country's
     Biggest Spy Center (Watch What You Say)." *WIRED* (March, 2012). Accessed May 29,
     2015, http://www.wired.com/2012/03/ff_nsadatacenter/).
50   McGowan, *Psychoanalytic Film Theory*.
51   Mazumdar, "Terrorism, Conspiracy," 145.
52   See Rao, Vyjayanthi. "How to Read a Bomb: Scenes from Bombay's Black Friday."
     Public Culture 19 (2007): 567–592.
53   Mazumdar, "Terrorism, Conspiracy," 145.
54   Ibid., 150; see also Rao's reading of the film ("Read a Bomb").
55   Mazumdar, "Terrorism, Conspiracy," 150, 151.
56   Ibid., 155.
57   Mitra, Smita. "On '*Black Friday*.'" *Economic & Political Weekly* 42 (2007): 1409.
58   Ibid., 1409.
59   Mazumdar, "Terrorism, Conspiracy," 152.
60   Mitra, "On Black Friday," following Roland Barthes.
61   Mazumdar, "Terrorism, Conspiracy," 157.
62   Ibid., 165.
63   Ibid., 168.
64   See, Deutsch, Sarah Ketorah and Gray Cavender. "*CSI* and Forensic Realism." *Journal
     of Criminal Justice and Popular Culture* 15 (2008): 34–53; Harrington, Ellen Burton.
     "Nation, Identity, and the Fascination with Forensic Science in Sherlock Holmes and
     CSI." *International Journal of Cultural Studies* 10 (2007): 365–382.

Chapter 5

1   Cf. Dovey, Jon. *Freakshow: First Person Media and Factual Television*. London: Pluto,
    2000.
2   Dovey, *Freakshow*, 64.
3   Baudrillard, *Simulations*, 50.
4   Dovey, *Freakshow*.
5   Baudrillard, *Simulations*, 50.
6   Ibid.
7   Quoted in Baudrillard, *Simulations*, 50.
8   Ibid., 25.
9   Deleuze, however, sees television as a means of control. "[T]elevision is the
    form in which the new powers of 'control' become immediate and direct"
    (*Negotiations*, 75).

10 Barthes, Roland. *Camera Lucida: Reflections on Photography*, translated by Richard Howard. New York: Hill and Wang, 1981, 76.

11 Barthes, *Camera Lucida*, esp. 88–89; Sontag, *On Photography*.

12 Levin, "Rhetoric of the Temporal."

13 Dovey, *Freakshow*, 55.

14 Ibid.

15 Raphael, Chad. "The Political Economic Origins of Reali-TV." In *Reality TV: Remaking Television Culture* (2nd edition), edited by Susan Murray and Laurie Ouellette, 123–140. New York: New York University Press, 2008.

16 Levin, "Rhetoric of the Temporal," 585.

17 Dovey, *Freakshow*, 67.

18 Levin, "Rhetoric of the Temporal," 589–590.

19 Ibid., 589.

20 The next turn in the quest for authenticity in the surveillance image is through the surveillance of the brain itself, capturing its experiences and memories. See such films as *Strange Days* (1995), *The Final Cut* (2004), *Sleep Dealer* (2008), and the television series *Black Mirror*. See, e.g., Catherine Zimmer's analysis of *Strange Days* in "Surveillance and Social Memory" as well as in *Surveillance Cinema*.

21 A list on IMDB.com includes 370 such films.

22 Others are pornographic. See Bell, "Surveillance Is Sexy," Martin, *Sexy Thrills*, and Dovey, *Freakshow*.

23 Levin, "Rhetoric of the Temporal," 584.

24 Ibid., 589.

25 Denzin, *The Cinematic Society*, 34–35.

26 Bombay was renamed Mumbai in 1995.

27 Harris, Andrew. "The Metonymic Urbanism of the Twenty-First-Century Mumbai." *Urban Studies* 49 (2012): 2967; Mazumdar, Ranjani. *Bombay Cinema: An Archive of the City*. Minneapolis: University of Minnesota Press, 2007.

28 Rao, "Read a Bomb," 575.

29 Dovey, *Freakshow*, 57.

30 Virilio, Paul. *The Information Bomb*, translated by Chris Turner. New York: Verso, 2000.

31 Heron, Christopher. "Surveillance Camera Cinema." *The Seventh Art*, 2012. Accessed April 9, 2016. http://www.theseventhart.org/dailies/2012/02/04/surveillance-camera-cinema-faceless-der-riese-influenza-video-essay-issue-1/.

32 Dovey, *Freakshow*, 66.

33 Hoberman, James. "The Giant." In *CTRL Space: Rhetorics of Surveillance from Bentham to Big Brother*, edited by Thomas Levin, Ursula Frohne, and Peter Weibel, 82. Cambridge: MIT Press, 2002 [Originally 1984].

34 Ibid.

35 Ibid.

36 Ibid., 83.

37 McGowan, *Psychoanalytic Film Theory*.

38 Dovey, *Freakshow*, 66.

39 Hoberman, "The Giant."

40 Virilio, Paul. *The Vision Machine*, translated by Julie Rose. London: BFI, 1994, 47, emphasis in original.

41 McLuhan, Marshall. *Understanding Media: The Extensions of Man*. New York: Signet, 1964.

42 Wise, "Webcams Surveillance."

43 Turner, John S. "Collapsing the Interior/Exterior Distinction: Surveillance, Spectacle, and Suspense in Popular Cinema." *Wide Angle* 20 (1998): 97.

44 Ellis, *Visible Fictions*.

45 *Surveillance 24/7* (2007) is a less successful attempt at this genre. The film opens with the statement, "The footage in this film is taken from surveillance cameras and CCTV." However, the opening shot is of the protagonist reflected in the lens of a CCTV camera. So unless surveillance cameras are focused in on other cameras, the stated premise seems immediately undermined. The film does blend cinematic and surveillance-type footage, often showing a shot in what looks like standard cinematic format, but then it takes on the markers of CCTV (with additional graininess and a burn-in). The second shot of the film also undermines the stated premise: it is of a train approaching a station, but filmed from the level of the tracks. As the train approaches the camera rises up to not-quite surveillance height and looks down on the protagonist getting on the train. Perhaps Sergio Leone programmed the CCTV camera?

46 Baudrillard, *Simulations*, 52.

47 This is what the director Adam Rifkin called it when pitching the idea of the film. See the Behind the Scenes feature on the DVD.

48 Baudrillard, *Simulations*, 52.

49 Virilio, *Information Bomb*.

50 Baudrillard, *Ecstasy*, 20–21.

51 Berger, John. *Ways of Seeing*. Harmondsworth: Penguin, 1990.

52 See Bell, "Surveillance Is Sexy."

53 McGowan, *Psychoanalytic Film Theory*.

Conclusion

1   See www.theguardian.com/world/interactive/2013/nov/01/snowden-nsa-files-surveillance-revelations-decoded#section/1. Accessed April 23, 2016.

2   Ibid.; HBO's John Oliver mocked the public's lack of concern and knowledge about Snowden and the NSA in his April 5, 2015 episode of *Last Week Tonight* on surveillance. www.youtube.com/watch?v=XEVlyP4_11M. But see the Pew Research Center's report on "Public Perceptions of Privacy and Security in the Post-Snowden Era," which shows some increasing concern.

3   Campbell, "Inside Echelon"; and Hager, *Secret Power*.

4   Bamford, "Spy Center."

5   Holpuch, Amanda and Ruth Spencer. "NSA on TV and Film: The Shows that Predicted the Surveillance Revelations." *The Guardian*, September 27, 2013. Accessed May 18, 2015. http://www.theguardian.com/tv-and-radio/2013/sep/27/nsa-tv-film-homeland-relations.

6   See Zimmer's discussion of the "reactionary narrative formation" (p. 173) of *Déjà Vu* and similar films, such as *Source Code*, in *Surveillance Cinema*.

7   Mumford, Lewis. *The Myth of the Machine: The Pentagon of Power*. New York: Harcourt, Brace, Jovanovich, 1970, 274–275. On Mumford's point about "no dream" escaping the surveillant eye, see Wim Wender's 1991 film *Until the End of the World*, where a device has been invented to record and play back dreams. In *Final Cut* it is mentioned that some of the implanted microchips malfunction and record dreams and daydreams as well as what is actually perceived by the individual.

8   These themes about AI and the loss of humanity are taken up in another body of films, from Fritz Lang's *Metropolis* (1927) to Steven Spielberg's *A.I.* (2001) to Alex Garland's *Ex Machina* (2015).

9   But see Packer, Jeremy and Joshua Reeves. "Decentralized Execution: Media Swarms and Military Command." Paper presented at the National Communication Association Conference, Las Vegas, 2015.

10 Mirzoeff, *The Right to Look*.

11 Gan, Vicky. "How TV's 'Person of Interest' Helps Us Understand the Surveillance Society." Smithsonian.com October 24, 2013. Accessed May 18, 2015. http://www.smithsonian.com/smithsonian-institution/how-tvs-person-of-interest-helps-us-understand-the-surveillance-society-5407171/no-ist.

12 See Carlson, Scott. "On the Record, All the Time." *Chronicle of Higher Education*, February 9, 2007; Pedersen, Isabel. "MyLifeBits, Augmented Memory, and a Rhetoric of Need." *Continuum* 22 (2008): 375–384; Allen, Anita. "Dredging Up the Past: Lifelogging, Memory and Surveillance." *University of Chicago Law Review* 75 (2008): 47–74; and Bell, Gordon and Jim Gemmell. *Total Recall: How the E-Memory Revolution Will Change Everything*. New York: Dutton Adult, 2009.

13 Mann and Niedviecki, *Cyborg*.

14 Bell and Gemmell, *Total Recall*, 166.

15 Stone, n.d., lindastone.net/qa/continuous-partial-attention.

16 Mittell, "All in the Game."

17 Slack and Wise, *Culture and Technology*.

18 Lyon, *Electronic Eye*.

Filmography

8mm (dir. Joel Schumacher, 1999)
The 1,000 Eyes of Dr. Mabuse (dir. Fritz Lang, 1960)
1984 (dir. Michael Anderson, 1956)
1984 (dir. Michael Radford, 1984)
Aamir (dir. Raj Kuman Gupta, 2008)
A.I. (dir. Steven Spielberg, 2001)
Battle Royale (dir. Kinji Fukasaku, 2000)
Black Friday (dir. Anurag Kashyap, 2004)
Black Widow (dir. Bob Rafelson, 1987)
The Blair Witch Project (dir. Daniel Myrick and Eduardo Sánchez, 1999)
Blowup (dir. Michelangelo Antonioni, 1966)
Blue Velvet (dir. David Lynch, 1986)
Bob le Flambeur (dir. Jean-Pierre Melville, 1955)
Body Double (dir. Brian De Palma, 1984)
Body Heat (dir. Lawrence Kasdan, 1981)
Brazil (dir. Terry Gilliam, 1985)
Caché (dir. Michael Haneke, 2005)
Cam-Girl (dir. Curt Wiser, 2012)
Cam Girl (dir. Mirca Viola, 2014)
Captivity (dir. Roland Joffé, 2007)
Chinatown (dir. Roman Polanski, 1974)
Cloverfield (dir. Matt Reeves, 2008)
Cold Eyes (dir. Kim Beyong-seo and Jo Eui-seok, 2013)
Colossus: The Forbin Project (dir. Joseph Sargent, 1970)
The Conversation (dir. Francis Ford Coppola, 1974)
Déjà Vu (dir. Tony Scott, 2006)
Demon Seed (dir. Donald Cammell, 1977)
The Departed (dir. Martin Scorsese, 2006)
Der Riese (dir. Michael Klier, 1984)
Dhobi Ghat (Mumbai Diaries) (dir. Kiran Rao, 2010)
Disconnect (dir. Henry-Alex Rubin, 2012)
Disturbia (dir. D.J. Caruso, 2007)
Eagle Eye (dir. D.J. Caruso, 2008)
The Echelon Conspiracy (dir. Gary Markus, 2009)
EDtv (dir. Ron Howard, 1999)
Election (dir. Johnnie To, 2005)
Election 2 [Triad Election] (dir. Johnnie To, 2006)
The End of Violence (dir. Wim Wenders, 1997)
Enemy of the State (dir. Tony Scott, 1998)
Escape to Witch Mountain (dir. John Hough, 1975)
Ex Machina (dir. Alex Garland, 2015)

Eye in the Sky (dir. Yau Nai Hoi, 2007)
Fatal Attraction (dir. Adrian Lyne, 1987)
The Final Cut (dir. Omar Naim, 2004)
Gattaca (dir. Andrew Niccol, 2007)
Gigante (dir. Adrián Biniez, 2009)
The Good Thief (dir. Neil Jordan, 2002)
Halloween (dir. John Carpenter, 1978)
The Handmaid's Tale (dir. Volker Schlöndorff, 1990)
He Got Game (dir. Spike Lee, 1998)
He Walked by Night (dir. Alfred L. Werker, 1948)
Hostel (dir. Eli Roth, 2005)
The House on 92nd Street (dir. Harry Hathaway, 1945)
The Hunger Games (dir. Gary Ross, 2012)
Infernal Affairs (dir. Andrew Lau and Alan Mak, 2002)
Infernal Affairs 2 (dir. Andrew Lau and Alan Mak, 2003)
Infernal Affairs 3 (dir. Andrew Lau and Alan Mak, 2003)
I-See-You.com (dir. Eric Steven Stahl, 2006)
I've Heard the Mermaids Singing (dir. Patricia Roezma, 1987)
The Lipstick Camera (dir. Mike Bonifer, 1994)
The Lives of Others (dir. Florian Henkel von Donnersmark, 2006)
The Long Goodbye (dir. Robert Altman, 1973)
Look (dir. Adam Rifkin, 2007)
Lost Highway (dir. David Lynch, 1997)
The Matrix (dir. The Wachowski Brothers, 1999)
Metropolis (dir. Fritz Lang, 1927)
Minority Report (dir. Steven Spielberg, 2002).
La Mirada Invisible (dir. Diego Lerman, 2010)
Munich (dir. Steven Spielberg, 2005)
My Little Eye (dir. Marc Evans, 2002)
The Naked City (dir. Jules Dassin, 1948)
The Net (dir. Irwin Winkler, 1995)
Night Eyes 2 (dir. Rodney McDonald, 1992)
Oceans 11 (dir. Lewis Milestone, 1960)
Oceans 11 (dir. Steven Soderbergh, 2001)
Old Boy (dir. Chan-wook Park, 2003)
One Eight Seven (dir. Kevin Reynolds, 1994)
One Hour Photo (dir. Mark Romanek, 2002)
Overheard (dir. Felix Chong and Alan Mak, 2009)
Overheard 2 (dir. Felix Chong and Alan Mak, 2011)
Overheard 3 (dir. Felix Chong and Alan Mak, 2013)
Panic Room (dir. David Fincher, 2002)
Paranormal Activity (dir. Oren Peli, 2007)
Peeping Tom (dir. Michael Powell, 1960)
The Player (dir. Robert Altman, 1992)
PTU (dir. Johnnie To, 2003)
Rear Window (dir. Alfred Hitchcock, 1954)
Red (dir. Krzysztof Kieslowski, 1994)

Red Road (dir. Andrea Arnold, 2007)
Rififi (dir. Jules Dassin, 1954)
The Running Man (dir. Paul Michael Glaser, 1987)
Saw (dir. James Wan 2004)
Seven (dir. David Fincher, 1995)
A Short Film About Love (dir. Krzysztof Kieslowski, 1989)
Silence of the Lambs (dir. Jonathan Demme, 1991)
Sleep Dealer (dir. Alex Rivera, 2008)
Sliver (dir. Phillip Noyce, 1993)
Snake Eyes (dir. Brian de Palma, 1998)
Source Code (dir. Duncan Jones, 2011)
Sparrow (dir. Johnnie To, 2008)
Strange Days (dir. Kathryn Bigelow, 1995)
Super 8 (dir. J.J. Abrams, 2011)
Surveillance 24/7 (dir. Paul Oremland, 2007)
The Terminator (dir. James Cameron, 1984)
THX 1138 (dir. George Lucas, 1971)
The Truman Show (dir. Peter Weir, 1998)
Unfriended (dir. Leo Gabriadze, 2014)
Until the End of the World (dir. Wim Wenders, 1991)
V for Vendetta (dir. James McTeigue, 2005)
A Wednesday (dir. Neeraj Pandey, 2008)
Westworld (dir. Michael Crichton, 1973)
Wings of Desire (dir. Wim Wenders, 1987)
Zero Dark Thirty (dir. Kathryn Bigelow, 2012)
La Zona (dir. Rodrigo Plá, 2009)

Television Series

An American Family (PBS, 1973)
Are You Being Served (BBC, 1972–1985)
Big Brother (Veronica, 1999–2011)
Big Brother (CBS, 2000–)
Black Mirror (Channel 4, 2011–)
Cops (Fox, 1989–)
Criminal Minds (CBS, 2005–)
CSI (CBS, 2000–2015)
Dexter (Showtime, 2006–2013)
Dragnet (NBC, 1951–1959)
Homeland (HBO, 2011–)
Law and Order (NBC, 1990–2010)
Loft Story (M6, 2001)
Murder, She Wrote (CBS, 1984–1996)
The Naked City (ABC, 1958–1963)
NYPD Blue (Fox, 1993–2005)
Person of Interest (CBS, 2011–)
The Prisoner (ITV, 1967–1968)
The Real World (MTV, 1992–)
Survivor (CBS, 2000–)
The Wire (HBO, 2002–2008)

Works Cited

Albrechtslund, Anders. "Surveillance and Ethics in Film: *Rear Window* and *The Conversation*." *Journal of Criminal Justice and Popular Culture* 15 (2008): 129–144.

Allen, Anita. "Dredging Up the Past: Lifelogging, Memory and Surveillance." *University of Chicago Law Review* 75 (2008): 47–74.

Andrejevic, Mark. *Reality TV: The Work of Being Watched*. Lanham: Rowman and Littlefield, 2003.

Andrejevic, Mark. *iSpy: Surveillance and Power in the Interactive Era*. Lawrence, KS: University Press of Kansas, 2007.

Andrejevic, Mark. "Foreword." In *Feminist Surveillance Studies*, edited by Rachel E. Dubrofsky and Shoshana Amielle Magnet, ix–xvii. Durham, NC: Duke University Press, 2015.

Ang, Ien. *Watching Dallas: Soap Opera and the Melodramatic Imagination*. New York: Routledge, 1985.

Ascherson, Neal. "Beware, the Walls Have Ears." *The Guardian*, March 11, 2007. Accessed June 15, 2009, http://www.guardian.co.uk/film/2007/mar/11/germany.features.

Ash, Timothy Garton. "The Stasi on Our Minds." *The New York Review of Books*, May 31, 2007.

Atwood, Margaret. *The Handmaid's Tale*. New York: Anchor Books, 1998.

Ball, Kirstie, Kevin D. Haggerty, and David Lyon (eds). *Routledge Handbook of Surveillance Studies*. New York: Routledge, 2012.

Bamford, James. "The NSA Is Building the Country's Biggest Spy Center (Watch What You Say)." *WIRED*, March, 2012. Accessed May 29, 2015, http://www.wired.com/2012/03/ff_nsadatacenter/.

Barthes, Roland. *Camera Lucida: Reflections on Photography*, translated by Richard Howard. New York: Hill and Wang, 1981.

Baudrillard, Jean. *Simulations*, translated by Paul Foss, Paul Patton, and Philip Beitchman. New York: Semiotext(e), 1983.

Baudrillard, Jean. *The Ecstasy of Communication*, translated by B. and C. Schutze, edited by Sylvère Lotringer. New York: Semiotext(e), 1988.

Baudrillard, Jean. "Telemorphosis." In *CTRL Space: Rhetorics of Surveillance from Bentham to Big Brother*, edited by Thomas Levin, Ursula Frohne, and Peter Weibel, 480–485. Cambridge: MIT Press, 2002.

Bell, David. "Surveillance Is Sexy." *Surveillance and Society* 6 (2009): 203–212.

Bell, Gordon and Jim Gemmell. *Total Recall: How the E-Memory Revolution Will Change Everything*. New York: Dutton Adult, 2009.

Benjamin, Walter. "The Work of Art in the Age of Mechanical Reproduction." In *Illuminations*, edited by Hannah Arendt, translated by H. Zohn. New York: Schocken, 1969.

Berda, Yael. "Managing Dangerous Populations: Colonial Legacies of Security and Surveillance." *Sociological Forum* 28 (2013): 627–630.

Berger, John. *Ways of Seeing*. Harmondsworth: Penguin, 1990.

Bernstein, Matthew. "The Lives of Others." *Film Quarterly* 61 (2007): 30–36.

Bogard, William. *The Simulation of Surveillance: Hypercontrol in Telematic Societies.* New York: Cambridge University Press, 1996.

Boorstin, Daniel. *The Image: A Guide to Pseudo-Events in America.* New York: Vintage, 1961.

Bradsher, Keith. "Hong Kong Surveillance Law Passes." *The New York Times*, August 6, 2006. Accessed April 20, 2015, http://www.nytimes.com/2006/08/06/world/asia/06cnd-hong.html.

Broe, Dennis. "Genre Regression and the New Cold War: The Return of the Police Procedural." *Framework* 45 (2004): 81–101.

Browne, Simone. "Race and Surveillance." In *The Routledge Handbook of Surveillance Studies*, edited by Kirstie Ball, Kevin D. Haggerty, and David Lyon, 72–79. New York: Routledge, 2012.

Browne, Simone. *Dark Matters: On the Surveillance of Blackness.* Durham, NC: Duke University Press, 2015.

Burgin, Victor. "Jenni's Room: Exhibitionism and Solitude." In *CTRL Space: Rhetorics of Surveillance from Bentham to Big Brother*, edited by Thomas Levin, Ursula Frohne, and Peter Weibel, 228–235. Cambridge: MIT Press, 2002.

Calvert, Clay. *Voyeur Nation: Media, Privacy, and Peering in Modern Culture.* Boulder, CO: Westview Press, 2000.

Campbell, Duncan. "Inside Echelon: The History, Structure, and Function of the Global Surveillance System Known as Echelon." In *CTRL Space: Rhetorics of Surveillance from Bentham to Big Brother*, edited by Thomas Levin, Ursula Frohne, and Peter Weibel, 158–169. Cambridge: MIT Press, 2002.

Carey, James and J.A. Game. "Communication, Culture, and Technology: An Internet Interview with James W. Carey." *Journal of Communication Inquiry* 22 (1998): 117–130.

Carlson, Scott. "On the Record, All the Time." *Chronicle of Higher Education*, February 9, 2007.

Chu, Yiu-Wai. "Toward a New Hong Kong Cinema: Beyond Mainland-Hong Kong Co-productions." *Journal of Chinese Cinemas* (2015). Accessed 10 March, 2015. doi: 10.1080/17508061.2014.994352.

Clissold, Bradley D. "Candid Camera and the Origins of Reality TV: Contextualizing a Historical Precedent." In *Understanding Reality Television*, edited by Su Holmes and Deborah Jermyn, 33–53. New York: Routledge, 2004.

Corber, R.J. "Resisting History: Rear Window and the Limits of the Postwar Settlement." *boundary 2* (19) (1992): 121–148.

Darnton, Robert. *Berlin Journal: 1989–1990.* New York: WW Norton and Company, 1991.

Davis, Susan. "The Theme Park: Global Industry and Cultural Form." *Media, Culture and Society* 18 (1996): 399–420.

De Lauretis, Teresa. *Alice Doesn't: Feminism, Semiotics, and Cinema.* Bloomington: Indiana University Press, 1984.

Deleuze, Gilles. *Negotiations*, translated by Martin Joughin. New York: Columbia University Press, 1995.

Deleuze, Gilles and Félix Guattari. *Anti-Oedipus: Capitalism and Schizophrenia*, translated by Robert Hurley, Mark Seems, and Helen R. Lane. Minneapolis: University of Minnesota Press, 1983.

Denzin, Norman "The Conversation." *Symbolic Interactionism* 15 (1992): 135–150.

Denzin, Norman. *The Cinematic Society: The Voyeur's Gaze.* Thousand Oaks, CA: Sage, 1995.

Deutsch, Sarah Ketorah and Gray Cavender. "*CSI* and Forensic Realism." *Journal of Criminal Justice and Popular Culture* 15 (2008): 34–53.

Doane, Mary Ann. *The Desire to Desire: The Women's Film of the 1940s.* Bloomington: Indiana University Press, 1987.

Dovey, Jon. *Freakshow: First Person Media and Factual Television.* London: Pluto, 2000.

Dubrofsky, Rachel E. and Shoshana Amielle Magnet (eds). *Feminist Surveillance Studies.* Durham, NC: Duke University Press, 2015.

Ebert, Roger. "*Rififi.*" Accessed April 9, 2016. http://www.rogerebert.com/reviews/great-movie-rififi-1954, 2002.

Ebert, Roger. "*Caché*: A Riddle, Wrapped in a Mystery, Inside an Enigma." *Roger Ebert's Journal, Chicago Sun-Times,* January 18, 2010.

Elkins, James. *The Object Stares Back: On the Nature of Seeing.* New York: Harcourt, 1996.

Ellis, John. *Visible Fictions: Cinema, Television, Video* (2nd edition). New York: Routledge, 1992.

Faludi, Susan. *Backlash.* New York: Crown Publishing, 1993.

Foucault, Michel. *Discipline and Punish,* translated by Alan Sheridan. Harmondsworth: Penguin, 1977.

Foucault, Michel. *The History of Sexuality, Volume 3: The Care of the Self,* translated by Robert Hurley. New York: Vintage, 1988.

France24. "The Paris Massacre that Time Forgot, 51 Years On." Accessed January 23, 2015. http://www.france24.com/en/20121017-paris-massacre-algeria-october-17-1961-51-years-anniversary-historian-einaudi.

Funder, Anna. "Tyranny of Terror." *The Guardian,* May 5, 2007. Accessed June 15, 2009. http://www.theguardian.com/books/2007/may/05/featuresreviews.guardianreview12.

Funder, Anna. *Stasiland: Stories from Behind the Berlin Wall.* New York: Harper Perennial, 2011.

Gan, Vicky. "How TV's 'Person of Interest' Helps Us Understand the Surveillance Society." *Smithsonian.com,* October 24, 2013. Accessed May 18, 2015. http://www.smithsonianmag.com/smithsonian-institution/how-tvs-person-of-interest-helps-us-understand-the-surveillance-society-5407171.

Gandy, Oscar. *The Panoptic Sort: A Political Economy of Personal Information.* Boulder, CO: Westview, 1993.

Gandy, Oscar. "It's Discrimination, Stupid!" In *Resisting the Virtual Life: The Culture and Politics of Information,* edited by James Brook and Iain Boal. San Francisco: City Lights, 1995.

Gates, Kelly. *Our Biometric Future: Facial Recognition Technology and the Culture of Surveillance.* New York: New York University Press, 2011.

Goldhaber, Michael. "The Attention Economy and the Net." *First Monday* 2 (1997). Accessed April 9, 2016, http://firstmonday.org/article/view/519/440.

Graham, Stephen. "Spaces of Surveillant-Simulation: New Technologies, Digital Representations, and Material Geographies." *Environment and Planning D: Society and Space* 16 (1998): 483–504.

Greenleaf, Graham. "Country Studies B.3 – Hong Kong." In *Comparative Study on Different Approaches to New Privacy Challenges, in Particular in the Light of Technological Developments,* edited by Douwe Korff European Commission

Directorate-General Justice, Freedom and Security, 2010. Accessed April 9, 2016, http://ec.europa.eu/justice/data-protection/document/studies/files/new_privacy_challenges/final_report_country_report_b3_hong_kong.pdf.

Greenwald, Glenn. "Why Privacy Matters." *TEDGlobal*, October 2014. TED.com.

Griffiths, Alison. *Wondrous Difference: Cinema, Anthropology, and Turn-of-the-Century Visual Culture*. New York: Columbia University Press, 2002.

Guynn, Jessica. "Rear Window on Justin.tv." *SFGate*, April 11, 2007. Accessed May 3, 2015. http://blog.sfgate.techchron/2007/04/11/rear-window-on-justin-tv/

Hager, Nicky. *Secret Power*. Nelson, NZ: Craig Potton Publishing, 1996.

Hall, Stuart. "Notes on Deconstructing the Popular." In *People's History and Socialist Theory*. London: Routledge, 1981.

Hardt, Michael. "The Global Society of Control." *Discourse* 20 (1998a): 139–152.

Hardt, Michael. "The Withering of Civil Society." In *Deleuze and Guattari: New Mappings in Politics, Philosophy, and Culture*, edited by E. Kaufman and K.J. Heller, 23–39. Minneapolis: University of Minnesota Press, 1998b.

Harrington, Ellen Burton. "Nation, Identity, and the Fascination with Forensic Science in Sherlock Holmes and *CSI*." *International Journal of Cultural Studies* 10 (2007): 365–382.

Harris, Andrew. "The Metonymic Urbanism of the Twenty-First-Century Mumbai." *Urban Studies* 49 (2012): 2955–2973.

Hawthorn, Jeremy. "Morality, Voyeurism, and 'Point of View': Michael Powell's *Peeping Tom* (1960)." *Nordic Journal of English Studies* 2 (2003): 303–324.

Heron, Christopher. "Surveillance Camera Cinema." *The Seventh Art*, 2012. Accessed April 9, 2016, http://www.theseventhart.org/main/videos/issue-1-surveillance-camera-cinema.

Herzog, Todd. "The Banality of Surveillance: Michael Haneke's *Caché* and Life After the End of Privacy." *Modern Austrian Literature* 43 (2010): 25–40.

Hoberman, James. "The Giant." In *CTRL Space: Rhetorics of Surveillance from Bentham to Big Brother*, edited by Thomas Levin, Ursula Frohne, and Peter Weibel, 82–83. Cambridge: MIT Press, 2002. Originally 1984.

Holpuch, Amanda and Ruth Spencer. "NSA on TV and Film: The Shows that Predicted the Surveillance Revelations." *The Guardian*, September 27, 2013. Accessed May 18, 2015. http://www.theguardian.com/tv-and-radio/2013/sep/27/nsa-tv-film-homeland-relations.

Howe, Lawrence. "Through the Looking Glass: Reflexivity, Reciprocality, and Defenestration in Hitchcock's *Rear Window*." *College Literature* 35 (2008): 16–37.

Howell, Philip. "Crime and the City Solution: Crime Fiction, Urban Knowledge, and Radical Geography." *Antipode* 30(4) (1998): 357–378.

Ingham, Mike. *Johnnie To Kei-Fung's PTU*. Hong Kong: Hong Kong University Press, 2009.

Institute for Precarious Consciousness. "We Are All Very Anxious." Accessed April 9, 2016, http://www.weareplanc.org/blog/we-are-all-very-anxious.

Kammerer, Dietmar. "Video Surveillance in Hollywood Movies." *Surveillance and Society* 2 (2004): 464–473.

Kammerer, Dietmar. *Bilder der Überwachung*. Frankfurt: Suhrkamp Verlag, 2008.

Kammerer, Dietmar. "Surveillance in Literature, Film, and Television." In *Routledge Handbook of Surveillance Studies*, edited by Kirstie Ball, Kevin D. Haggerty, and David Lyon, 99–106. New York: Routledge, 2012.

Kaplan, Martha. "Panopicon in Poona: An Essay in Foucault and Colonialism." *Cultural Anthropology* 10 (1995): 85–98.

Kawashima, Kentaro. "An Image of the Control Society: On Kinji Fukasaku's *Battle Royale.*" In *Public Enemies: Film Between Identity Formation and Control*, edited by Winfried Pauleit, Christine Rüffert, Karl-Heinz Schmid, and Alfred Tews, 110–124. Berlin: bertz+fischer, 2011.

Koo, Se-woong. "South Korea's Invasion of Privacy." *The New York Times*, April 2, 2015. Accessed April 20, 2015. http://nyti.ms/1MF6i2W.

Korghan, Frank and Douglas Rushkoff. "Generation Like." *Frontline*, Public Broadcasting Corporation, February 18, 2014.

Koskela, Hille. "Webcams, TV Shows, and Mobile Phones: Empowering Exhibitionism." *Surveillance and Society* 2 (2004): 199–215.

Kundnani, Arun and Deepa Kumar. "Race, Surveillance, and Empire." *International Socialist Review* 96 (2015). Accessed April 9, 2016, http://isreview.org/issue/96/race-surveillance-and-empire.

Lague, David, Greg Torode, and James Pomfret. "Special Report: How China Spies on Hong Kong's Democrats." *Reuters*, December 14, 2014. Accessed April 20, 2015. http://www.reuters.com/article/2014/12/15/US-Hong-Kong-Surveillance.

Lake, Jessica. "*Red Road* (2006) and Emerging Narratives of 'Sub-Veillance.'" *Continuum: Journal of Media and Cultural Studies* 24 (2010): 231–240.

Lalvani, Suren. *Photography, Vision, and the Production of Modern Bodies.* Albany, NY: SUNY Press, 1996.

Law, W.S. "The Violence of Time and Memory Undercover: Hong Kong's Infernal Affairs." *Inter-Asia Cultural Studies* 7 (2006): 383–402.

Lefait, Sébastien. *Surveillance on Screen: Monitoring Contemporary Films and Television Programs.* Lanham, MD: Scarecrow Press, 2013.

Levin, Thomas Y. "Rhetoric of the Temporal Index: Surveillant Narration and the Cinema of 'Real Time.'" In *CTRL Space: Rhetorics of Surveillance from Bentham to Big Brother*, edited by Thomas Levin, Ursula Frohne, and Peter Weibel, 578–593. Cambridge: MIT Press, 2002.

Luhr, William. *Film Noir.* Malden: Blackwell, 2012.

Lyon, David. *The Electronic Eye: The Rise of Surveillance Society.* Minneapolis: University of Minnesota Press, 1994.

Lyon, David. *Surveillance Society: Monitoring Everyday Life.* Philadelphia, PA: Open University Press, 2001.

Lyon, David. *Surveillance After September 11.* Malden: Polity, 2003.

Lyon, David. *Surveillance Studies: An Overview.* Malden: Polity, 2007.

Lyon, David. "The Emerging Surveillance Culture." In *Media, Surveillance and Identity: Social Perspectives*, edited by André Jansson and Miyase Christensen, 71–88. New York: Peter Lang, 2014.

MacMurdo-Reading, Margaret Ann. "The Spectacle and the Witness: An Historical and Critical Study of Surveillance in Visual Culture from 1920 to 2008." PhD diss., University of Otago, 2013.

Mann, Steve and Hal Niedzviecki. *Cyborg: Digital Destiny and Human Possibility in the Age of the Wearable Computer.* Toronto: Doubleday of Canada, 2001.

Mann, Steve, Jason Nolan, and Barry Wellman. "Sousveillance: Inventing and Using Wearable Computing Devices for Data Collection in Surveillance Environments." *Surveillance and Society* 1 (2003): 331–355.

Marchetti, Gina. *Andrew Lau and Alan Mak's Infernal Affairs—The Trilogy*. Hong Kong: Hong Kong University Press, 2007.

Marchetti, Gina. "Chinese Cinema at the Millennium: Defining 'China' and the Politics of Representation." In *The International Encyclopedia of Media Studies, Vol. III: Content and Representation*, edited by Sharon Mazzarella, 322–342. Malden: Blackwell, 2013.

Martin, Nina K. *Sexy Thrills: Undressing the Erotic Thriller*. Urbana: University of Illinois Press, 2007.

Marx, Gary T. *Undercover*. Berkeley: University of California Press, 1988.

Marx, Gary T. "Electric Eye in the Sky: Some Reflections on the New Surveillance in Popular Culture." In *Computers, Surveillance, and Privacy*, edited by David Lyon and Elia Zureik, 193–233. Minneapolis: University of Minnesota Press, 1996.

Marx, Gary T. "A Tack in the Shoe: Neutralizing and Resisting the New Surveillance." *Journal of Social Issues* 59 (2003): 369–390.

Marx, Gary T. "Soul Train: The New Surveillance and Popular Music." In *Lessons from the Identity Trail: Anonymity, Privacy, and Identity in a Networked Society*, edited by Ian Kerr, Carole Lucock, and Valerie Steeves, 377–397. New York: Oxford University Press, 2009.

Marx, Gary T. "Coming to Terms and Avoiding Information Techno-Fallacies." In *Privacy in the Modern Age: The Search for Solutions*, edited by Marc Rotenberg, Julia Horowitz, and Jeramie Scott, 118–126. New York: The New Press, 2015.

Massumi, Brian. "The Autonomy of Affect." *Cultural Critique* 31 (1995): 83–109.

Mazumdar, Ranjani. *Bombay Cinema: An Archive of the City*. Minneapolis: University of Minnesota Press, 2007.

Mazumdar, Ranjani. "Terrorism, Conspiracy, and Surveillance in Bombay's Urban Cinema." *Social Research* 78 (2011): 143–172.

McCoy, Alfred. "Surveillance Blowback." *The Nation*, July 16, 2013. Accessed October 26, 2015. www.thenation.com/article/surveillance-blowback.

McGowan, Todd. *Psychoanalytic Film Theory and the Rules of the Game*. New York: Bloomsbury Academic, 2015.

McLuhan, Marshall. *Understanding Media: The Extensions of Man*. New York: Signet, 1964.

Mirzoeff, Nicholas. *The Right to Look: A Counterhistory of Visuality*. Durham, NC: Duke University Press, 2011.

Mitra, Smita. "On 'Black Friday.'" *Economic & Political Weekly* 42 (2007): 1408–1410.

Mittell, Jason. *Genre and Television: From Cop Shows to Cartoons in American Culture*. New York: Routledge, 2004.

Mittell, Jason. "All in the Game: *The Wire*, Serial Storytellers, and Procedural Logic." Accessed February 24, 2015. http://www.electronicbookreview.com/thread/firstperson/serial, 2011.

Modleski, Tania. "The Master's Dollhouse." In *The Women Who Knew Too Much: Hitchcock and Feminist Theory*. New York: Routledge, 1998.

Modleski, Tania. *The Women Who Knew Too Much: Hitchcock and Feminist Theory* (2nd edition). New York: Routledge, 2005.

Monahan, Torin. "Surveillance as Cultural Practice." *The Sociological Quarterly* 52 (2011): 495–508.

Monahan, Torin and Rodolfo D. Torres (eds). *Schools Under Surveillance: Cultures of Control in Public Education*. New Brunswick, NJ: Rutgers University Press, 2009.

Moore, Burness E. and Bernard D. Fine. *Psychoanalytic Terms and Concepts*. New Haven, CT: American Psychoanalytic Association and Yale University Press, 1990.

Mulvey, Laura. "Afterthoughts on 'Visual Pleasure and Narrative Cinema' Inspired by King Vidor's *A Duel in the Sun* (1946)." In *Feminist Film Theory: A Reader*, edited by Sue Thornham, 122–130. Edinburgh: Edinburgh University Press, 1999.

Mulvey, Laura. "Visual Pleasure and Narrative Cinema." In *Film Theory and Criticism: Introductory Readings*, edited by Leo Braudy and Marshall Cohen, 833–844. New York: Oxford University Press, 2004.

Mumford, Lewis. *The Myth of the Machine: The Pentagon of Power*. New York: Harcourt, Brace, Jovanovich, 1970.

Nellis, Mike. "News Media, Popular Culture and the Electronic Monitoring of Offenders in England and Wales." *The Howard Journal* 42 (2003): 1–31.

Ng, Kang-chung and Clifford Lo. "Hong Kong Police Now Less Popular Than China's PLA, After Occupy Clashes." *South China Morning Post*, December 10, 2014. Accessed April 9, 2016, http://www.scmp.com/print/news/hong-kong/article/1659238/police-now-less-popular-pla-hku-poll-finds.

Niedzviecki, Hal. *The Peep Diaries: How We're Learning to Love Watching Ourselves and Our Neighbors*. San Francisco, CA: City Lights, 2009.

Norris, Clive and Gary Armstrong. *The Maximum Surveillance Society: The Rise of CCTV*. Oxford: Berg, 1999.

Orwell, George. *Nineteen Eighty-Four*. New York: Everyman's Library, 1992. Originally Harcourt, Brace and Company, 1949.

Ott, Brian. "The Visceral Politics of *V for Vendetta*: On Political Affect in Cinema." *Critical Studies in Media Communication* 27 (2010): 39–54.

Ouellette, Laurie. "'Take Responsibility for Yourself': Judge Judy and the Neoliberal Citizen." In *Reality TV: Remaking Television Culture* (2nd edition), edited by Susan Murray and Laurie Ouellette, 223–242. New York: New York University Press, 2008.

Ouellette, Laurie and James Hay. *Better Living Through Reality TV: Television and Post-Welfare Citizenship*. Malden: Blackwell, 2008.

Packer, Jeremy and Joshua Reeves. "Decentralized Execution: Media Swarms and Military Command." Paper presented at the National Communication Association Conference, Las Vegas, 2015.

Paik, Peter Y. *From Utopia to Apocalypse: Science Fiction and the Politics of Catastrophe*. Minneapolis: University of Minnesota Press, 2010.

Parenti, Christian. *The Soft Cage: Surveillance in America from Slavery to the War on Terror*. New York: Basic Books, 2003.

"The Paris Massacre That Time Forgot, 51 Years On." *France24*, October 18, 2012. Accessed January 23, 2015. http://www.france24.com/en/20121017-paris-massacre-algeria-octover-17-1961-51-years-anniversary-historian-einaudi/.

Pecora, Vincent. "The Culture of Surveillance." *Qualitative Sociology* 25 (2002): 345–358.

Pedersen, Isabel. "MyLifeBits, Augmented Memory, and a Rhetoric of Need." *Continuum* 22 (2008): 375–384.

Pew Research Center. "Public Perceptions of Privacy and Security in the Post-Snowden Era." November 12, 2014. Accessed April 9, 2016, http://www.pewinternet.org/2014/11/12/public-privacy-perceptions/.

Pugliese, Joseph. *Biometrics: Bodies, Technologies, Biopolitics*. New York: Routledge. 2012.

Pugsley, Peter C. "Hong Kong Film as Crossover Cinema: Maintaining the HK Aesthetic." In *Crossover Cinema: Cross-Cultural Film from Production to Reception*, edited by Sukhmani Khorana, 51–65. New York: Routledge, 2013.

Rancière, Jacques. *The Politics of Aesthetics: The Distribution of the Sensible*, translated by Gabriel Rockhill. New York: Bloomsbury Academic, 2013.

Rao, Vyjayanthi. "How to Read a Bomb: Scenes from Bombay's Black Friday." *Public Culture* 19 (2007): 567–592.

Raphael, Chad. "The Political Economic Origins of Reali-TV." In *Reality TV: Remaking Television Culture*, edited by Susan Murray and Laurie Ouellette, 123–140. New York: New York University Press, 2008.

Rapping, Elayne. *Law and Justice as Seen on TV*. New York: New York University Press, 2003.

Rist, Peter. "Scenes of 'In-Action' and Noir Characteristics in the Films of Johnnie To (Kei-Fung)." In *Hong Kong Film, Hollywood and the New Global Cinema: No Film Is an Island*, edited by Gina Marchetti and Tan See Kam, 159–163. New York: Routledge, 2007.

Rodley, Chris. "A Very British Psycho." Channel 4 International. Available on *Peeping Tom* (DVD) The Criterion Collection, 1999.

Rose, Nicolas. *Powers of Freedom: Reframing Political Thought*. New York: Cambridge University Press, 1999.

Rule, James B. *Private Lives, Public Surveillance: Social Control in the Information Age*. London: Allen Lane, 1973.

Sa'di, Ahmad H. "Colonialism and Surveillance" In *The Routledge Handbook of Surveillance Studies*, edited by Kirstie Ball, Kevin D. Haggerty, and David Lyon, 151–158. New York: Routledge, 2012.

Scholz, Trebor (ed.). *Digital Labor: The Internet as Playground and Factory*. New York: Routledge, 2012.

Senft, Theresa. *Camgirls: Celebrity and Community in the Age of Social Networks*. New York: Peter Lang, 2008.

Singha, Radhika. "Punished by Surveillance: Policing 'Dangerousness' in Colonial India, 1872–1918." *Modern Asian Studies* 42 (2015): 241–269.

Slack, Jennifer Daryl and J. Macgregor Wise. *Culture and Technology: A Primer* (2nd edition). New York: Peter Lang, 2015.

Sontag, Susan. *On Photography*. New York: Picador, 2001.

Stam, Robert. *Reflexivity in Film and Literature: From Don Quixote to Jean-Luc Godard*. New York: Columbia University Press, 1995.

Staples, William G. *Everyday Surveillance: Vigilance and Visibility in Postmodern Life* (2nd edition). Lanham: Rowman and Littlefield, 2014.

Stewart, Garrett. *Closed Circuits: Screening Narrative Surveillance*. Chicago: University of Chicago Press, 2015.

Strain, Ellen. "Exotic Bodies, Distant Landscapes: Touristic Viewing and Popularized Anthropology in the Nineteenth Century." *Wide Angle* 18 (1996): 70–100.

Sun, Yi. "Crossing Genres: A Study of Johnnie To's Stylized Films." *Asian Cinema* 22 (2011): 74–110.

Sun, Yi. "Shaping Hong Kong Cinema's New Icon: Milkyway Image at International Film Festivals." *Transnational Cinemas* (2015). Accessed 9 March, 2015. doi: 10.1080/20403526.2014.1002671

Teo, Stephen. *Director in Action: Johnnie To and the Hong Kong Action Film*. Hong Kong: Hong Kong University Press, 2007.

Tiziallas, Evangelos. "Torture Porn and Surveillance Culture." *JumpCut* 52 (2010).

Truffaut, Francois, Alfred Hitchcock, and H.G. Scott. *Hitchcock* (Rev. Ed.). New York: Simon and Schuster, 1984.

Turner, Dennis. "The Subject of 'The Conversation.'" *Cinema Journal* 24 (1985): 4–22.

Turner, John S. "Collapsing the Interior/Exterior Distinction: Surveillance, Spectacle, and Suspense in Popular Cinema." *Wide Angle* 20 (1998): 93–123.

Villasenor, John. "Recording Everything: Digital Storage as an Enabler of Authoritarian Governments." Brookings, December 14, 2011. Accessed May 29, 2015. http://www.brookings.edu/research/papers/2011/12/14-digital-storage-villasenor.

Virilio, Paul. *The Vision Machine*, translated by Julie Rose. London: BFI, 1994.

Virilio, Paul. *The Information Bomb*, translated by Chris Turner. New York: Verso, 2000.

Williams, Hubert and Patrick V. Murphy. "The Evolving Strategy of Police: A Minority View." *Perspectives on Policing* 13 (1990): 1–15.

Williams, Raymond. "Culture Is Ordinary." In *Resources of Hope*, edited by Robin Gable. New York: Verso, 1989. Originally 1959.

Williams, Raymond. *The Long Revolution*. London: Chatto and Windus, 1961.

Williams, Tony. "Transcultural Spaces of a Vanishing Hong Kong: Johnnie To's *Sparrow*." *Asian Cinema* 21 (2010): 113–123.

Willis, Andy. "Hong Kong Cinema Since 1997: Troughs and Peaks." *Film International* 40 (2006): 6–17.

Willsher, Kim. "France Remembers Algerian Massacre 50 Years On." *The Guardian*, October 17, 2011. Accessed January 23, 2015. http://www.theguardian.com/world/2011/oct/17/france-remembers-algerian-massacre.

Wise, J. Macgregor. "'An Immense and Unexpected Field of Action': Webcams, Surveillance, and Everyday Life." *Cultural Studies* 18 (2004): 424–442.

Wise, J. Macgregor. "A Hole in the Hand: Assemblages of Attention and Mobile Screens." In *Theories of the Mobile Internet: Materialities and Imaginaries*, edited by Andrew Herman, Jan Hadlaw, and Thom Swiss, 212–231. New York: Routledge, 2014.

Yim, Tsz-kit. "Post-1997 Hong Kong Cinema, Masculinity Crisis, and Generational Hegemony: The Baby-Boomers, Post-70s Generation and Beyond." MA Thesis, University of Hong Kong, 2012.

Zimmer, Catherine. "Surveillance and Social Memory: Strange Days Indeed." *Discourse* 32 (2010): 302–320.

Zimmer, Catherine. "Surveillance Cinema: Narrative Between Technology and Politics." *Surveillance and Society* 8 (2011): 427–440.

Zimmer, Catherine. *Surveillance Cinema*. New York: New York University Press, 2015.

Zureik, Elia. "Colonial Oversight." *Red Pepper* October/November (2013): 46–49.

Index

Note: Locators with letter 'n' refer to notes.